THE LIBRARY OF
PHILOSOPHY AND THEOLOGY

Edited by
JOHN MCINTYRE and IAN T. RAMSEY

———————————

PAUL TILLICH: AN APPRAISAL

PAUL TILLICH
AN APPRAISAL

J. HEYWOOD THOMAS

SCM PRESS LTD

BLOOMSBURY STREET LONDON

FIRST PUBLISHED 1963
© SCM PRESS LTD 1963
PRINTED IN GREAT BRITAIN BY
THE CAMELOT PRESS LTD
LONDON AND SOUTHAMPTON

PIAE PATRIS MEMORIAE

CONTENTS

PREFACE

BEFORE going to Union Theological Seminary in 1952 I knew
but little of Paul Tillich, and so I was grateful for the opportunity of hearing him expound his theological system and of
sitting at his feet. On my return to Britain I wrote a little
article entitled 'Introducing Paul Tillich' (*London Quarterly
Review*, January 1956). Several months after it appeared one
reader was good enough to thank me for it and to express the
hope that I should attempt a more thorough introduction in
the form of a book. Thus the idea of this book was born, and for
a long time I did nothing about it. However, after Volume 2 of
Systematic Theology appeared I set to work, and the first draft of
the book was finished in 1960. It was not published then because
the publication of the third and final volume of *Systematic
Theology* was thought to be imminent, but two years have now
passed and it still has not appeared. To delay further the
publication of this attempt at introduction and evaluation
would not only involve postponing its final appearance but
indeed make this exceedingly difficult; for even now books on
Tillich have begun to appear. Father Tavard's *Paul Tillich
and the Christian Message* is an example. This excellent study of
Tillich's Christology appeared too late for me to make really
full use of it, but I have tried to indicate the extent of my
agreement with his searching criticisms of Tillich in the
appendix on Catholic criticism which I have added. However,
even if it had appeared some time ago I should still have felt
that some such study as mine was needed. For, though Father
Tavard is amazingly sympathetic and tries to present some
portrait of Tillich the theologian, yet his book is essentially the
examination of one aspect of Tillich's thought—and that, too,

9

from a viewpoint which made it inevitable that Tillich's thought should prove unsatisfactory in his eyes.

The same may be said of Professor Kenneth Hamilton's book, *The System and the Gospel*, which is to be published concurrently with mine. It seems that Professor Hamilton wants to argue much the same thesis as Father Tavard—that the demands of the system militate against the proper expression of the Gospel. He does many things that I also wish to do—such as criticizing the ambiguity of Tillich's thought—but always for the sole purpose of showing the reader the error of Tillich's ways. My aim has been to try and show the bare bones of the system and the way in which they are so richly clothed with flesh, and only then to point out confusions and errors. In short, I have attempted an introduction and evaluation rather than a simple critique. True, Tillich needs to be criticized with all the power and penetration we can muster, but we also need to understand what he is saying. I have sought, above all, to repay a pupil's double debt—to say what I have learned and to pull my teacher's work to bits. And now I am very conscious of having attempted far more than I have been able to achieve.

Many people have shown me much kindness and I must indicate my gratitude. My friend, Dr H. Cunliffe-Jones, read the entire manuscript and made several useful criticisms. Professors Ramsey and McIntyre, the editors of the SCM Press Library of Philosophy and Theology, also encouraged me with constructive criticism. I am grateful to them for having saved me from infelicities, inaccuracies and errors, and if any such faults remain the responsibility is, of course, entirely mine. Thanks are also due to the editors of *The Scottish Journal of Theology* and *The London Quarterly Review* for their permission to use material that has appeared in their journals, to the editorial staff of the SCM Press for their patience, and to Miss June Hogg who typed the manuscript.

J. H. T.

LIFE AND DEVELOPMENT

LIKE many a distinguished figure before him, Paul Tillich was born the son of a clergyman in a village manse. He was born on 20th August 1886 in Starzeddel, a village in the province of Brandenburg. Four years later the family moved to Schönfliess-Neumark where Paul's father was superintendent of the diocese. The young boy was sent to the common school at first, but he received private lessons in Latin so that later he went to a humanistic 'gymnasium' in the nearby city of Königsberg-Neumark. These medieval towns in which he spent the first fourteen years of his life made a profound impression on him as did also the country which surrounded his home. Though he has never harboured a romantic hostility towards technical civilization the ties with the country remained deep in his soul. Nearly all his great memories and strong longings, he tells us, are linked with the soil, weather, wind and woods. However, during this time the boy made regular visits to Berlin, his father's birthplace; and these visits were for him a source of excitement which was as strange and mysterious as is seeing the sea for a child brought up in the country. When in 1900 his father was called to an important position in Berlin Paul was overjoyed. There he resumed his classical education in a gymnasium, passing his final examination in 1904 and matriculating in the theological faculties of Berlin, Tübingen and Halle. In 1909 he took his first and in 1911 his second theological examination. Even before entering the University he had studied philosophy and gained a good knowledge of the history of philosophy and a working knowledge of Fichte and Kant. Next he became acquainted with the work of Schleiermacher, Hegel and Schelling. In 1910 he presented a thesis on Schelling for the degree of Doctor of Philosophy of Breslau,[1] and two years later he wrote another thesis on Schelling for the degree of Licentiate of Theology from Halle.[2]

In 1912 he was ordained a minister of the Evangelical Lutheran Church of the province of Brandenburg. Two years later the First World War broke out, and he joined the Army as a chaplain, serving for four years. When the war was over, he became a Privatdozent of Theology in the University of Berlin, and so began his long academic career.

During the war he had sought relief from the ugly gruesomeness and destructiveness of war in painting, and he studied both reproductions of paintings and the history of art. This adventure reached its climax in his seeing a picture by Botticelli in Berlin on his last furlough of the war. 'The discovery of painting', he says, 'was for me an experience of decisive importance.'[3] So significant indeed was this that from reflection upon this experience and from the interpretation of art he gained the fundamental categories of his philosophy of religion. His interest in art also led him to a profounder sympathy with the Roman Catholic Church. Thus he says, 'My growing inclination towards the old Church and her solutions of the problems of "God and the world", "state and Church", were nourished by the overwhelming impression made upon me by early Christian art in Italy. What no amount of Church history had brought about was accomplished by the mosaics in ancient Roman basilicas.'[4] A more important consequence—for Tillich has never regarded Roman Catholicism as a possible spiritual home—was his growing interest in a 'theology of culture'. This is what he taught in the historical and systematic courses he gave between 1919 and 1924. The lectures covered such subjects as the relation of religion to politics, art, philosophy, psycho-analysis and sociology. All this was an attempt at apologetic theology which would speak to the cultural

---

[1] *Die religionsgeschichtliche Konstruktion in Schellings positiver Philosophie, ihre Voraussetzungen und Prinzipien*, Breslau, Fleischmann, 1910.
[2] *Mystik und Schuldbewusstsein in Schellings Entwicklung*, Gütersloh, Bertelsmann, 1912.
[3] *The Interpretation of History*, p. 15.   [4] *Ibid.*, p. 16.

upheaval of post-war Berlin, the excitement of which Tillich enjoyed to the full.

After some five years in Berlin he moved to Marburg, where he was Professor of Theology. Marburg presented him with a completely different cultural situation from that of Berlin inasmuch as he found the students deeply influenced by the neo-orthodox theology. The result was that all cultural problems were banned from theology and theologians such as Schleiermacher and Harnack regarded as really useless. At first Tillich was very much depressed by this, but later he came to feel that this too was a challenge to find a new apologetic theology. And in 1925 he began his *Systematic Theology*, the first volume of which was not to appear until over twenty-five years later. The existentialism of this first volume reveals the influence of Marburg, for it was there that Tillich met with existentialism in its twentieth-century form. Of it he says, 'I resisted, I tried to learn, I accepted the new way of thinking more than the answers it gave.'[1] In some ways it was not a new way of thinking, for its dialectical pattern is something which takes us as far back as Hegel. It may well be that Tillich's 'existentialism' is no more than the expression of what he had learnt from Schelling and his teacher, Martin Kähler, in language learnt from Heidegger. At any rate Kähler certainly influenced his theological method profoundly.[2] Tillich's dialectical method was a point of contact with his pupils, and it is worth noting that his view of dialectics is not the same as Barth's. 'Dialectics', he says, 'is the way of seeking for truth by talking with others from different points of view, through "Yes" and "No", until a "Yes" has been reached which is hardened in the fire of many "No's" and which unites the elements of faith promoted in the discussion. It is most unfortunate that in recent years the name "dialectical theology" has been applied to a theology that is strongly opposed to any kind of dialectics.'[3]

[1] 'Autobiographical Reflections', *The Theology of Paul Tillich* (ed. C. W. Kegley and R. W. Bretall), New York, Macmillan, 1952, p. 14.
[2] See *The Protestant Era*, London, Nisbet, 1951, pp. xxviii-xxx. Cf. Ch. Rhein, *Paul Tillich, Philosoph und Theologe*, Stuttgart, Evangelisches Verlagswerk, 1957, pp. 21f.
[3] *Op. cit.*, p. xxviii.

In 1928 he accepted the call to Dresden as Professor of the Philosophy of Religion and Social Philosophy. Here he enjoyed once more the life of a big city which had always appealed so much to him. Culturally Dresden was very much alive, being a centre of visual art, architecture, opera and ballet. All of this Tillich once more savoured to the full. His move to Frankfurt in 1929 took him to a very similar cultural situation. The University there had no theological faculty, but Tillich's occupation of the Chair of Philosophy tended to fill that gap. He felt impelled to make philosophy a living issue for his pupils and so his lectures were concerned with the boundary between philosophy and theology. This, together with his public speaking, brought Tillich into conflict with the growing Nazi movement. When Hitler became German Chancellor Tillich was instantly dismissed from his post. Fortunately Reinhold Niebuhr happened to be in Germany that summer and he invited Tillich to Union Theological Seminary, New York. In November 1933 he and his family left Germany and emigrated to the United States of America. The greater part of his academic career has thus been spent in the U.S., and this has been mostly in New York where he was Professor of Philosophical Theology at Union Seminary. On reaching retiring age he was invited by Harvard University to become one of its University Professors. In 1955, therefore, he began his second American career.

This bare outline of his life-story helps us to understand the development of Tillich's theological thought. He has been called a romantic and he has admitted the justice of this description because of his 'relationship to nature' and his relation to history. His relationship to nature, he says, is expressed in a predominantly aesthetic-meditative attitude rather than a scientific-analytical or technical relation. This attitude, which has profound implications for his theology, has its roots in his biography. His actual experience of nature was one of these roots, while the influence of romantic poetry and that of Lutheran theology also combined to effect this romantic attitude towards nature. His early life—and probably his later life as well—seems to have been characterized by a

Wordsworthian attachment to nature, indeed a sort of nature-mysticism. As Leibrecht says:

'Though he prefers to call himself an "ecstatic naturalist", there is quite a bit of the romanticist in Tillich. Let him but speak of a tree and his romantic strain at once becomes apparent. He does not belittle the scientist, but yet avows that the latter can describe only the biological and chemical processes of the tree's growth. He cannot explain what any particular tree is as such, for itself. To see nature in its creative ground requires a poet or a philosopher.'[1]

Doubtless this Wordsworthian attitude was strengthened by his reading of German literature with its abundance of poetry all of which has a mystical flavour. 'There are', he says, 'verses of Goethe, Holderlin, Novalis, Eichendorff, Nietzsche, George and Rilke which never have ceased to move me as deeply as they did when I first heard them.'[2] The Lutheran insistence on the doctrine that the finite is capable of the infinite put a theological seal on this nature mysticism which had been the joint product of his experience and his reading of poetry. His attitude towards history was just as inevitably romantic. Having spent the earliest years of his life in some of the most historic places in Germany, Tillich could not avoid having a feeling for history as a living and ever-present reality. More specifically in his profound appreciation of the European Middle Ages through which romanticism influenced the intellectual history of the later nineteenth and early twentieth centuries Tillich displays a romantic attitude towards history. Indeed he freely admits that his theology of history could not have been conceived without this influence. His early life as son of a Lutheran manse amidst the beauties of Gothic churches gave Tillich what he has called an experience of the 'holy' as an understandable good. This influenced his method in philosophical theology so that he began 'with the experience of the holy and advanced towards the idea of God, and not the reverse way'. Four further respects in which Tillich may be

[1] W. Leibrecht, 'The Life and Mind of Paul Tillich', *Religion and Culture* (ed. Leibrecht), New York and London, Harper and SCM Press, 1959, p. 7.
[2] 'Autobiographical Reflections', *Theology of Paul Tillich*, p. 5.

described as a romantic are mentioned by Leibrecht.[1] The first is his great interest in myth, symbol and sacrament—myth he regards as the expression of the relationship between man's ecstatic reason and the power of being. Secondly, he 'shares with the romantics a passion for creativity'. The basis of his theological evaluation of culture as the form of religion is the conviction that creative work of every kind is infinitely important. Thirdly, he has a romantic contempt for 'the bourgeois world of self-sufficiency and easy satisfaction'. Leibrecht elaborates this rather whimsically by saying: 'Tillich has something of the romantic Bohemian in him: he never wears a conventional hat; he loves his wine, especially shared with his friends.'[2] Finally, he shares the romantic's respect and admiration for Greek culture and thought and his thought is full of echoes of Hellenism.

Life in Berlin did not encourage this romantic strain, though the influence of his parents' strong personalities tended to increase the pressure of the sociological and psychological restrictions of his early life. Consequently Tillich soon realized that the balance of the romantic and revolutionary motives was one of the basic problems of his thought and life. The same kind of tension was produced by the intellectual forces which influenced him during his university careers. The decisive lesson he learned was that Protestant theology far from being stagnant was able to incorporate strictly scientific methods without losing its Christian foundations. The other dynamic influence was that of Kierkegaard whom Tillich discovered during this period. Kierkegaard's dialectic shook but did not break Tillich's nineteenth-century conservatism. And despite the impact of both Biblical Criticism and of Kierkegaard, Tillich and his contemporaries still hoped that the great synthesis between Christianity and humanism could be achieved with the help of German classical philosophy. This is not to say, however, that Kierkegaard's influence on Tillich has been negligible; for it is easy enough to show the Kierkegaardian origin of much of his thought. What it does mean is that Kierkegaard's thought remained for Tillich in a very

[1] *Op. cit.*, p. 7.   [2] *Ibid.*

16

real sense enclosed in its nineteenth-century expression. It is significant that he regards the philosophy of Schelling's second period as being the beginning of Existentialism.[1] Tillich's first published work was on the subject of Schelling's philosophy of religion, and there can be little doubt that his own philosophical position is to a very large extent derived from Schelling. He acknowledges a profound affinity with Schelling's personality and thought. It is well known that there are at least two periods in Schelling's philosophical career and it is work of the later, more theological, period which influenced Tillich. This was an attempt to formulate a 'philosophy of revelation', to understand revelation in terms of its own immanent concepts. Religion was the pivot of philosophy, said Schelling. He attacked the speculative philosophy of Hegel from which he distinguished his own 'positive' philosophy which had its principle in the practical interests of man. From the beginning the central concept of his philosophy was that of freedom. Sin is born of the actualization of freedom. As Schelling's later philosophy reflects the influence of von Baader and Boehme so Tillich's philosophy reflects the influence of Schelling. We shall see in our discussion of his interpretation of philosophy how close he is to Schelling (and also Hegel); for the moment it is sufficient that we see the tradition from which he emerged and that we appreciate that this is the tradition of Schelling rather than Kierkegaard. For Tillich Kierkegaard does not represent a new force in philosophy but the continuation of the kind of break with Hegel which had been effected in Schelling's 'positive philosophy'. One final point on this subject must be mentioned. In so far as Tillich can be said to be in the 'existentialist' tradition he must also reflect the influence of Husserl whose phenomenological philosophy forms the link between Kierkegaard and contemporary philosophy. The popularity of this philosophical school in Germany a generation ago makes it extremely probable that this was the kind of philosophy

[1] In his 'Autobiographical Reflections' (*op. cit.*, p. 11) he writes 'Here [i.e. in Schelling's second period] lies the philosophically decisive break with Hegel, and the beginning of that movement which today is called Existentialism.' Cf. *Theology of Culture*, New York and London, Oxford University Press, 1959 and 1960, pp. 76-7.

Tillich was taught. In which case the influence of Husserl (which will be discussed later) came from two directions.

One final influence must be mentioned—that of the socialist movement in Germany after the First World War. Tillich has described how after a few weeks in the army he had lost his original enthusiasm and saw that the apparent unity of the nation was an illusion and that in the class struggle the Church was looked upon as being an ally of the ruling groups. His sympathy with the social side of the revolution which ensued was nothing new—he had always been sympathetic to social struggle. The great social upheaval which Germany witnessed in the postwar years brought this latent socialism to the forefront of Tillich's mind and he was an ardent advocate of a religious socialism. He has emphasised the central importance of this doctrine in his development. His doctrine of *kairos* is an expression of the religious disparity he perceives in the secular struggle for social justice, and he has gone so far as to say that if the prophetic message is right then there can be nothing 'beyond religious socialism'.

Tillich's early work reveals the dialectical character of his theology, full as it is of Barthian ideas. Like Barth he insists on Kierkegaard's 'infinite qualitative difference' between the temporal and the eternal, on the necessity of revelation and the inevitability of paradox when human language tries to express the divine revelation. However, Tillich was too liberal-minded to follow Barth entirely, and increasingly his work became sharply distinguished from 'dialectic theology'. Against Barth's denial of any revelation within the order of nature as such, Tillich has insisted on God's revelation as well his hiddenness. Whereas Barth resists what has been called the apologetic task of interpreting or translating the Christian message into the language of the contemporary situation, Tillich has made this the essential character of his theological method. This method of correlation also makes him systematic in a way that Barth had never been. This made him a congenial theologian for his American audience.

His work made its first impact on American theology from his book, *The Religious Situation*, which was translated from the

German by Richard Niebuhr. The result was that he was accepted into the united front of 'realistic' theologians,[1] much in the same way as he was regarded earlier as belonging to the School of dialectic theologians and just as he distinguished his theology from that of Barth so Tillich has made clear where he differs from other American realistic theologians. Nowadays it is widely recognized that he occupies a unique place in American theology, and it is not unjust to describe a great part of American theology as a commentary on his work.

What we have seen in this introductory survey of Tillich's thought is that Tillich mirrors very effectively some of the major movements of thought in the twentieth century, and is indeed a link between this and the nineteenth century. His theology is not so much an amalgam as a new creation which uses as its materials the tremendously varied influences which we have seen were at work in his early life—social, artistic, philosophical, theological and political. Not surprisingly then it has been necessary to indicate this background so that we have a clue to the understanding even of the strictly theological themes of the system. To the exposition and examination of the main features of the system we now turn.

[1] This term was used to characterize the work of Reinhold Niebuhr (a politico-economic realism) and that of H. N. Wieman (empirical realism).

I

THE NATURE AND METHOD OF THEOLOGY

TILLICH tells us in the Preface to volume I of *Systematic Theology* that his purpose is 'to present the method and the structure of a theological system written from an apologetic point of view and carried through in a continuous correlation with philosophy'.[1] Thus it is clear from the outset that for Tillich the purpose of the theology is essentially apologetic. A theological system, he says, must serve two different needs— 'the statement of the truth of the Christian message and an interpretation of this truth for every generation'. The weakness of fundamentalism, for example, is that it does not concern itself sufficiently with the situation whereas apologetic theology, on the other hand, has all too often gone to the other extreme of being prepared to surrender points of Christian doctrine in an effort to find common front with the secular situation. The weakness of the fundamentalist type of kerygmatic theology should serve to remind us that kerygmatic theology must be completed by apologetic theology which speaks to the special 'situation' if it is not to become narrow and irrelevant. On the other hand, apologetic theology must be 'based on the *Kerygma* as the substance and criterion of each of its statements' if it is not to lose its Christian character. Tillich's theology attempts to combine both these elements despite the fact that his purpose in writing theology is primarily apologetic. Yet he is so impressed by the kerygmatic character of theology that he insists that the theologian must work within the 'theological circle'. This is what distinguishes the theologian's task from that of the philosopher of religion. Whereas the latter is 'general and abstract' in his concepts the theologian seeks to be 'specific

[1] *Systematic Theology*, vol. I, London, Nisbet, 1953, pp. ix-x.

and concrete', entering the theological circle 'with a concrete commitment' and 'as a member of the Christian Church'.

Tillich recognizes two formal criteria of every theology. 'The object of theology is what concerns us ultimately. Only those propositions are theological which deal with their objects in so far as it can become a matter of ultimate concern for us.'[1] The purpose of this first criterion is to enable us to distinguish between ultimate and preliminary concerns and so that we do not confuse theological questions with scientific, historical or political questions or any other which concern our relation to the world of existence. The second formal criterion of every theology is that 'only those statements are theological which deal with their object in so far as it can become a matter of being or not-being for us.'[2] For only that which has 'the power of threatening or saving our being', 'the structure, the meaning and the aim of existence' is of ultimate concern to us. These two criteria express Tillich's existentialist approach to the theology, and it is the character of this approach which determines his conception of the method of theology. Thus, for example, he seeks in theology for answers to the questions raised by man's situation. The starting point of his theology, however, is the analysis of the human situation and not the answers of the Christian message.

Before we examine the method of Tillich's theology as such it will be worth our while to notice what he says about the organisation of theology.[3] Tillich regards the classical tradition of natural theology as a section of systematic theology and the nineteenth-century idea of the philosophy of religion as the substitute for this section of classical systematic theology as equally unsatisfactory. For there is no natural means of verifying any of theology's affirmations—no such thing as the demonstration of God's existence. Tillich wants to replace this separation of natural and revealed theology by an incorporation of the philosophical element in natural theology into the structure of the system itself, 'using it as the material out of which questions are developed'. Similarly Tillich suggests that

[1] *Systematic Theology*, vol. I, p. 15.
[2] *Ibid.*, p. 17.   [3] *Ibid.*, pp. 32ff.

apologetic should not be regarded as a separate element of natural theology, but should rather be regarded as an omnipresent element of systematic theology. Finally, no more than apologetics should moral theology be made a special section of theology—an existential theology implies ethics in such a way as to make that unnecessary. For in every theological statement, Tillich thinks, the ethical is a necessary and often a fundamental element.

Furthermore, we inherit the basic structure of our theology since the task of systematic theology is to explain the contents of the Christian faith. Three questions immediately arise, therefore: What are the sources of systematic theology? What is the place of 'experience' in systematic theology? What is the norm by which these sources are to be interpreted? In addition to these questions there is the question of the general characterization of his method as 'method of correlation'.

Dealing with the sources of systematic theology, Tillich rejects what he calls 'the assertion of neo-orthodox biblicism' that the Bible is the *only* source. He maintains that the biblical message could not be understood and could never have been received had there not been preparation for it in human history. Since therefore, the biblical message embraces more than the biblical books, systematic theology has sources other than the Bible. This rejection of radical biblicism is welcome; for such a position opens the door to subjectivism and also denies the speculative character of theology. Yet the Bible, Tillich admits, is the basic course of systematic theology because it is the 'original document' about the events on which the Christian Church is founded. By 'original document' he seems to mean a document which is the testimony of an eyewitness inspired by his response to the happenings thus perceived as revealing events. But if it is true that his theology makes the Bible the chief source of doctrine why is it that the biblical affirmations are so little used? The biblical material is made available as a source of systematic theology by the biblical theologian who is concerned not with pure historical facts but with 'theologically interpreted facts'. In so far as the Bible is an event in Church history the systematic theologian

23

implicitly uses Church history when he uses the Bible. He must do this explicitly as well as implicitly. The relation of systematic theology to Church history is definite and direct, since our understanding of the Bible is founded on the understanding of previous generations. Together with Church history there is another historical source of systematic theology—the history of religions and culture, which is an analysis and exposition of the motives and types of religious expression, showing how these expressions follow from the nature of religious concern and how cultural phenomena are to be understood theologic-ally. The sources of systematic theology have, therefore, almost unlimited richness. The degree of importance which any particular source possesses corresponds to the directness or indirectness of its relationship to the central event on which the Christian faith is based, namely the appearance of Jesus Christ.

The medium through which we receive these sources is 'experience'. The question of experience has, therefore, been a central question whenever the nature and method of theology have been discussed. The early Franciscan theologians were, Tillich says, strictly experiential theologians; and the principle of experience survived in various forms until it received its classical expression in the theology of Schleiermacher. The crucial question for theology at the moment is whether the neo-orthodox abandonment of Schleiermacher's method is justified. Tillich does not accept a psychological interpretation of Schleiermacher's famous definition of religion as 'feeling of absolute dependence' and suggests that 'feeling' here is to be interpreted in the light of Schleiermacher's Augustinian herit-age in Moravianism and the philosophy of Spinoza and Schelling. Even so he admits that in *The Christian Faith* Schleier-macher went too far in trying to 'derive all the contents of the Christian faith from what he called the "religious conscious-ness" of the Christian'.[1] Tillich distinguishes three uses of the word experience—the ontological, the scientific and the mystical.[2] It is not at all clear that he achieves anything by this distinction; for he explains the first sense by referring to

[1] *Systematic Theology*, vol. I, pp. 47-8.
[2] *Ibid.*, p. 48.

philosophical positivism which would regard empirical data
as the only source of meaningful assertions but admits that in so
far as empirical theology makes 'experience' its criterion of
meaning it uses the word in the mystical sense. Similarly if the
second concept of experience as experimentally tested observations is used this presupposes the mystical sense. Therefore the
real problem for empirical theology is experience in the sense
of mystical experience. Here the danger is that of asserting that
the source of systematic theology is a religious experience which
transcends the Christian message as bound to the unique event
of Jesus the Christ. Tillich does not want to say this, but neither
does he want to adopt the neo-orthodox position of denying
that experience has any place in the method employed by
systematic theology. Experience is doubtless in some sense a
source but it is not the only source, and so he prefers to describe
it as the medium through which we are aware of the sources of
systematic theology. Christian theology, says Tillich, 'is based
on the unique event of Jesus the Christ'[1] and this event is
given to experience but is not derived from it.

If these are the sources of theology, what is its norm? The
necessity of such a norm is obvious in view of the variety of the
sources and the indefiniteness of the medium through which
they are received. The question of the norm of Christian doctrine is an old one which received what Tillich calls its material
answer in the creed. The formal answer was given in the
hierarchy of ecclesiastical authorities who were supposed to
safeguard the norm against heretical distortions. The Lutheran
Reformation broke with the Roman system by unearthing as
the material norm the Pauline doctrine of 'justification through
faith' and the biblical message as the formal norm. The growth
of norms is a historical process which is, for the most part,
unconscious. The norm must never be merely the private
opinion of a theologian but the expression of an encounter of
the Church with the Christian message. To the present situation which man experiences in despair and self-estrangement,
the Christian message comes as an answer in terms of what can
overcome such self-alienation, a reality of reconciliation and

[1] *Ibid.*, p. 52.

creativity. Therefore the norm of theology for our situation should be 'the New Being' in Jesus as the Christ.

Though it is not possible for us at this point to discuss Tillich's comments on the organization of theology in any detail, we can raise some general questions. For many of his readers Tillich seems to be avoiding the issue of natural theology by saying that it should be incorporated into the structure of the system. The problem in connection with natural theology is surely whether any exposition of theological statements does not commit a fallacy like that of naturalistic ethics. The same problem is raised by the suggestion about the place of apologetics, for it is open to question whether Tillich's use of philosophical notions in his explanation of Christian doctrine does not lead to this kind of fallacy. If apologetics means the translation of the Christian message into philosophical terms then it seems to be doing the same thing as the naturalistic fallacy. The third suggestion is more difficult to understand. It is clear that any Christian ethic rests upon a theological foundation, and every attempt to formulate principles of Christian morality independently of such a foundation has led to error. However this does not imply that there is no need for a special section of a systematic theology dealing with Christian ethics. Tillich's suggestion seems to be born of the confusion between saying that you cannot have Christian ethics without theology and that since you have theology you do not need Christian ethics. But could one not just as well say that as any Christian theology must imply consistent reference to the Incarnation we do not need a special section of theology which deals with Christology? Tillich's uneasiness at this point is evident from his admission that 'reasons of expediency may, nevertheless, justify the preservation of departments of Christian ethics'.[1] This seems to indicate that he is not prepared to legislate on this particular point of organization.

It is worth emphasizing that among the sources of theology reason was not included, because despite its important rôle in systematic theology it is not a source. Theology is rational, but is derived from reason. There are three senses of the word

[1] *Systematic Theology*, vol. I, p. 36.

'rational' in which it is true to say that theology is rational—the semantic, the logical and the methodological. The language that the theologian uses cannot be a sacred or revealed language and he must use whatever language is available. But he must make the meaning of the terms he uses clear. This seems to be what Tillich wants to say when he says that theology should be semantically rational. What his concept of meaning is he does not tell us. Nor does the following enunciation of this primary rationality of theology make it clearer: 'The principle of semantic rationality involves the demand that all connotations of a word should consciously be related to each other and centred around a controlling meaning.'[1] All we can safely say is that for Tillich the theologian is obliged to use language carefully and consistently, but it is most likely that more than this rather tame assertion is involved in his concept of semantic rationality.[2] Theology is also rational in the sense of being logical. Theology, says Tillich, 'is as dependent on formal logic as any other science'. He would defend this position against both philosophical and theological criticism. For such criticism would seem to imply that dialectical thinking is perforce opposed to formal logic; and this, thinks Tillich, is not the case. What happens, he says, is that a static ontology gives way to a dynamic one. It is very doubtful whether this way of putting things is either clear or useful. Indeed what Tillich seems mainly concerned with is the two different types of paradox which we may distinguish as material and metaphysical. A material paradox is such a sentence as 'It is raining and it isn't', spoken by someone on a showery day when it is not *really* raining and yet we would get wet if we went out of doors. This is the situation when there is no logical contradiction whereas in the metaphysical paradox there is logical contradiction. Tillich would say that all theological paradox is of the former type. Finally, theology is rational in so far as it is methodical. Once the method of theology is established it must be carried

---

[1] *Ibid.*, p. 62.
[2] Cf. the discussion of Tillich's view of philosophy later in this chapter and the fuller discussion of this point in my article, 'Some notes on the Theology of Paul Tillich', *Hibbert Journal*, April 1959.

through consistently and rationally. That is to say, theology must be systematic. Tillich defends the idea of a system by which he means something 'between *summa* and essay' against the many-sided attack to which it has been exposed.[1] First of all, he denies that 'system' must mean 'deductive system'. Such a system would be impossible in the case of theology because of the existential character of the Christian truth. He returns to this point at the beginning of the second volume of *Systematic Theology* where he describes the unity of the system as dynamic rather than deductive.[2] What this means is hard to say, but we may concede that a system need not be deductive and that what is necessary is that it should be a totality of consistent assertions. Similarly we can agree that a system need not be an obstacle to further research and that it can indeed stimulate research.

Tillich's description of experience as the medium through which we receive the sources of systematic theology, while in some ways a most commendable emphasis, is rather ambiguous. We cannot but agree when he says that to make experience a source of systematic theology would be to open the door to all kinds of heresy. For if our theology is Christian we are committed to the declaration that the revelation in Christ is final. Moreover, if we become too empirical in our theology we are in danger of making theological assertions something other than they are—to empty them, in fact, of their specifically theological content. Thus it is a sound instinct that makes Tillich describe experience as a medium rather than a source of systematic theology. Even so, one wonders what he means when he admits that the act of receiving the sources transforms them and goes on to say that, while the transformation must not be too great, it must not be so small as to result in a mere 'repetition'. This seems to give experience a degree of importance in relation to the sources of systematic theology which would tend to destroy the position that experience is not itself a source. What does Tillich mean when he says that experience 'transforms' the sources and that they should not be merely 'repeated'? The

[1] *Systematic Theology* I, p. 66.
[2] *Systematic Theology*, vol. II, London, Nisbet, 1957, pp. 3-4.

only thing we can suppose he means is that any doctrinal source must never be used merely as a source of information and to the extent that personal appropriation of the truth is necessary it is transformed. But this is a trivial point—as if we said that the sounds I hear now are in my ear and not outside on the street. This confusion is a result of Tillich's love of abstract formulations and his way of throwing in important qualifications of his position at the end of his discussion. In his exposition of these concise abstract formulations he is all too brief. Thus he does not give us sufficient illumination about the use of the norm in systematic theology. What does it mean to say that 'the New Being in Jesus as the Christ' is the norm of our theology? We can understand that Christology is a central doctrine, a doctrine indeed to which all other elements of Christian doctrine must by definition be related. But even so this does not make it the norm. That there should be a norm is obvious, and he does well to show that the development of theology is the history of the development of the various norms. Again, the brevity with which he enumerates his principle of the semantic rationality of theology leaves his notion of meaning unclear and does but hide the confusion in his thinking. He asserts that the principle demands that the various connotations of a word should be centred upon the controlling meaning. Now what 'controlling meaning' signifies it is hard to say. What it seems to mean is some kind of highest common factor of the connotations which thereby becomes the meaning of the terms. Semantic rationality is then assumed because all the connotations of the word will centre around this focus. This seems to be Tillich's position as far as we can gather from his description and the example he gives of how the term 'history' is employed in theology.[1] The rationality of this procedure, however, is a sheer illusion born of the confusion of similarity or identity of language with similarity or identity of meaning.

In his little book on biblical religion[2] Tillich sets himself to

[1] *Systematic Theology* I, p. 62.
[2] *Biblical Religion and the Search for Ultimate Reality*, Chicago and London, Univ. of Chicago Press and Nisbet, 1955 and 1956.

meet the criticism voiced by more than one reader—that the metaphysical character of his theology militates against the biblical emphases. The book is particularly interesting inasmuch as one feels that Tillich tries hard to put this objection in an even more radical form than that given it by his critics. Even so, one cannot help feeling that the whole thing is a sham battle, that the critics' problem is caricatured rather than admitted, that the argument moves inexorably towards its predetermined conclusion. What gives rise to this feeling is both the method of meeting the criticism—that is, the technique of calling for definitions—and the actual content of his definition of philosophy. One would search this book in vain for any mention of the discussion of religious problems which has figured prominently in English philosophy since 1950. Rather, Tillich avoids the concrete encounter of philosophers and theologians and asks how to define philosophy. The definition he gives—'that cognitive endeavour in which the question of being is asked'[1]—is very important because it is one of the two premises in his argument that philosophy and theology are necessarily related. The other premiss is his description of the philosophical attitude. This, he says, engages two aspects of man's mind. First, man philosophizes because of his thirst for knowledge—he discovers things, describes them and abandons descriptions in the light of further investigation. The philosopher seeks those abiding principles called categories and ultimately he seeks Being itself. However, the second element or aspect is the driving force—the existential element. 'It is always a driving force in the depths of his being that makes the philosopher a philosopher.'[2] This existential element is, for Tillich, some kind of religious impulse.

Having exposed the bare bones of the book let us see how Tillich clothes them with flesh. He begins with an analysis of the biblical religion. Since it is essentially mysterious it expresses the distance between God and man—God calls man into being. Thus it is a personal religion where God's will is always revealed to man through persons. When man encounters

[1] *Biblical Religion and the Search for Ultimate Reality*, p. 5. Cf. p. 13.
[2] *Ibid.*, p. 19.

God it is a Person who is encountered. This Person is active in history, and the stories of his activity make up the Bible. Because the Bible is interested in the history of salvation the picture of history that is presented therein is neither the expression of man's potentialities nor the fateful development and decline of man but rather the new creation; for in Christ the New Being manifested itself in the world and through this history has meaning. The biblical picture of the human situation is that man faces a choice: to decide for or against Christ. In this way the Bible recognizes our personal nature. God's purpose in history is the redemption of individuals—not as individuals but as citizens of his Kingdom. Man's moral existence and his social existence, according to the Bible, are based on his religious existence, on faith. 'Faith is the concern about our existence in its ultimate "whence" and "whither".'[1] It is the activity within us of the Divine Spirit—not believing something incredible but an act of the whole personality. The faith spoken of in the Bible is always the faith of a society or nation or church. Anyone who wishes to belong must accept faith's assertions, that is, the society's creed, before he can be a member. This can mean a real personal submission or merely an intellectual assent. Thus the word 'faith' diminishes in meaning from being the state of being grasped by an ultimate concern to be a number of doctrines. Such a tendency can be seen within the Bible because it represents the faith of a particular community, namely the early Church. However, if this is what is meant by 'faith' there is no possibility of achieving a synthesis between it and the scepticism that is characteristic of ontology. Thus there seems to be no room for the Bible in ontology and so Tillich argues that we must ask once more whether it is possible to harmonize these two different ways. So unlikely seems the possibility that it looks as if we are forced to choose between them. However, neither is sufficient of itself— neither irrational religion nor irreligious reason is a service to truth. Therefore we must try again, and Tillich suggests that the quest of a new synthesis is unavoidable. The way to do this is to ask whether the biblical ideas and attitudes have

[1] *Ibid.*, p. 51.

consequences which not only admit but even demand this synthesis. The other side of this problem is the question whether the consequences of ontology do not lead it to the concern of biblical religion. It is at this point that Tillich's definition of philosophy plays an important rôle. Philosophy contains an existential element—the philosopher is driven forward by an infinite anxiety about Being. But does not this reveal faith? For does not faith also mean such an ultimate concern? This is indeed what the biblical faith is. Therefore the search for ultimate reality and faith are identical in this respect. Faith is thus on the path of the question concerning ultimate reality whether it does actually ask the question or not. Only if he is Ultimate Reality can God be an ultimate concern. Finally, faith and doubt are not opposed but faith includes doubt, and so once more ontology and the biblical religion meet.

This discussion of *Biblical Religion and the Search for Ultimate Reality* has revealed the method of correlation that Tillich employs. The reason why he adopts this method is that he wishes to combine kerygmatic and apologetic theology. This method, he says, 'explains the contents of the Christian faith through existential questions and theological answers in interdependence'.[1] The analysis of the 'situation' constitutes a 'philosophical task'. The answers cannot be inferred from the questions but must be provided by the Christian message; 'they are "spoken" to human existence' from beyond it—from the final revelation in Jesus as the Christ. However, if the *content* of the answers is derived from revelation, their *form* is dependent on the structure of the questions which they answer. Since the form of the 'answers' is determined by the philosophical analysis of the situation, the way in which that analysis is conceived is important for any evaluation of Tillich's method. What then is Tillich's view of philosophy and its relation to theology? He begins by noting that 'there is no generally accepted definition of philosophy'. The fact that he should be concerned to obtain a definition of philosophy is a clue as to the method he considers appropriate in philosophy and

[1] *Systematic Theology* I, p. 68.

reveals his belief that clarity is obtained by definition. So he proposes his own definition of philosophy—'that cognitive approach to reality in which reality as such is the object'. On this view, then, philosophy is a description of reality as such. It is not exactly the view of philosophy that Tillich would have been taught as a student. For at that time the 'phenomenology' of Edmund Husserl was the dominant fashion in German philosophy.[1] Husserl was profoundly influenced by Brentano, who gave him the courage to choose philosophy as a profession, and the influence of Brentano's logical theories can be seen from Husserl's early opposition to symbolic logic.[2] It was from Brentano's psychology that Husserl derived his important doctrine of intentionality, with its guiding principle that 'consciousness is always consciousness of something.' Husserl rejects psychology as the basis of logic and stresses the autonomous ideal of logic.[3] Yet he holds that the meaning of logical propositions can only be revealed by going back to those acts of consciousness in which this meaning is 'constituted'. That is, these acts of consciousness are held to be correlated with objective contents, the essences or 'structures' of which may be revealed to disinterested reflection. Thus these structures are known by a pure act of understanding. Philosophy is a science of essences which, though it is *the* universal science and, in a radical sense, an exact science, does not preserve the common-sense point of view of empirical science. Husserl distinguishes between transcendental phenomenology and descriptive

---

[1] Edmund G. A. Husserl was born at Prossnitz in Moravia in 1859, and was educated at the Universities of Berlin and Vienna. Originally a student of mathematics he became increasingly interested in philosophy. He returned to Berlin in 1882 to be an assistant to Weierstrass. When the latter became sick in 1883 Husserl was left free and he seized the opportunity to study philosophy. He returned to Vienna and there came under the influence of Brentano, and from Vienna went to Halle where in 1887 he became a Privatdozent of Philosophy and Professor in 1894. He moved to Gottingen in 1901 and to Freiburg in 1916. His *Ideas* (1931) forms a general introduction to Phenomenology, but his *Meditations Cartésiennes* (1931) is the best introduction to his thought as a whole.

[2] 'Die Folgerungscalcul und die Inhaltslogik', *Vierteljahrsschrift fur Wissenschaftliche Philosophie*, 15, pp. 168-89.

[3] See *Logische Untersuchungen*, vol. I.

(phenomenological) psychology.[1] Philosophy, as a science of essences, is a production of the anonymous consciousness containing the foundation of all our experience and all science. So Husserl describes his philosophy as a kind of idealism which declares 'every form of current philosophical realism to be in principle absurd, as no less every idealism to which in its own arguments that realism stands contrasted'.[2] The influence of this kind of philosophy on Tillich is seen in his vision of philosophy as indeed some kind of exact science.[3] But he cannot be called a Phenomenologist. What he does in his interpretation of philosophy is to fuse the phenomenological view of philosophy with some kind of Absolute Idealism. So without abandoning his phenomenological heritage Tillich can maintain that philosophy is an understanding of 'being as such' or 'reality as a whole'. These very terms reveal how Tillich fuses different philosophical traditions; for the former is Aristotelian whereas the latter is borrowed from nineteenth-century Idealism. All these various traditions are then harmonized in this view of philosophy as a systematic exposition of the nature of reality. Thus he says:

> 'Philosophy asks the ultimate question that can be asked, namely, the question as to what being, simply being, means. Whatever the object of thought may be, it is always something that *is* and not *not is*. But what does this word "is" mean? What is the meaning of being? . . . This question and the shock with which it holds us . . . is . . . the root of philosophy. For philosophy asks the question concerning being itself. . . . Therefore, all philosophers have developed a "first philosophy", as Aristotle calls it, namely, an interpretation of being.'[4]

He proceeds to defend this representation of philosophy against three possible criticisms.[5] First, it may be said that this implies a return to old-fashioned metaphysics. This criticism, says

---

[1] Cf. *Ideas*, p. 13. [2] *Ibid.*, p. 19.
[3] Thus Rhein says (*op. cit.*, pp. 42-3) that Tillich follows a phenomenological tradition and that a phenomenological element is constantly found in his work.
[4] *Protestant Era*, pp. 95-6. [5] *Ibid.*, pp. 96-7.

Tillich, would seem to regard metaphysics as being something beyond human experience, a product of purely arbitrary imagination. To preserve our intellectual good name, however, let us abandon the term metaphysics so that we may show that the question of being is the question of 'what is nearer to us than anything else'. Secondly, it might be argued that this picture of philosophy is untrue in so far as it fails to recognize the primacy of epistemology in the field of philosophy. This criticism Tillich admits to be correct to a certain extent, but he contends that epistemology is impossible without an ontology. 'Epistemology is wrong only if it pretends that it can exist without an ontological basis.' Lastly, it might be said that 'there is no approach for man to the structure and meaning of being, that what being is, is revealed to us in the manifoldness of beings and in the world in which they are all united and inter-related to one another'.

Let us consider these three criticisms and Tillich's answers. It is interesting to see him anxious to repudiate the charge that he is reverting to old-fashioned metaphysics. The sin of any philosophy is not so much that it is wrong as that it is out of date, and it had become a commonplace of our philosophical talk to say that metaphysics is out of date. But will Tillich's remedy do? What can he hope to achieve by abandoning the name if the business he carries out is the same? What we need is not only a new proprietor for our philosophical shop but also a new method of business. We must recognize that to call metaphysics old-fashioned or nonsensical is worse than a cliché—it is itself nonsense. Nevertheless, it will not do to imagine that we have escaped the charge of transcendentalism if we say that the object of philosophy is 'we ourselves as far as we are and . . . able to ask what it means that we are'. McTaggart defined metaphysics as 'the systematic study of the nature of ultimate reality'.[1] This has been the intention of all the classical metaphysicians from Plato to Bradley, and Tillich seems to be undertaking exactly the same task.

The second criticism is likewise left unanswered in the end. For what Tillich does here is to take the point of the criticism

[1] McTaggart, *Some Dogmas of Religion*, p. 1.

and turn it upon itself as its rebuttal. This point is that if ontological assertions are true, epistemological ones are also true. We might say that they have the same logic, and by this we would mean that there is no evidence relevant to the first which is not relevant to the second. If therefore we say that philosophy is primarily concerned with questions of epistemology as against ontology we are not denying that knowledge-statements imply reality-statements. Rather what we are doing is making the point once more that questions of philosophy are not decided by more information, that philosophy is not concerned with the description of the real. Tillich's remarks about the 'breakdown of the epistemological period of philosophy in the last decades' serve only to reveal his ignorance of the fruitful work done as a result of the 'revolution in philosophy'. His answer therefore makes no point against the criticism.

The third criticism and answer are difficult to handle because it is not very clear what the point is here. As far as we can see, what the imaginary critic means is that you cannot speak of being itself but only of particular beings. If this is indeed what is meant then it must be admitted to be true. The only use that the phrase 'being itself' can be said to have is that of a shorthand expression for the manifoldness of beings. Therefore to speak of 'being-itself' as something over and above particular beings is to commit a category mistake. It is very like the man who, on being shown the Colleges of Cambridge, asks, 'But where is the University?' Therefore Tillich's answer to this criticism does not meet the real point at all. What is revealed here is something we have seen in dealing with Tillich's answer to the first criticism, namely the confusion in Tillich's understanding of this fundamental concept in his philosophical theology, the concept of being. He is right in saying that the meaning of being is man's basic concern if this means that we are driven to ask the question, 'What is the meaning of our existence?'; but he is quite wrong in his assumption that this makes statements about the being 'in' man or the world at all meaningful.[1] Again he is quite wrong when he accuses his critic of being a dictator because the critic denies him the right

[1] *Protestant Era*, p. 97.

to use this form of language until he admits that it is not ordinary language.

That there is an object which philosophy studies is the fallacy which is revealed again in Tillich's more recent publications. For example, when he discusses the question of the relation between theology and philosophy in volume I of *Systematic Theology*, he begins by saying that theology deals with a special object, and this claim to the status of a realm of knowledge places it under the obligation of giving an account of its relation to other forms of knowledge. That we are right in assuming this to imply that philosophy too has an object becomes evident when we see that he proposes to '*call philosophy that cognitive approach to reality in which reality as such is the object*'. This refusal to see that philosophy is to be distinguished from other arts or sciences by its method rather than its subject-matter, that indeed there is no special subject-matter to philosophy, is the basic fallacy in Tillich's understanding of the nature of philosophy. His notion of what philosophy is results from the domination of the model of science which leads him to imagine that philosophy is concerned with information just as science is. The scientist is concerned with giving us the best explanation of phenomena, that is, the most economical description of them. The philosopher according to Tillich's view does very much the same thing, for he too describes reality. The difference is that he does this job in a bigger and better way than the scientist. It is the whole of reality that he describes. This domination of the model of science is the source of a double confusion because of Tillich's strange view of the nature of scientific method. In so far as he is guided by a passion for truth, says Tillich, the philosopher is no different from the scientist. But the scientist is not interested in truth; his business is to find the most likely and useful hypothesis to explain certain phenomena. The criterion by which we judge a hypothesis is that of range of predictability. If two theories are equally good from this point of view what makes us accept the one rather than the other is elegance. The philosopher collaborates with the scientist, says Tillich, and is to a certain extent dependent on what the scientist does. He admits that

the philosopher neither criticises nor augments the knowledge provided by the sciences. Yet the knowledge thus gained
is 'the basis of his description of the categories, structural laws,
and concepts which constitute the structure of being'. Now this
is very strange indeed, and one can only believe that we are
now once more faced with this picture of the philosopher as the
super-scientist. Professor John Wisdom once said that if he were
asked which was the more important for philosophy—science
or fairy-tales—he would have no hesitation in replying that
fairy-tales were. By this beautifully eccentric remark Wisdom
sought to make clear that philosophy is not at all like science.
What the scientist does is to reduce the description of facts to
as few concepts as possible, but this sort of explanation does
not concern the philosopher. The sort of 'explanation' he is
concerned with is more like a logical analysis. Tillich is aware
of a difference between science and philosophy which is
connected with this opposition of logic and fact, but he is too
fascinated by the model of science to abandon the view that
philosophy is a matter of hypothesis and proof. This tendency
is seen again in the distinction he draws between philosophical
assertions and theological ones, saying that the former are
cosmological whilst the latter are soteriological. 'The philosopher deals with the categories of being in relation to the
material which is structured by them.' It is not very clear to us
what this means. The only meaning we can see in this is that
if one speaks about the categories of being then one must speak
of the way in which concrete language is used and how this
language fits into other languages making one common world
of experience. We have already seen, however, that Tillich
would deny this, and so once more we are back with transcendentalism. The philosopher looks at 'the whole of reality in
order to discover the structure of reality as a whole'. How 'the
whole of reality' differs from 'reality as a whole' it is difficult to
say. Tillich speaks of an identity or at least an analogy 'between
the *logos* of reality as a whole and the *logos* working in (the philosopher)'. This is some unintelligible form of idealism. What is
so very baffling about this is that Tillich goes on to say that the
place where philosophy stands is no place at all—it is pure

reason. But if the work of philosophy is one of pure reason, what has the philosopher to do with the identity that he has mentioned? The clear intention of that remark is that of indicating the rationality of reality as a whole which is meant to be the discovery of the philosopher. The philosopher looks at the universal *logos*, we are told. And once again the strange confusion of logic and fact in Tillich's interpretation of philosophy comes to light. 'It seems to me', he says, 'that the oldest definition given to philosophy is, at the same time, the newest and that which always was and always will be valid: Philosophy is that cognitive endeavour in which the question of being is asked. . . . It is the simplest, most profound, and absolutely inexhaustible question—the question of what it means to say that something *is*. This word "is" hides the riddle of all riddles, the mystery that there is anything at all.'[1] He contends that ontology is not the creation of imaginary worlds or trans-empirical realities. But if the philosopher 'looks at' something which is neither transempirical nor any special being then we must confess that we are at a loss to understand what Tillich means. It seems to us that he is forced to describe philosophy then either as an empirical science or as some peculiar *a priori* science. The fallacy of this position is what we have singled out before, namely the misconception that philosophy has a special object of study and is in essence like science though it is more general. It is true that one of the most difficult problems of philosophy is that of seeing what we mean when we say that something is real. To grasp the nature of the question 'Is the sense-datum real?' and again the nature of the question asked by a man in the desert 'Is the water I see over there real?'— this is indeed philosophy. But what exactly are we doing? Are we describing the real? Only in a very odd way, for our description will not fill out any description which we already have. The point of talking about philosophy as concerned with reality is threefold. First, it reminds us that language always points to a concrete situation. In discussing anything in philosophy there is little progress made unless we realize that words are not depositories of hypostatic meaning but refer to the

[1] *Biblical Religion and the Search for Ultimate Reality*, p. 5.

concrete situations in terms of which words must always be 'cashed'. This is what Wittgenstein meant by his now famous injunction, 'Do not ask for the meaning. Ask for the use.' Secondly, it does not follow from the fact that philosophical theories are not tested by observation and are therefore neutral with regard to matters of fact that philosophy is concerned with facts. Finally, besides the critical, puzzle-mongering aspect of philosophy, there is a synoptic and constructive aspect as well. The philosopher is not content to investigate the questions that puzzle the experts each on its own merits. He is anxious to find connections between them, to generalize, to build bridges between various fields of study and between various areas of human interest such as art, morality and religion and science. And this not only can be done but must be done by the philosopher in the fulfilment of his task. Generalizing the methods proved successful in one field may suggest ways of tackling problems in very different fields, as for example Descartes found.

If we talk of philosophy as description, however, we shall have to admit that it is a description of a particular kind. To this Tillich might reply that it is indeed this—that particular kind of description which is a description of reality as a whole. The question is, then, what we mean when we talk of 'reality'. The noun 'reality' is a word we learn to use only after we have become familiar with such words as 'real' and 'really'. Moreover, there are various contexts in which we meet the expression 'really this'—e.g., the scientific, the moral and the artistic. Let us look at these uses of the word so that we shall be able to come back to the definition of philosophy as a study of reality and estimate its significance. The scientist will say that the stick which in water looks as if it were bent is 'really' straight. The moralist will say that even though giving money to an alcoholic beggar appears to be an act of kindness it is not 'really' good or right. Then the artist will say that though we may think Gauguin's use of colour is wild it is 'really' a beautiful colour effect that is achieved. It would be a mistake to imagine that the word had the same meaning in these three contexts. Nor again can we as it were obtain a lowest common denominator by saying that what a thing is really is what it is like as a part of reality. For the reality in one context differs from the reality in another context. If we walk through the woods with two friends one of whom is an artist and the other a scientist and we discuss the colour of the sky we shall find that the two cannot agree about the 'reality'. 'Look at the sky through this foliage', says the artist, 'and you will see that it is a deeper blue than is the sky yonder'. Here the physicist interjects, 'But look here, you don't mean to say that the sky here is a deeper blue than it is over there. It is simply an optical illusion.' The artist will not have this and replies, 'Can't you see that it is a deeper blue? If this is not a deeper blue than that then I don't khow what is.' We see at once the completely different standpoints of the artist and the scientist. For the former it is what he *sees* that is of decisive importance whereas for the scientist how the thing looks is precisely what he discounts as irrelevant. Therefore the way in which the artist draws the distinction between what is 'really' and what is not 'really' something is very different from the way in which the scientist draws the distinction. And since they draw the distinction on different grounds it is nonsense to say that either the artist is right or the scientist is. In this way the demand for an unambiguous answer as to what is really so-and-so can lose all meaning. And as with 'really' so with 'reality'. As has been well said, reality is a blessed word, and did we not possess it in our language we should have had to invent it; but when the philosopher looks at it closely, tears it from its context and asks himself 'Now what is reality?' he has successfully manoeuvred himself into an impossible position.

The importance of this definition of philosophy in Tillich's thought is that it enables him to go on to show that philosophy and theology are therefore necessarily correlated if not indeed identical—at least in some respects.[1] This is what he says:

'Philosophy necessarily asks the question of reality as a whole, the question of the structure of being. Theology necessarily asks the same question, for that which concerns us ultimately must

[1] Cf. Rhein's discussion of this as 'The question of reality in both [philosophy and theology]' (*op. cit.*, pp. 76f.).

belong to reality as a whole; it must belong to being. . . . The structure of being and the categories and concepts describing this structure are an implicit or explicit concern of every philosopher and of every theologian.'[1]

What Tillich has done here is to define both philosophy and theology in the same way and then to deduce that every theologian must be concerned with the basic question of philosophy. But this is really nothing more than a tautology, since the truth of the statement follows from the definition of the terms. It is exactly like a mathematical formula such as 'X = Y and Z = Y so that X = Z.' The correlation that Tillich wants to establish has been put beyond all doubt; for if anything is theology then what makes it theology also makes it philosophy. It may be suggested that we are doing violence to Tillich's argument since it is not so completely formal and empty as we make it. True, his next step in the argument of this section is to show how philosophy and theology are related and how they differ. But even within this attempt to give the iautology content we have the same recourse to the cast-iron certainty of the tautology. He says that 'every creative philosopher is a hidden theologian.' The reasons Tillich gives for this statement are the following: (i) the philosopher 'exists' and he is conditioned by his psychological, sociological and historical situation. (ii) He exists in the power of 'an ultimate concern, whether or not he is fully conscious of it, whether or not he admits it to himself and to others'. (iii) His intuition of the universal *logos* of the structure of reality as a whole is 'formed by a particular *logos* which appears to him in his particular place and reveals to him the meaning of the whole'. (iv) This particular *logos* is a matter of active commitment within a special community. If we examine these reasons we see that Tillich interprets the philosopher's 'existence' as being essentially a religious matter, for otherwise the first reason is not at all relevant. But if he does so interpret it then he is saying nothing more than that a philosopher who has a religious concern will be likely to hide (or he may reveal) in his metaphysics a theology. However, this does not mean that this is essential to philosophy. The same

[1] *Systematic Theology* I, p. 24.

movement of argument by definition is revealed in the third and fourth reasons, for here again the point is that the definition of the philosopher corresponds with that of the theologian. The meaning of the remarks about active commitment is not clear, but as far as we can judge what Tillich is saying is something like this. Since theology is the study of reality which has as its object the real which is related to it existentially, then philosophy which is also the study of reality becomes theology whenever it has any existential concern. But this is true only as a matter of definition, and one wonders whether Tillich is prepared to maintain the converse of this thesis and say that when he expounds Christianity sometimes he is expounding universal and philosophical truths. Furthermore, the meaning of these terms has been legislated unnecessarily so that it is misleading rather than helpful. Jean-Paul Sartre is a philosopher who would reveal all these characteristics. But if we call Sartre a theologian then we must introduce so many caveats when we go on to say that Karl Barth and Emil Brunner are theologians that our language becomes complicated beyond reason. It is therefore best that the term be not defined in this way. It is like saying that a dog is an animal with four legs, a furry coat and a tail, and that in so far as a cat has these characteristics, it is a dog!

Tillich's definition of theology likewise gives erroneous expression to a valuable emphasis. His existentialist emphasis (to use a not very elegant term) is clearly both important and valuable. Theology has always had to face this question since the New Testament; even so, theologians have not been willing to go over the dead bones of their scholarship to search diligently for that life which was to bring them together. They have been so loath to discuss the nature of their undertaking that recently philosophers have evinced almost more interest in the nature of theology than have the theologians. In this situation Tillich's work is very welcome, for not only does he show enough courage to ask what the nature and method of theology is but he emphasises the necessity for commitment in theological undertaking. Where his emphasis goes wrong is in its metaphysical colouring, because he forces it into the logical mould of the deduction he makes. Thus he brings about a correlation which is nothing more than a linguistic *tour de force*. It is also important to notice a danger that lies hidden in this wholesome emphasis. If theology is possible only when there is commitment then it might become a series of assertions whose main reference is to the theologian. This is not quite the criticism that Karl Barth levelled against Schleiermacher and Ritschl though that is a perfectly good point in its original context and may even be a proper criticism of Tillich's description of theology as the theologian expressing his 'ultimate concern'. The point here is that theology is as intellectual and rational a discipline as any other. To say that the theologian is determined by his faith can thus be misleading, for though it is true that the theologian uses concepts which have a tremendous personal significance for him, he is concerned to talk some kind of sense with them and certainly to talk sense about them. Thus Anselm's formula '*Credo ut intelligam*' has always been characteristic of the mood of theology and an expression of its essential movement, the movement from pure personal concern to understanding. So long as a man is simply committed, so long he need not be a theologian. To risk a dangerous statement, let us say that he is a theologian when he turns his attention to the concepts.

One other point must be discussed before we leave this subject, and that is what Tillich has to say about the possibility of a conflict between philosophy and theology. He denies the necessity of such a conflict. 'A conflict', he says, 'presupposes a common basis on which to fight. But there is no common basis between theology and philosophy.'[1] This is very difficult to understand in view of what Tillich has to say about the correlation of the two subjects, and anyway it seems very odd. When the theologian says something about God he is claiming that he knows something, and the philosopher who is concerned with the puzzle of knowledge instantly recognizes that the theologian's knowledge is different from any other. Tillich may say that he is quarrelling with the theologian (assuming that there is a conflict) about a philosophical matter. This is really

[1] *Systematic Theology* I, p. 30.

too simple—for the nature of the theologian's knowledge is as much his concern as it is the philosopher's. Tillich himself has given an instance of the possibility of skirmishing on the border-line of philosophy and theology in his discussion of the nature of theology and its proper method. The whole question of theological discourse and its relation to religious language is the No Man's Land where theologians and philosophers meet and either agree or conflict.

The method of correlation, then, is a courageous attempt to bring philosophy and theology closer together; but it is an attempt that is vitiated by certain fundamental confusions which we have tried to lay bare.[1] Nevertheless, Tillich has made us raise once more in a pointed way the question 'What is theology and how is it related to the philosopher's task?' Despite the difficulties there is something refreshing about Tillich's bold conception of philosophy in the classical manner and this view of philosophy is a healthy emphasis. Tillich is assuredly right in thinking that there is more to philosophy than logical analysis of language, and it is regrettable that his refusal to see that this is nevertheless part of the description of philosophy blunts the edge of this criticism.

[1] Rhein rather strangely asserts the impossibility of understanding Tillich's theology without accepting Tillich's assumption that philosophy and theology cannot conflict (see *op. cit.*, p. 180). The inadequacy of Tillich's attempt to maintain this has been very forcefully pointed out by Marvin Fox in his article, 'Tillich's Ontology and God' (*Anglican Theological Review*, July 1961, p. 267): 'Tillich seems to me to be striving mightily to walk on two fences at once. One fence is named "ontology" and the other "Christianity". Unhappily while these fences are occasionally at a close and manageable distance, they are more often far apart and even turn in opposite directions. Tillich, with all his agility, cannot help falling in between. He struggles, with desperation, to hold on to both fences, at least with his finger-tips. But, having failed, he tries to build a new fence which will be easier to walk along. I am not sure what this new fence should be named. I only know that none of the old names fits.'

II

THE DOCTRINE OF GOD AND REVELATION

As we have seen, Tillich's method in theology is empirical in the sense that he does not approach the central problem of theology by asking 'What is God?' but rather by asking 'What is holy?' According to his own method of correlation his starting-point must be the question developed by an analysis of the human situation. So he begins by analysing man's cognitive situation, his 'cognitive rationality' and the question implied in the finitude, self-estrangement and the ambiguities of reason. Then he seeks to give the answer to this question, which is Revelation.

Tillich distinguishes two concepts of reason[1]—the ontological and the technical, of which the former predominates in 'the classical tradition from Parmenides to Hegel' while the latter has been predominant since the breakdown of German classical idealism. According to the classical philosophical tradition reason is 'the structure of the mind which enables the mind to grasp and to transform reality'.[2] The technical concept of reason reduces it to the capacity for 'reasoning'. Only the cognitive side of the classical concept of reason remains and 'the non-cognitive sides of reason have been confined to the irrelevance of pure subjectivity.'[3] Technical reason, says Tillich, is adequate and meaningful only as an expression of metaphysical reason and as its companion. So theology is not forced to make a decision for or against one of these two concepts of reason. It uses technical reason in its method but it rejects the confusion of technical with ontological reason. The traditional

[1] *Systematic Theology* I, pp. 79-83. 'Ecstatic reason' (see below, p. 49) is not a 'concept of reason' but a 'state of reason'.
[2] *Ibid.*, p. 80.   [3] *Ibid.*, p. 81.

46

question of the relation of reason to revelation should not, therefore, be discussed on the level of technical reason, for where technical reason prevails religion is 'superstition . . . foolishly supported by reason or rightly removed by it'.[1] It is only on the level of ontological reason, of reason in the sense of *logos*, that there is a genuine problem of the relation of reason to revelation. However, to distinguish ontological reason from technical reason is not enough for theology. It is also necessary to distinguish ontological reason in its essential perfection from ontological reason within life and history. 'From the time of Parmenides' says Tillich, 'it has been a common assumption of all philosophers that the *logos*, the word which grasps and shapes reality, can do so only because reality itself has a *logos* character.'[2] But reason in its objective and subjective structure points to something which appears in these structures but which transcends them in power and meaning. So Tillich talks of the 'depth of reason', and again he speaks of 'ecstatic reason' which is one's capacity for receiving revelation rationally.

It is these last two senses of 'reason' that are most important for Tillich's discussion of revelation and we shall now examine these more closely. What Tillich means by the depth of reason is indicated by what he says about Kant's doctrine of the categories which he describes as a doctrine of human finitude.

> 'By analysing the categorical structure of reason man discovers the finitude in which he is imprisoned. He also discovers that his reason does not accept this bondage and tries to grasp the infinite with the categories of finitude, the really real with the categories of experience, and that necessarily fails. The only point at which the prison of finitude is open is the realm of moral experience, because in it something unconditional breaks into the whole of temporal and crucial conditions. But this point which Kant reaches is nothing more than a point, an unconditional command, a mere awareness of the depth of reason.'[3]

Tillich is not any more willing a prisoner of finitude than Kant because like Kant he has the sense of the importance of the unconditioned. This haunting claim cannot be identified with the importance of any *object*, and is connected with what

[1] *Systematic Theology* I, p. 82.   [2] *Ibid.*, p. 83.   [3] *Ibid.*, p. 91.

Tillich calls 'the ground of our being'. He uses the term 'ground', he says, because he does not want to use words like 'cause' and 'substance' which suggest categories of the human mind. What he has to say about the 'depth of reason' is relevant here:

> 'The depth of reason is the expression of something that is not reason, but which precedes reason and is manifest through it. Reason in both its objective and its subjective structures points to something which appears in these structures but which transcends them in power and meaning. This is not another field of reason which could progressively be discovered and expressed, but it is that which is expressed through every rational expression. It could be called the "substance" which appears in the rational structure, or "being-itself" which is manifest in the *logos* of being, or the "ground" which is creative in every rational creation, or the "abyss" which cannot be exhausted by any creation or by any totality of them, or the "infinite potentiality of being and meaning" which pours into the rational structures of mind and reality, actualizing and transforming them. All these terms which point to that which "precedes" reason have a metaphorical character. "Preceding" is itself metaphorical. This is necessarily so, because if the terms were used in their proper sense they would belong to reason and would not precede it.'[1]

Tillich's point in this paragraph is far from clear. He seems only to be making a point often made—that reality is beyond reason and cannot be summed up even in an infinite number of propositions. Yet there may be something more than this trite observation here. When he talks of the 'depth of reason' he may mean that there is something about rational expressions which indicates a meaning beyond what it expresses. There is also a quest for perfection in reason which could only be achieved in an intuitive union with reality. Tillich holds that 'essentially' this should be possible; reason and reality should be one. But under the conditions of human knowledge we cannot have this intuitive union. 'Essentially reason is transparent towards its depths in each of its acts and processes. In existence this transparency is opaque and is replaced by myth

---

[1] *Systematic Theology* I, p. 88.

and cult.' But if we were to ask how we know that there is essentially this union, that the law of reason is the law of nature within mind and reality, it does not seem that Tillich has any answer other than that this is what was held by the philosophers in the 'classical tradition'. Tillich never discusses this central epistemological difficulty and seems to be content to justify his position by appealing to the classical tradition as an authority. Yet when he contrasts philosophy with theology he says that the 'autonomous' reason rightly rejects any alien authority, but he does not admit that when reason thus asserts its autonomy it denies the 'depth of reason'. A reason which was subject to no alien authority, but which, instead of just following its own internal laws, expressed in passionate devotion the nature of reality beyond itself would be not autonomous or heteronomous but 'theonomous'. Why the term 'theonomous' is appropriate here it is difficult to understand. The only reason seems to be that the term 'being' is used both of the object of philosophy and of the nature of God, as we saw in our discussion of the method of correlation.

Tillich holds that the 'ontological reason' contains at least two unresolved conflicts within itself. There is the conflict between the demand for theoretical detachment and the demand for some kind of union with the object of knowledge, the conflict, that is, between detached knowledge and cognitive participation. This is the result of his interpretation of philosophy on the model of science and is really an exaggeration. For there is no reason to suppose that philosophy should essentially be a dispassionate study. It is even possible for the philosopher to be passionately engaged in the task of being dispassioned; and, after all, philosophy is a matter of the heart and not only the head. The second conflict in a way includes the first but is by far the more significant. This conflict is the split between the autonomy of reason, its demand for completion, and the recognition in the depth of reason that whatever we say about reality is said in abstractions and always leaves more to be said. We discover this, says Tillich, by a scrutiny of the actual conditions under which our reason works. This conflict is never finally soluble under these conditions. The question it raises is that of the selectiveness of our thinking, because of the limitations of the actual situations in which we think and which form the basis of our thinking. When Tillich says that a philosophy is creative in so far as it is driven by feeling, he is pointing at something more important than any superficial conflict of thought and feeling. He is really saying that there are certain experiences about which we get excited because they are somehow metaphysically significant. The question then is how we are to recognize such significance, why these experiences rather than some others should be thus selected. This is the question of the relation of reason to the 'depth of reason' and it may become a question of the competence of any form of reason other than the technical reason. Putting the question in another way, what we are asking is whether we can by our thinking know anything about reality. In this context the idea of revelation is relevant.

Revelation is the occurrence of an event which evokes 'numinous astonishment', by which term he means the feeling of being in the grip of a mystery, yet elated with awe. This kind of experience Tillich calls 'ecstasy', a state of reason rather than emotion, in which reason transcends its normal subject-object structure. Ecstatic reason is not the destruction of reason, but reason raised to a more creative level, in which there is no distinction between detached knowing and cognitive participation. The ecstatic reason is the subjective side of a situation in which some event occurs which evokes it and which we may then call a 'sign event'. The occurrence of this whole situation is revelation. The vehicle of revelation is an experience which is charged with the sense of the mystery of existence. The sign event may be historical happenings, happenings in nature, or in the lives of saints 'whose faith and love can become sign events for those who are grasped by their power of creativity'. In one sense the sign event is an empirical fact, but the ecstatic reason finds a particular significance in it because it is somehow linked with our 'ultimate concern'. This phrase not only indicates the mystery of our continued existence but also what is fundamental or ultimately important in the character of our existence. Revelation, then, consists in the whole constellation of sign events as grasped by ecstatic reason, conveying a sense of ultimate concern.

Tillich distinguishes between original and dependent revelations.[1] An original revelation 'is a revelation which occurs in a constellation that did not exist before'. This miracle and this ecstasy are 'joined for the first time'. In a dependent revelation the two factors are not pure miracle on the one hand and its pure ecstatic reception on the other, but rather the original miracle, together with its original reception, form the first element, while the second is a variable factor changing as new individuals and groups receive the revelation. Tillich takes as an example the confession of Jesus as the son of the living God which Peter made. This, he says, was an original revelation; but the confession of following generations has been a confession of the Jesus who had been received as the Christ by Peter and the other Apostles. There is continuous revelation in the history of the Church, but it is dependent revelation. The relation of Church history to revelation, therefore, is very similar to the relation of experience to the sources of systematic theology. 'Jesus Christ . . . the same yesterday, today and for ever' is indeed the unchanging point of reference, but the act of referring changes with each new generation. The history of the Church is not therefore a *locus* of the original revelation in addition to the one on which it is based, but is the *locus* of continuous dependent revelation. A dependent revelatory situation exists in every moment in which the divine Spirit moves the human spirit. Whether it is original or dependent, revelation has revelatory power only for those who participate in it. But if the correlation of revelation is changed by every new reception we may wonder whether infinite reception will not substantially alter or even exhaust the original revelation. History has indeed shown, says Tillich, how a revelatory correlation came to an end by a complete disappearance of the unchanging point of reference or by a complete loss of its power to create new revelatory situations. Yet how can a revelation come to an end? If revelation is indeed the activity of God how can this ever come to an end? And if it is not God's

[1] *Systematic Theology* I, pp. 140-2.

work then is it really 'revelation'? Tillich's answer is that every revelation is mediated by one of the several media of revelation, and what happens in the cessation of a revelation correlation is the breakdown of the medium's idolatrous claim of power for itself. That which was revelatory in it is preserved as an element in more embracing and more purified revelation.

While Tillich emphasises the cognitive character of revelation he insists that the knowledge it mediates cannot be separated from the situation of revelation and cannot be introduced into the context of ordinary knowledge as an addition.[1] Knowledge of revelation does not increase our knowledge about the structures of nature, history and man, any claim whatsoever to knowledge on this level must be verified in the usual way. Knowledge of revelation is knowledge about the revelation of the mystery of being to us, not information about the nature of beings and their relation to one another. And just as knowledge of revelation does not interfere with ordinary knowledge so ordinary knowledge cannot interfere with revelatory knowledge. There is, however, one limit to the independence of the knowledge of revelation from all forms of ordinary knowledge, namely the presence of revelatory elements within assertions of ordinary knowledge. Should it come about, says Tillich, that matters of ultimate concern are discussed under the cover of ordinary knowledge, theology must protect the truth of revelation against attacks from distorted revelations. This, however, is a religious struggle and not a struggle between knowledge of revelation and ordinary knowledge.

The truth of revelation is judged according to criteria which are themselves revelatory.[2] What these criteria are we can gather if we ask what there is about the revelation in Jesus as the Christ which marks this off as a final revelation. A revelation is final if it has the power of negating itself without losing itself. Every revelation is conditioned by the medium in and through which it appears. The question of the final revelation is the question of a medium of revelation which overcomes its own finite conditions by sacrificing them and itself with them.

[1] *Systematic Theology* I, p. 143.   [2] *Ibid.*, p. 145.

'He who is the bearer of the final revelation must surrender his finitude—not only his life but also his finite powers and knowledge and perfection. In doing so he affirms that he is the bearer of final revelation . . . He becomes completely transparent to the mystery he reveals. But, in order to be able to surrender himself completely, he must possess himself completely. And only he can possess—and therefore surrender—himself completely who is united with the ground of his being and meaning without a separation and disruption'.[1]

Tillich's discussion of the nature of revelation must strike everyone as a courageous attempt to meet some of the main philosophical difficulties in the concept of revelation as cognitive. One theological point can be made briefly before we pass on to the more philosophical analysis of this discussion. If it is true, as Tillich has insisted here and elsewhere,[2] that Christian revelation is absolute and so includes the criterion of every revelation, it would seem as if we are saying that the notion of 'revelation' transcends Christianity. It is almost as if revelation were described as a religious rather than a Christian concept. I am not saying that there is not any other revelation, but I do question the value and the propriety of saying that Christian revelation includes all others when in Christian theology the term 'revelation' is synonymous with 'Jesus Christ'. The question which now arises, however, is the relation of the technical reason by which we know in the ordinary discursive sense and the ecstatic reason by which we know the revelation. Similarly we must be told what is the epistemological status of the empirical aspect of an event which is regarded as a 'sign event'. He has insisted that knowledge of revelation cannot prejudice any piece of scientific or historical knowledge, and correspondingly that no scientific or historical knowledge will determine the question of revelation. 'Knowledge of revelation, although it is mediated primarily through historical events, does not imply factual assertions, and it is therefore not exposed to critical analysis by historical research.'[3] Now, if it is true

[1] *Systematic Theology* I, p. 148.
[2] See *ibid.*, pp. 18-19, 52, 152; vol. II, pp. 100, 174-6.
[3] *Systematic Theology* I, p. 144.

53

that the utterances of the ecstatic reason are simply expressions of 'numinous astonishment' then clearly they do not entail factual assertions. Yet does Tillich really want to empty these statements of factual content in this way? He can afford to say that the results of historical criticism are irrelevant because in fact he is taking for granted that the main historical outline is correct. If revelation is a constellation of which one element is a particular event the knowledge of that event by technical reason cannot be completely independent of the knowledge of revelation. It is surely necessary for Christian philosophical theology in particular to take empirical knowledge seriously even though we should agree with Tillich if he wants to insist that this will never add up to knowledge of revelation. Saying this, however, does not imply the complete logical independence of knowledge of revelation and the various types of ordinary empirical knowledge. And if Tillich wants to maintain the latter position it is difficult to see how he can justify the purely historical assertions which are made in the statements concerning revelation. Also it is not easy to understand how we are to justify the claim of ecstatic reason to possess knowledge. For if we completely dissociate revelatory knowledge from empirical knowledge we remove it from the sphere where the word 'knowledge' has its typical use. What is more fruitful is to show how this typical use in some cases can be stretched to meet a case that is not so typical so that the oddity of the revelatory knowledge from the empirical standpoint does not preclude the possibility that it is genuine knowledge. Even then we have the further task of showing how such knowledge is checked—that is, how the appropriate situations are selected.

We must now attempt to summarize what Tillich has to say about the doctrine of God. God, he says, is that which ultimately or unconditionally concerns us.[1] This is Tillich's philosophical translation of the first commandment—'Thou shalt love the Lord thy God with all thy heart.' Apart from reference to our religious life we can only say that God is 'being-itself' or 'the power of being whereby it resists nonbeing'. All descriptions of God other than this are symbolical

[1] *Systematic Theology* I, p. 14, *et passim*.

and not literal, though it must be said that Tillich often speaks of such terms as 'eternity', 'absolute', 'unconditioned' as if they were synonymous with 'being-itself'.[1] Among non-literal or symbolic statements about God the central ones are that he is 'living' and 'personal', that he is 'the creative and abysmal ground of being' and that he is 'Spirit' or 'Love'. Life is 'the process in which potential being becomes actual being'. But since God 'transcends' the distinction between potential and actual, God is 'not living in the proper or non-symbolic sense'. God is living in so far as he is the ground of life. 'Ground' does not mean cause or substance taken literally but something which underlies all things in some way or other which we can only symbolically describe as causation or substantiality. A cause is also always an effect, a link in the causal chain, but God is not thus conditioned. Substance and accidents are related to each other in a logically necessary way which is different from the free relation of God to man asserted by Christianity. God is not a thing or an object; he has selfhood. But 'self' implies 'separation from and contrast to everything which is not self' whereas God, since he is 'being-itself' is separate from nothing. He is the 'absolute participant' so that we cannot understand the assertion of his selfhood literally. He is superpersonal but we necessarily speak of him symbolically as 'personal'.[2] God is free and yet has a destiny—again in a non-literal sense since in God destiny is 'an absolute and unconditional identity' with freedom. In no sense can we say that God exists because existence necessarily implies being subject to space, time and causality.[3]

Though most of these assertions seem to agree with those of classical or orthodox Christian doctrine Tillich's interpretation of them is rather novel. This is because he carries his doctrine of the symbolical nature of these assertions to much greater lengths than theologians have normally done. Whereas the classical theologian might also say that God transcends the difference between potentiality and actuality, meaning by this that he was actuality without potentiality, Tillich means that

---

[1] Cf. *Systematic Theology* I, pp. 217, 265, 304.   [2] *Ibid.*, p. 271.
[3] *Ibid.*, p. 227.

we must use both sides of the polar descriptions—'potential' and 'actual'. The doctrine of pure actuality, God as *actus purus*, is mistaken, says Tillich, since God is symbolically to be described as living, and 'life is actualisation, not actuality'. Again, 'if we say that God is being-itself, this includes both rest and becoming.'[1] Nor is creation to be understood in terms of the concept of cause to the exclusion of that of effect. For Tillich talks of 'divine self-creation' and says that the finite creatures are taken up into the divine life and that what is positive in time is included in that life. God is therefore to be described not by one of these polar symbols but by both.

There is a fundamental confusion in his discussion of religious language. Once more he raises our hopes by insisting that everything we say about God is symbolic, but this clear emphasis is marred by a fruitless discussion of the necessity of at least this one non-symbolic assertion about God. I fail to see that this is an assertion about God. What he says can be understood if we understand what we mean by the word 'symbol'. It is, however, clear that Tillich wants to make this a non-symbolic assertion about God because he understands his definition of God as Being-itself to be non-symbolic as well. Presumably he feels justified in formulating this definition since he has demonstrated both the necessity and the possibility of a non-symbolic anchor. Here we meet this paradoxical character of Tillich's thought that I have mentioned already—namely, the way in which its fruitfulness is covered over with a disconcertingly antiquated and forbidding terminology. The necessity of a non-symbolic anchor which he has shown thus turns out to be not only a trivial matter but also a confusion which would not have been possible had he used the insights of modern logic. Even so it is worth reflecting on this concept, because what it leads on to is the whole problem of the verification of theological assertions which is so vital an issue in contemporary debates between philosophers and theologians. For if we have non-symbolic anchors to theological statements which are themselves symbolic it follows that the

[1] *Systematic Theology* I, p. 273.

theological statements are meaningful only because of these other statements. Therefore, the ultimate verification of the theological statement is an empirical verification. The question which this concept raises then is whether theological statements are in fact verified in this way. It seems clear to me that the analysis of theological statements by philosophers gives a negative answer. What is more important perhaps, I do not think Tillich himself would want to say that this is the appropriate verification.

When we began this *résumé* of Tillich's doctrine of God we said that for Tillich 'being-itself' was the sum-total of our knowledge of God apart from the religious concern. This concern is a 'total concern'. To say this does not, however, mean that there can be no other object of our love. Tillich recognizes that love of God includes all legitimate love whatsoever. The sacred is not an interest alongside secular interest, and that it should seem thus to man is for Tillich another symptom of the 'disrupted' character of human existence. Since it is a religious imperative to be interested in the finite and changeable and conditioned—my neighbour and his welfare—the religious interest must be in a God who embraces the finite, relative and unchangeable. This is not at all clear and seems even to suggest that Tillich is holding some doctrine of God as being the Absolute of the metaphysicians. Certainly, he says that God is the answer to the philosophical question. He says further that theology today must deal with the controversy between the classical philosophies or theologies of being according to which becoming is an inferior order of reality and the philosophies or theologies of process developed for the most part in modern times. According to the latter, being is an aspect of becoming or process which is reality itself. Tillich tries to do justice to both sides in the controversy. It is impossible, he thinks, to speak of being without also speaking of becoming and, *vice versa*, becoming would be impossible if nothing were preserved in it as the measure of change. Being is further described in terms of freedom and destiny. Man is free because he has a destiny. Things have no destiny because they have no freedom. God has no destiny

57

because he is freedom. The doctrine of God must face also the dialectical problem of non-being.

> 'If God is called the living God, if he is the ground of the creative processes of life, if history has significance for him, if there is no negative principle in addition to him which could account for evil and sin, how can one avoid positing a dialectical negativity in God himself?'[1]

Being limited by non-being is finitude; finitude in awareness is anxiety. The categories express the union of being and non-being in everything finite. They 'articulate the courage which accepts the anxiety of non-being'. The question of God is the question of the possibility of this courage.

Tillich regards the discussion or controversy concerning the arguments for God's existence as a remarkable fact. Ever since Plato there have been attempts on the part of theologians to prove the reality of God and in the Middle Ages it was widely held that the existence of God was a demonstrable fact. Yet there have never been lacking voices raised in protest against this idea. Neither group prevailed over the other; and this says Tillich, can only be because 'the one group did not attack what the other group defended.'[2] The notion of an argument for God's existence is fallacious on two counts. 'Both the concept of existence and the method of arguing to a conclusion are inadequate for the idea of God.' Tillich repudiates the idea that God can be spoken of as in any sense existing.

> 'However it is defined, the "existence of God" contradicts the idea of a creative ground of essence and existence. . . . The scholastics were right when they asserted that in God there is no difference between essence and existence. But they perverted their insight when in spite of this assertion they spoke of the existence of God and tried to argue in favour of it.'[3]

The scholastics did not really mean what they said, thinks Tillich, but really meant to assert 'the reality, the validity, the truth of the idea of God, an idea which did not carry the connotation of some*thing* or some*one* who might or might not exist'.[4] The only sense in which it could be true to say that God

[1] *Systematic Theology* I, p. 210.   [2] *Ibid.*, p. 227.   [3] *Ibid.*   [4] *Ibid.*

existed is the Christological paradox. Otherwise God does not exist. He is being-itself beyond essence and existence and therefore 'to argue that God exists is to deny him'. Again, the method of arguing to a conclusion contradicts the idea of God. For such a method must derive the idea of God from the world—some characteristics of the world make the conclusion 'God' necessary; and in that case God cannot be that which transcends the world infinitely. Tillich refers to the Cartesian, the Thomist and the Whiteheadian methods of proof and maintains that in 'each of these cases God is "world", a missing part of that from which he is derived in terms of conclusions'. This is as remote from the idea of God as is the concept of existence. The classical proofs, then, are neither proofs of nor arguments for the existence of God. They are 'expressions of the *question* of God which is implied in human finitude'. The way in which systematic theology must deal with the proofs, then, is to remove this argumentative character and 'eliminate the combination of the words "existence" and "God".' Thus understood the arguments are analyses of the human situation which show that the question of God is both possible and necessary.

The ontological argument points to the ontological structure of finitude whereby the awareness of the infinite is included in man's awareness of finitude.[1] The question of God is possible because an awareness of God is present in the question of God. Man is aware of an infinity which belongs to him as he is aware of his actual finitude. The various forms of the ontological argument are various descriptions of the way in which potential infinity is present in actual finitude. The validity of the argument is the validity of this description or analysis. The unconditional element appears theoretically as *verum ipsum* and practically as *bonum ipsum*, both being manifestations of *esse ipsum*. Despite the obvious limitations of the ontological argument there is nothing, thinks Tillich, more important for philosophy and theology than the truth it contains, 'the acknowledgement of the unconditional element in the structure of reason and reality'.[2]

The possibility of the question of God having been illustrated

[1] *Systematic Theology* I, p. 228.   [2] *Ibid.*, p. 231.

by the ontological argument, its necessity is revealed by the cosmological arguments. 'The question of God *must* be asked because the threat of non-being, which man experiences as anxiety, drives him to the question of being conquering non-being and of courage conquering anxiety.'[1] This question is what traditionally has received its inadequate formulation in the so-called cosmological and teleological arguments. The validity of these arguments again is not the validity of the logical demonstration of the existence of a highest being but the validity of their analysis of reality which indicates that the cosmological question of God is unavoidable. The first type of argument (the cosmological argument) has moved from the finitude of being to an infinite being whereas the teleological has moved 'from the finitude of meaning to a bearer of infinite meaning'. The first type of argument is determined by the categorical structure of our knowledge of the finite. 'From the endless chain of causes and effects it arrives at the conclusion that there is a first cause, and from the contingency of all substances it concludes that there is a necessary substance.'[2] Tillich raises again the central objection which Kant made against this argument, that these two concepts of cause and substance were categories of finitude. So he describes 'first cause' and 'necessary substance' as 'hypostatized questions'. They are symbols which express the question implied in finite being, 'the question of that which transcends finitude and categories, the question of being-itself, embracing and conquering non-being, the question of God'. The teleological argument moves from finite and threatened meanings to an infinite and unthreatened cause of meanings. 'The basis for the so-called teleological argument for the existence of God is the threat against the finite structure of being, that is, the unity of its polar elements. The *telos* from which this argument has received its name, is the "inner aim", the meaningful, understandable structure of reality.'[3] This again is invalid as an argument; but as the question it is not only valid but inescapable because anxiety about meaninglessness is the characteristically *human* form of ontological anxiety. The task of a theological treatment of the traditional arguments

[1] *Systematic Theology* I, p. 231.   [2] *Ibid.*, p. 232.   [3] *Ibid.*, p. 233.

for the existence of God is twofold: 'to develop the question of God which they express and to expose the impotency of the "arguments", their inability to answer the question of God'.

Whilst one must agree with Tillich that the arguments for God's existence are unable to answer the question of God one wonders whether they are really as useless as he makes them out to be. It seems to me highly doubtful that the medieval theologians who argued concerning the demonstrability of God's existence 'were not divided by a conflict over the same matter.'[1] Certainly the word 'proof' has more than one use. What is accepted as proof in a mathematical problem, a philosophical discussion and in a court of law is in each case a different matter. Yet it is not clear that this is the only reason for the diversity of opinion amongst theologians concerning this matter of proof. Gaunilo, for instance, was not discussing anything different from what Anselm had discussed when he made his famous criticism of the ontological argument. There were many things said by means of this argument which escaped Gaunilo's attention; but the point he attacked has been regarded as an essential part of the argument. Therefore it is not true to say as Tillich does that the whole argument about proofs is due to a mutual misunderstanding of positions.

There is another point in Tillich's argument which strikes me as somewhat dubious. 'However it is defined', he says, 'the existence of God contradicts the idea of a creative ground of essence and existence. . . . The scholastics were right when they asserted that in God there is no difference between essence and existence. But they perverted their insight when in spite of this assertion they spoke of the existence of God and tried to argue in favour of it.'[2] Let us turn to St Anselm and see what he means. He seems to mean quite clearly what Tillich says he did not; for he uses the word 'existit' where he has used the word 'est' and states the conclusion of his argument quite roundly in these words—'existit ergo procul dubio aliquid quo maius cogitari non valet, et in intellectu et in re'.[3] Now if *existentia in re* is not existence what is it? It is tempting to dismiss

[1] *Systematic Theology* I, p. 227.　　[2] *Ibid.*, p. 227.
[3] Anselm, *Proslogion c.* 2.

61

Tillich's assertion that 'to argue that God exists is to deny him'[1] as a purely logical truth and thus empty of information since its truth is derived from the definition of 'existence' as spatio-temporal existence. However, the assertion that God exists is such a hoary philosophical problem and there are so many difficulties in it that we cannot discuss this paradox. It has been pointed out more than once in recent years that the necessity which this assertion is said to possess makes the truth of the assertion a linguistic matter but this will not satisfy the claim that it makes a 'real difference' as well. Even so, these are arguments which can be turned against Tillich's development of the question and should not therefore carry any weight in a justification of his paradox which I repeat is little more than a tautology. The value of it is that it leads us to look at the complexity of religious assertions with their logical air of certainty and factual appearance of synthetic truth.

Tillich says rightly that 'the method of arguing through to a conclusion . . . contradicts the idea of God'. For if we make God the conclusion of a process of argument then he is on the same level as the other elements of the argument. As Tillich expresses it, in these arguments 'God is "world", a missing part of that from which he is derived in terms of conclusions'.[2] Therefore he denies that these arguments are either arguments or proofs. This means to us to be saying too much. That they are not proofs is beyond doubt. The idea of God is incapable of proof in the strict sense (of logical demonstration)—just as it is incapable of disproof. Yet what does this mean? No more can we prove the existence of other persons or the existence of the material world. But we would not for that reason say that either of these is dubitable. The point about God is that we cannot assume the same communicability as we can in the case of the external world and other persons. Therefore though these proofs be not proofs they can be arguments. If we are right in our assumption then they serve quite an important purpose in theology—and that is to show the *rationale* of the hypothesis or assumption that God is real.

The ontological argument fails as a logically necessary

---

[1] *Systematic Theology* I, p. 227.   [2] *Ibid.*, p. 228.

argument because it proceeds from a necessity of thought to a necessity of fact. To say that if one thinks of God one must think of an existent God is true, but it does not follow that what is necessary to the consistency of one's thought must be regarded as existing in any sphere outside thought. That God is a being follows from the definition of God; but the synthetic proposition 'God exists' is still open to doubt. It is necessary to think of a triangle under the Euclidean geometry as having certain properties, but such a triangle cannot exist in fact if we are to accept the modern idea of a curving in space. The argument remains entirely in the sphere of thought, and though we cannot think of God except as existing, it does not follow that such existence is independent of my thinking. Now it is not at all clear that Tillich says anything more than this when he says that the 'ontological argument in its various forms gives a description of the way in which potential infinity is present in actual finitude'.[1] This is the true itself, *verum ipsum*. It seems to us that in this talk of *verum ipsum* and *bonum ipsum* as manifestations of *esse ipsum* Tillich is making a series of logical leaps. What is this unconditional element implied by thinking? Is it not simply logical consistency? If we define space in the Euclidean way then the shortest distance between two points is the straight line. A triangle must be a space bounded by three straight lines with angles whose sum makes 180 degrees. This must be—by the laws of logic. Yet this is no *verum ipsum*. All that is implied by thought is the principle of non-contradiction. What Tillich has done however is to make thought imply some hypostatic *verum* and *bonum ipsum* which in turn are the shadows of *esse ipsum*. Once again we are back in Plato's cave where the real world is the world behind the world. The late Professor John Laird said in his Gifford lectures that the ontological argument was true in so far as it expressed the ontological principle of the identity of thought and reality.

[1] *Ibid.*, p. 229. It may be remarked here that Tillich does not seem to appreciate the complexity of Anselm's argument in *Proslogion* 1-4. Nor does he even state it properly when he speaks (*ibid.*, p. 230) of 'the Anselmian statement that God is a necessary thought and that therefore this idea must have objective as well as subjective reality'. The criticism made of the Ontological Argument in the text above does not apply to Anselm.

Thought and being are identical. This is the Hegelian error so clearly exposed by Kierkegaard. So we would say that the ontological argument fails not only when put in the form of an axiomatic proof of God but also when it is used to express some idealistic assumption about the identity of thought and reality. If, however, it is interpreted as supporting the religious man's conviction that the God he meets in the heart must be real and the greatest reality, it still remains, and always will remain, stripped of its scholastic garments, as the expression, however faulty technically, of a conviction that is unshakeable.

The second deductive argument, the cosmological argument, is the expression of one of the fundamental common-sense convictions of mankind. Young children, as soon as they learn to make things for themselves, begin to ask questions about the making of the world. The creative 'high gods' of many primitive peoples point to the same line of thinking amongst them, for whatever may have been the origin of the idea, now at any rate the high god serves as an explanation of the making of things. It is the conviction that the universe is the work of some Power not ourselves that underlies the cosmological argument. Tillich says the argument comes out of the threat of non-being which is 'logical and non-logical'. All that this can mean is that the argument coincides with a habit of our thought; for we do assume that the world's existence has some meaning. Locke said indeed that its evidence was equal to mathematical certainty—'there is no truth more evident than that something must be from eternity'. Kant was constrained to admit that it had certain persuasive force not less with the speculative than with the common intellect. The chief limitation to the argument lies in a word Locke uses, 'something'. As Lotze said, it yields no metaphysical personal God but an Absolute—to identify God with the Absolute or First Cause is very questionable procedure. At best the argument asserts really no more than that the ordinary nexus of cause and effect does not give us the explanation of existence that we desire. This will not help theism very much. For it does not even follow that Tillich is right in saying that the question of God is implied in finite being and must therefore be asked.

64

Tillich's interpretation of the teleological argument does not seem any more illuminating than his interpretation of the other two arguments. His description of it as 'anxiety about meaningfulness' only reveals a limited idea of meaning as purpose. The argument was described by Kant as 'the clearest, oldest and best suited to human reason'. It seems to me that the teleological argument reveals perhaps not so much a way of coming to know the reality of God as a way of confirming our faith in him. For it is certain that when we do believe in God, nature contributes to that belief, and few things strengthen it more than to see how manifold are his works. The appeal of the argument in fact lies in that sense of God in nature from which Darwin could never divest himself and which was to Wordsworth the most evident of religious truths.

The doctrine of God receives further elaboration in *The Courage to Be* where Tillich reaches the conclusion that the courage of the Reformation, the courage of confidence, 'transcends both the courage to be as a part and the courage to be as oneself'.[1] It is based on God, on God alone, and he is experienced in a unique and personal encounter. In its centre is 'the courage to accept acceptance in spite of the consciousness of guilt'.[2] Referring to Luther, the representative of ecclesiastical Protestantism, and Thomas Münzer, the representative of evangelical radicalism, Tillich remarks:

> 'Both men experienced the anxiety of meaninglessness and described it in terms which had been created by Christian mystics. But in doing so they transcended the courage of confidence which is based on a personal encounter with God. They had to receive elements from the courage to be which is based on mystical union.'[3]

Only at this point in his argument does Tillich introduce the concept of faith, for he believes that neither mystical union nor personal encounter 'fulfils the idea of faith'.[4] Faith, he says, is the state of being grasped by the power of being-itself; and since it is expressed in the courage to be, 'what "faith"

---

[1] *The Courage to Be*, London, Nisbet, 1952, p. 155.   [2] *Ibid.*
[3] *Ibid.*, p. 162.   [4] *Ibid.*, p. 163.

means must be understood through the courage to be'.[1] Faith is the experience of the power of being which is effective in every act of courage. But this experience is paradoxical in character—it is accepting and being accepted, accepting acceptance. This paradoxical character of faith is, for Tillich, metaphysical as well as 'moral' in origin—that is, it is not simply the Reformation emphasis of '*simul justus et peccator*' but an emphasis on the transcendence of the God in whom is my faith. 'Being-itself transcends every finite being indefinitely; God in the divine-human encounter transcends man unconditionally. Faith bridges this infinite gap by accepting the fact that in spite of it the power of being is present, that he who is separated is accepted.'[2] To the question whether faith can resist meaninglessness Tillich answers that there is a faith which makes 'the courage of despair' possible, and this is 'absolute faith'.[3] Absolute faith transcends the divine-human encounter since the radical doubt which such faith presupposes prevents this encounter and so the courage to be in its radical form, yields a new understanding of the idea of God.

> 'The courage to take meaninglessness into itself presupposes a relation to the ground of being which we have called "absolute faith". It is a *special* content, yet it is not without content. The content of absolute faith is the "God above God". Absolute faith and its consequence, the courage that makes the radical doubt, the doubt about God into itself, transcends the theistic idea of God.'[4]

Tillich distinguishes three meanings of the word 'theism'—the unspecified affirmation of God, the name of 'the divine-human encounter', and theological theism. 'Now theism in the first sense must be transcended because it is irrelevant, and theism in the second sense must be transcended because it is one-sided. But theism in the third sense must be transcended because it is wrong.'[5] What is wrong, apparently, is that in theological theism God is conceived as 'a being beside others and as such a part of the whole of reality'. Essentially

[1] *The Courage to Be*, p. 163.   [2] *Ibid.*
[3] *Ibid.*, p. 167. Cf. *The Theology of Culture*, pp. 27-9.   [4] *Ibid.*, p. 172.
[5] *Ibid.*, pp. 174-5.

this is nothing more than what we have already seen said in connection with the arguments for the existence of God. What gives it an air of saying something new is the claim that this transcendent God is required by this experience of absolute faith and the suggestion that calling God a part of the whole of reality is wrong. Taking the second point first we see here another instance of the confusion wrought by Tillich's use of the expression 'the whole of reality'. If by 'reality' we mean the sum-total of all that is then we must say God is part of it; but if by 'reality' we mean the discoverable universe obviously he is not part of this nor even like it. We are led to think that he must not be described as part of reality by the false picture of 'reality' as a collection of things on a particular thing. Hence to say that God cannot be a part of reality is in the end to say nothing. Similarly the claim that absolute faith requires an idea of a God above God can be shown to be an empty claim. In the first place, Tillich seems undecided about the relation between this faith and the courage to be, since at times he makes them synonymous and at others calls faith the cause of courage.[1] But whichever way it is regarded this faith can be said to require the God above God only because it is defined as 'undirected' and 'undefinable, since everything defined is dissolved by doubt and meaninglessness'.[2] That is, the characteristics of this experience are defined in advance and not obtained as a result of an analysis of the experience.

We have already seen how Tillich interprets the reality of God in terms of Being. God is being and God is living. A third characterization is 'God is creative'.[3] He is creative because he is God, and so it is meaningless, says Tillich, to ask whether creation is a necessary or a contingent act of God. Creation is neither necessary nor contingent inasmuch as God is not dependent on 'a necessity above him' and creation is 'identical with his life'. It is not a story of an event which took place 'once upon a time'. 'It is the basic description of the relation between God and the World.' This is symbolized by talking of creation

---

[1] Cf. *The Courage to Be*, pp. 165, 167, 172.   [2] *Ibid.*, p. 167.
[3] *Systematic Theology* I, p. 280.

as having taken place, as taking place and as the future fulfilment of God's *telos*—that is, originating creation, sustaining
creation and directing creation.

The first task of theology, says Tillich, is an interpretation of
the phrase *creatio ex nihilo* which expresses the classical Christian
doctrine of creation.[1] The obvious meaning of the words is a
rejection of dualism and as such distinguishes Christian thought
from any form of paganism. God has nothing presented to him
which either assists or hinders his creativity. 'That which
concerns man ultimately can only be that on which he ultimately depends.' But, though this negative meaning of *creatio
ex nihilo* is clear, the question is whether the phrase *ex nihilo*
points to more than the rejection of dualism. 'The word *ex*
seems to refer to the origin of the creative. "Nothing" is what
(or where) it comes from.' So this phrase, thinks Tillich, means
that the creature must take over 'the heritage of non-being'.
Being a creature means that one belongs not only to the sphere
of being but also that of non-being. There are two truths
expressed in the doctrine of creation out of nothing. The first
is that the tragic character of existence is not rooted in the
creative ground of being and so does not belong to the essential
nature of things. Secondly, there is an element of non-being in
creatureliness so that though the tragic is not necessary it is
potential. There are several points of interest in this interpretation of *creatio ex nihilo* but in this brief discussion I want to
consider the crucial question of whether it is a justifiable and
acceptable interpretation of the doctrine. There are, of course,
innumerable difficulties in this traditional formulation of the
Christian doctrine of creation; and with most of these we shall
not concern ourselves. We shall not discuss, for example,
whether *creatio ex nihilo* can in fact be used as a formulation of
the Christian doctrine. Dr Arnold Ehrhardt has pointed out
the fact that several instances of the use of this phrase are not
identical with, but largely contradictory of, the biblical idea of
creation.[2] But it is sufficient for our purposes that the phrase
has been used to mean just this idea, and we shall therefore

[1] *Systematic Theology* I, p. 281.
[2] A. Ehrhardt, 'Creatio ex nihilo', *Studia Theologica* IV, pp. 14ff.

assume that whenever a Christian theologian uses it this is what he wishes it to mean.

Tillich quite rightly says that the formula must be understood as the critical negation of dualism; but I wish to maintain that his picture is not monistic and that ultimately the way Tillich interprets '*creatio ex nihilo*' lands us back with the dualism it was meant to rebut. But first I shall examine the claim that '*creatio ex nihilo* is the mark of distinction between paganism, even in its most refined form and Christianity even in its most primitive form'.[1] If Tillich means this to refer to what we have called the biblical idea then we can agree. But it is not clear that this is what he does mean, and it seems more likely that he means to refer to the very expression *creatio ex nihilo*. At least he has never retracted the historical claim in the face of criticism. Now the only instance of the occurrence in biblical literature of the phrase *creatio ex nihilo*, as far as I am aware, is II Maccabees 7.28. The Maccabean mother says to her youngest son:

> 'I beseech thee, my son, look upon the heaven and the earth and all that is therein, and consider that God made them out of things that were not; and so was mankind made likewise. . . .'

For 'out of things that were not' the Greek text has οὐκ ἐξ ὄντων which the Vulgate translates as '*ex nihilo*'. Tillich might counter any argument from this evidence alone by saying that this source can hardly be called pagan. But, leaving aside the question of a possible philosophical influence on the language of this section of II Maccabees, the text is certainly pre-Christian and this must mean that Tillich's claim as it stands is not valid. We can also quote Philo on this; for though Philo's general tendency, as E. Bréhier has shown,[2] is the Hellenistic conception of God the Creator as an artificer, *De opificio Mundi* XVI. 4 and *De Somniis* I. 76 are notable exceptions, and as Bréhier points out the Armenian translator of *De Deo* VI represents matter as created by God.[3] More

---

[1] *Systematic Theology* I, p. 253.
[2] E. Bréhier, *Les idées philosophiques et religieuses de Philon de l'Alexandrie*, pp. 78-82.
[3] *Ibid.*, p. 81, note 2.

especially pagan sources in which there are references to the doctrine are Pseudo-Aristotle[1] and Plutarch.[2] It seems clear that in post-Aristotelian philosophy the doctrine of *creatio ex nihilo* gained considerable ground. Dr Ehrhardt points out that the starting-point of the doctrine can be seen in the early Greek philosophical concern with the definition of μὴ ὄν which meant not so much something which was not there as 'untruth, something which has no right to be there'. He also notes that this physical contrast is then turned into a moral contrast in Xeniades of Corinth.[3]

So much for Tillich's historical claim. The other point I want to raise is a systematic criticism. Tillich's assertion[4] that the word *ex* in the formula *creatio ex nihilo* refers to the 'origin of the creature' seems to me highly misleading. For it would suggest that the classical statement of the Christian doctrine of Creation is an affirmative statement rather than a negative one. It has been well said that the meaning of the creeds is always to be sought in what they denied rather than what they affirmed. 'God created the world out of nothing' though grammatically the same as 'Sybil Connolly has created some wonderful things out of Irish tweed' or 'Picasso has created a very mystifying art out of realism and cubism' is not logically parallel with either. It is much nearer the kind of thing we mean when we say 'Lord Nuffield made his fortune out of an idea.' Here the paradox is meant to remind us that Lord Nuffield did not start with a family fortune which he has now successfully multiplied. Thus it is not descriptive in a straightforward way, and the 'out of' is descriptive only in a very odd sense. If we want to know the origin of the Nuffield fortune we should want a very different kind of description. Similarly, the *ex* in *creatio ex nihilo* is not descriptive, and does not 'refer to' anything. This leads us on to Tillich's further statement— ' "Nothing" is what (or where) [the creature] comes from.' If what we have said is right then *a fortiori* the word *nihil* is not

---

[1] Pseudo-Aristotle, *De Gen. Animal.* I 97a, 8.
[2] Plutarch, *De Anim. Procr.*, v. 1014b.
[3] Ehrhardt, *op. cit.*, p. 25.
[4] *Systematic Theology* I, p. 281.

to be interpreted thus. It is quite useless then for Tillich to go on to try to define this *nihil*:

> 'Now "nothing" can mean two things. It can mean the absolute negation of being (*ouk on*), or it can mean the relative negation of being (*mē on*). If *ex nihilo* meant the latter, it would be a restatement of the Greek doctrine of matter and form against which it is directed. If *ex nihilo* meant the absolute negation of being, it could not be the origin of the creature. Nevertheless the term *ex nihilo* says something fundamentally important about the creature, namely, that it must take over what might be called "the heritage of nonbeing". Creatureliness implies nonbeing but creatureliness is more than nonbeing. It carries in itself the power of being, and this power of being is its participation in being-itself, in the creative ground of being.'[1]

I do not see how we can attach any meaning to this concept of nonbeing—at least, any such meaning as Tillich seems to think it does possess. It is, of course, clear to all who are familiar with Heidegger's work that this is the source of Tillich's use of the term 'Nonbeing'. Following Heidegger he takes nonbeing personally as '*das Nichts*'. Man, he says,

> 'must be separated from his being in a way which enables him to look at it as something strange and questionable. And such a separation is actual because man participates not only in being but also in nonbeing. . . . It is not by chance that historically the recent rediscovery of the ontological question has been guided by pre-Socratic philosophy and that systematically there has been an overwhelming emphasis on the problem of nonbeing.'[2]

But this emphasis has been characteristic only of Heidegger and the other existentialist philosophers, and this is one of the instances where the majority of philosophers would apply Occam's razor. His idea of nonbeing is in fact merely the hypostatization of a negation such as Lewis Carroll used in his humorous dialogue of the King and the Messenger.

> 'Who did you pass on the road?' the King went on, holding out his hand to the Messenger for some more hay. 'Nobody,' said the Messenger.

[1] *Ibid.*   [2] *Ibid.*, p. 208.

'That's right,' said the King: 'This young lady saw him too. So of course Nobody walks slower than you.'

'I do my best,' said the Messenger in a sullen tone. 'I'm sure nobody walks much faster than I do.'

'He can't do that,' said the King, 'or he'd have been here first.'

This dialogue reveals the peculiarity of the word 'nobody' as being a class rather than an individual like its opposite 'somebody'. It also reveals how natural a tendency it is to identify words as referring to objects, which is what lies behind Tillich's concept of nonbeing. The fallacy that the existence of a word means the existence of a thing results in a great deal of confusion in Tillich's thought. But it is quite fallacious to hold with Mill[1] that a significant proposition implies 'the real existence of the subject because in the case of a non-existent subject there is nothing for the proposition to assert', for we can significantly use descriptions which describe nothing, because these descriptions do not refer to any particular which is a constituent of the proposition. To see the error of Tillich's use of 'nonbeing' rather more clearly we may examine the hoary statement 'Unicorns exist'. Now we might think that there must be a sense of 'exist' or 'there are' in which it is true that there are unicorns and equally another sense in which it is true that there are no unicorns. The second assertion would then be equivalent to 'Unicorns are unreal.' This sense of 'are' must be such that we can describe 'being real' or 'being unreal' as a property like 'being yellow'. But this is not the case, and 'are unreal' is an expression which denies existence rather than asserts any special kind of existence. Similarly, the only meaning we can give to 'nonbeing' is the denial of the 'being' of something. Therefore to say that 'creatureliness implies nonbeing' either is a useless tautology or is meaningless. That is, we can give it meaning by defining the term 'being' as meaning only that existence is nonbeing, that being a creature will imply nonbeing. But this is not anything more than giving creatureliness another name and does not tell us anything about what it means to be a creature. And if we do not mean this then we are committed to a meaningless Manicheism, such as is

[1] J. S. Mill, *Logic*, Bk I vi, 2.

72

sometimes wrongly attributed to Augustine, for Augustine creation *de nihilo* is simply creation, and creatureliness means a being which is not God's and therefore not unchangeable.[1] Thus he says:

> 'When we say . . . that because it is made from nothing and not from God we do not give the Nothing any nature; but we do distinguish the nature of the Maker from the nature of the things that are made.'[2]

What Tillich has done is to make the 'nothing' out of which we come a something with fatal power. Hence, as I suggested, we are once more faced with Dualism.

The question of the nature of creation soon resolves into a question of the relation of creation to the categories of finitude. This is usually discussed as the question of the relation between creation and time. Symbolizing the originating creativity of God as we do by speaking of it as a past event, we are instantly faced with the question, what did God do before he created the world? This question Tillich regards as being both philosophically absurd and religiously repugnant, though the absurdity lies not so much in the question as in its presupposition, that creation is an event in the past. Traditionally theology has, since Augustine, met this difficulty by saying that the world was created *with* time and not *in* time. And where this formula has been suspected of implying an eternal creation, that creation is co-eternal with God though temporal in its content, theologians have asserted that creation is *in* time though they have agreed with Augustine that there is no pre-creation time. This, says Tillich, differs from the Augustinian position 'only in vocabulary, not in substance'. The answer to this problem must, he thinks, be sought in our understanding of the creative character of the divine life. Now if it is true, as we have said hitherto, that creativity is essential to the divine life then not only is the finite in some sense present *in* that life but the forms of finitude are also. The divine life therefore included temporality, but is not subject to it. God's eternity is not opposed to

[1] Mutability is inseparable from creatureliness, according to Augustine— vide *Contra Julianum opus imperfectum* V, 42.
[2] *Contra Julianum op. imp.* V, 44.

73

time but includes it and transcends it. The time of the divine life is determined by the present and not by the negative reference to the passage of time by which ours is. So it is meaningless to talk of pre-creation time, and to talk of creation *in* time can only mean 'the transformation of the time which belongs to the divine life into the time which belongs to creaturely existence'. So it is better to speak of creation *with* time.

Augustine's rebuttal of the Epicurean criticism of the Christian doctrine of creation by his famous formula has always been regarded as the way to understand the relation of creation to time. It is not surprising then that Tillich has followed it, but the peculiar twist it receives at his hands makes it a rather different theory from the traditional view. Two questions can be asked—(*a*) Is Tillich justified in his view of the divine nature as including temporality? (*b*) How valid is the inference whereby he arrives at this position? We shall take the second question first. It seems to me that the inference is illicit and is made possible only by the ambiguity of the terms he uses. From this perfectly valid assertion (a metaphorical one) that the creature is eternally hid in the creator's life he wrongly deduces that the forms of finitude are, in a literal sense, also present in that life. The argument is not obviously absurd because in it literal and metaphorical assertions jostle merrily together. If it is true that temporality is present in the divine life this is true only as a metaphorical or symbolical statement and will not yield the position Tillich wishes to maintain. It is indeed difficult to see why he should wish to maintain it, for he still insists on the Augustinian formula though now 'in time' is really as meaningful as 'with time'. So we return to the first question. It is true that the Bible displays little of the kind of outlook to be found in Plato where God and time are dramatically opposed. But does this mean that it regards the temporal as included in the divine? This can hardly be the case when it constantly speaks of the divine existence as neither subject to the ravages of time nor indeed as even related to time except by *Agape*. The eternity of God is indeed related to time but not as genus to species. When the Bible

74

talks of God sharing in time it does not suggest that he is 'temporal'. There seems little to be gained then from speaking of God as temporal in the way Tillich does.

As actualized freedom man is an independent being and this means that he can resist the possibility of returning to the ground of being. At the same time he is continuously dependent on the creative ground. 'Traditionally the relation of God to the creature in its actualized freedom is called the preservation of the world.'[1] The symbol of preservation can be adequately understood as continuous creativity 'in that God out of eternity creates things and time together'. This line of thought which takes us back through the Reformers to Augustine must be followed and made into 'a line of defence against the contemporary half-deistic, half-theistic way of conceiving God as a being alongside the world'.[2] But though God is essentially and therefore continually creative, there is a decisive difference between originating and sustaining creativity. The latter refers to 'the given structures of reality', that is to the unchanging or static elements within finitude. The modern sense of cosmic insecurity gives this symbol of God's sustaining creativity a new significance and power. Is this to be expressed in terms of immanence or transcendence? This question is usually answered, quite correctly but not very helpfully, by saying that both are necessary. But immanence and transcendence are spatial concepts, and here they point to a 'qualification relation: God is immanent in the world as its permanent creative ground and is transcendent to the world through freedom'. The meaning of this is the possible conflict and possible reconciliation of infinite and finite freedom.

Tillich rightly rejects any deistic understanding of the preservation of the world and adopts the Augustinian view of the preservation as continuous creativity. There is little in his understanding of this that is either novel or difficult despite the tortuous discussion and the frightening vocabulary. One point, however, must be mentioned. True to his insistence that God is being-itself and not a being, Tillich wants to develop this Augustinian view of preservation into an attack on the idea of

[1] *Systematic Theology* I, p. 290.   [2] *Ibid.*, p. 291.

God as a being alongside the world. Here again it is difficult to see how this can be consistently maintained together with the other parts of his doctrine of creation. If the creature is capable of actualizing the potentialism there is a sense, as Tillich admits, in which the creature is independent of the creator. In that case surely creator and creature are two separate beings. Anyhow, since creation means the bringing into existence of something which stands over against God it is hard to see how it is then impossible to say that God is a being alongside the world. He is not merely this, it is true. That is why we say he is transcendent and immanent.

Finally we must consider God's directing creativity. Creation, says Tillich, has no purpose beyond itself. He would therefore prefer to speak of the *telos* of creation—'the inner aim of fulfilling in actuality what is beyond potentiality and actuality in the divine life'. The divine creativity drives every creature toward such fulfilment, and this is traditionally called 'providence'. Faith in providence is always paradoxical in the sense that it asserts that things are not what they seem. In spite of the incessant experiences of meaninglessness yet it asserts that historical existence has meaning. There are two interpretations of Providence corresponding to its meaning as foreseeing and as foreordering. If the first is stressed God becomes the omniscient spectator who knows beforehand what will happen but never interferes with his creation. If the second is stressed then God becomes a planner who has ordered everything that will happen so that in the end he alone is an agent in the mechanism of history. Both these interpretations must be rejected. God is never a spectator but he is always active in and through the freedom of the creature. 'The man who believes in providence does not believe that a special divine activity will alter the conditions of finitude and estrangement. He believes and asserts with the courage of faith, that no situation whatsoever can frustrate the fulfilment of his ultimate destiny, that nothing can separate him from the love of God which is in Christ Jesus.' And what is true of the individual is true of history as a whole. Faith in historical providence means that we are certain that all history contributes to the ultimate fulfilment of creaturely existence. The Christian notion of providence is a personal one—providence is an element in the person-to-person relationship between God and man. And like Judaism Christianity adds to this idea of special providence faith in historical providence, for God establishes his Kingdom through history. Faith in providence does not seem to be verified by the facts of human existence. This raises the question of theodicy—'How can an almighty God be justified in view of realities in which no meaning whatsoever can be discovered?' The answer to this, says Tillich, is the paradoxical character of faith in providence. The first step in attempting to answer the question is the recognition that creation is creation of finite freedom, a risk which the divine creativity accepts. However, this does not answer the question why there is the great disparity between various persons' fulfilment. But the question of theodicy is existential, says Tillich, and this is forgotten if the question of theodicy is raised with respect to persons other than the questioner. That question can only be answered as we seek the point at which their destiny becomes our own. This point is the participation of their being in our own being. The question of theodicy finds its final answer in the mystery of the creative ground.

III

CHRISTOLOGY AND HISTORICAL CRITICISM

THOUGH Tillich begins his discussion of Christology with an examination of the various uses of the term Messiah or Christ in theology it will be as well for us to confine ourselves to what he says about 'the reality of Christ', since this is logically if not actually his point of departure. The Christian message, he says, is distinguished by its assertion that 'Jesus of Nazareth ... is actually the Christ, namely, he who brings the new state of things, the New Being.'[1] The first requirement in Christology, therefore, is an interpretation of the name 'Jesus Christ' preferably in the light of the story of Peter's confession 'Thou art the Christ' at Caesarea Philippi, which is the central story of the Gospel of Mark. The cruciality of this story for Tillich's Christology is due to the fact that it expresses the distinctively Christian claim that Jesus of Nazareth is the Christ and reveals this as both essentially a believing confession vis-à-vis a fact and the paradox that he who is the Christ has to die for his acceptance of the title, 'Christ'. Tillich takes up the point about the confession and emphasises the fact that there are two sides to this, both of which are equally important. 'Jesus as the Christ is both an historical fact and a subject of believing interpretation.'[2] If theology ignores the fact to which the name Jesus of Nazareth points, it ignores the basic Christian assertion that the new state of things has been ushered in by one who lived in the world. Only if there is this one point in history where man's estrangement from God is conquered can we have the Christian message that such estrangement has been overcome *in principle*. Yet, on the other hand, 'the believing

---

[1] *Systematic Theology* II, p. 112.   [2] *Ibid.*, p. 113.

reception of Jesus as the Christ' must receive equal emphasis. For without this reception the Christ would not have been the Christ. Without such a reception he would have been remembered in history perhaps, but he would be a prophetic anticipation of the New Being and not the final manifestation of the New Being itself. He would not have been the Christ even if he had claimed to be the Christ.[1] The reception is therefore as important as the fact, and 'only their unity creates the event upon which Christianity is based'. Does this mean that the validity of Christianity's central claim depends then on the continuance of the Church as the group which receives Jesus as the Christ? This is today a question of some urgency for we can imagine more easily than ever before in the history of the world that this historical tradition would break down completely. Indeed it is possible that a total catastrophe such as can now be conceived to be a result of total war would leave either no human civilization or a civilization in which there would be no record of the event 'Jesus as the Christ'. Such a possibility strikes Tillich as posing not only an interesting question because this state of affairs is 'neither verifiable nor refutable' but also a real question which now presses itself upon the consciousness of the contemporary Christian.[2] Would the suicide of mankind be a refutation of the Christian message? The answer of the New Testament, where the problem of the historical continuity is broached first, is that so long as there is human history the New Being in Jesus as the Christ is present and effective.

The question of the relation of Jesus as the Christ to history is the peculiarly modern theological question since theological problems which were always in some sense before the mind of the Church have now become intensified by the application of historical criticism to the biblical material. Tillich points out that it is the critical rather than the constructive aspect of historical research which has made such an impression on modern Christianity. Such biblical research was suspect from the beginning because it seemed to criticize not only the historical sources but the very revelation thus conveyed.

[1] *Ibid.*, p. 114. [2] *Ibid.*, p. 115.

79

Consequently historical research and rejection of biblical authority were identified. Historical criticism seemed then to cut the ground from beneath the feet of faith because revelation seemed to include the historical reports given in the biblical records and not simply separable revelatory content. However, Tillich regards the critical aspect of historical research as much less significant than the constructive aspect.[1] The facts behind the records, especially the facts about Jesus, were sought. The research for the 'historical Jesus' which thus began was a quest for a reality behind the traditions and was inspired by religious as well as scientific motives. But despite its numerous important theological consequences the attempt to find the empirical truth about Jesus of Nazareth was a failure. 'The historical Jesus, namely the Jesus behind the symbols of his reception as the Christ, not only did not appear but receded farther and farther back with every new step.'[2] The actual historical work done by the researchers is valid and has been corrected by later scholars, but the methodological situation remains the same. The result of all this, says Tillich, is 'not a picture of the so-called historical Jesus but the insight that there is no picture behind the biblical one which could be made scientifically probable.'[3] This is not an empirical statement but a logical one—this is so, says Tillich, because of the nature of the source itself. The reports are those of Jesus as the Christ, given by people who have received him as such. If the attempt to find the historical Jesus is to succeed we should have to separate what is factual from what belongs to faith, and with what has been discovered as the factual basis we can reconstruct a 'Life of Jesus'. Of such reconstructed biographies Tillich says that at best 'they are more or less probable results, able to be the basis neither of an acceptance nor a rejection of the Christian faith.'[4] Similarly, the attempt to formulate a *Gestalt* of Jesus by reducing the testimony of the essentials, leaving the particular details open to question, is doomed to failure; for the shape of the *Gestalt* depends on the valuation of these details which are assumed to be expendable. Neither a 'Life of Jesus' nor a

[1] *Systematic Theology* II, p. 117.   [2] *Ibid.*, p. 116.
[3] *Ibid.*, p. 118.   [4] *Ibid.*

'*Gestalt* of Jesus' is therefore possible.[1] This induced some theologians to confine themselves to the immediately given, namely, the words of Jesus, as the historical foundation of Christian faith. This has been done in two ways—either it makes the words general rules of human behaviour or it makes them concrete demands.[2] The first method reduces Jesus to the level of the Old Testament and therefore by implication denies his claim to have overcome the Old Testament context. The second method is a more fruitful and profound interpretation, and, according to it, the words emphasise Jesus' message that the Kingdom of God is 'at hand', and that those who want to enter it must decide for or against the Kingdom of God. This interpretation identifies the meaning of Jesus with that of his message so that he calls for a decision, the decision for God. Even this method, ingenious as it is in its avoidance of the historically impossible, cannot yield a historical foundation to the Christian faith.

What blinds us to this obvious impossibility of giving a foundation to the Christian faith through historical research, says Tillich, is 'the semantic confusion about the meaning of the term "historical Jesus" '.[3] The term ambiguously denotes the historical evidence concerning Jesus, that is, the result of the historian's research, and the factual character of the event 'Jesus as the Christ'. The more popular use of the term was the result of historical research into the character and life of the actual person, standing behind the Gospel story. But it is also used to signify the factual character of the event Jesus as the Christ—that is, it is simply a shorthand expression for the assertion that there is a fact of which this event is the name and interpretation. In this sense the question of the historical Jesus, says Tillich, is a question for faith and not for historical research.[4] What this seems to mean is that in order to make the purely doctrinal assertion faith must have the certainty of the historicity or factuality of the life of Jesus. This is not denied by a methodological scepticism, and Tillich sees no difficulty for faith in sceptical historical method. Not even the name

[1] *Ibid.*, p. 119.   [2] *Ibid.*, pp. 121-3.
[3] *Ibid.*, p. 123.   [4] *Ibid.*

'Jesus' can be regarded as guaranteed by faith—this with so many other things, must be left to the incertitude of our historical knowledge. Faith does, however, guarantee the factual transformation of reality in that personal life which the New Testament described in its picture of Jesus as the Christ. This is very puzzling and one really wants to know what kind of guarantee this is and how it is different from the first which has been so readily abandoned to the historical sceptic. But we shall leave this question as it will be necessary to discuss it again later, and we shall now continue with our exposition of Tillich's treatment of historical criticism and Christology.

His position with regard to 'an actual historical Jesus' has been interpreted by A. T. Mollegen[1] as the assertion of five points, and Tillich has agreed that these are a just summary of his position. These are the five points:

1. The incarnation was a fact.
2. The New Testament portrait of Jesus is the Jesus received as the Christ.
3. The historian's quest yields only probability which is not enough for religion.
4. The revelation portrayed in the New Testament is historical—i.e., the life of the historical person would verify the portrait.
5. Faith's certainty comes to the individual through his experience as a member of the Church.

First, then, the Incarnation was a fact. That is to say, if the technical devices now available for recording details of a person's life by means of film and sound-recording could have been used, we should have at our disposal a record of the person of Jesus Christ. As a matter of fact we do not have anything resembling this kind of evidence concerning him, since no one who recorded anything of his life had a merely historiographical interest in him. To this extent, then, he is unknown but the fact that we do not have a photographic record of him does not minimize the factuality of his existence.

Secondly, though we have no photograph we do have a portrait. This man was received as the Christ and is portrayed

[1] *The Theology of Paul Tillich*, pp. 231ff.

in the New Testament as Jesus who is the Christ, the Son of God, the Logos. Tillich also uses the term 'picture' of this account—'the Biblical picture of Jesus as the Christ'.[1] As we have already seen in the previous chapter, Tillich holds that revelation always occurs in the context of the history of revelation and that there can be no revelation without its reception by someone. So the New Testament picture of Jesus as the Christ is the result of the revelation of God which came, and could only come in the context of the Jewish expectation of the Messiah and receiving faith. Tillich calls this portrait the biblical historical Christ, and insists that this is the only historical evidence we have. Our information about him is due to people's reception of him as the Christ. Nothing can be known with any certainty about this man, apart from the portrait of him produced by faith. This does not rule out the possibility that he could have been received as the Prophet who was to come before the Christ and that such a reception produced evidence or data concerning him which was later incorporated into the portrait of faith. Identification of this evidence is a matter for the historical critic to decide. However, the only historically certain evidence that we now possess is the portrait of Christ in the New Testament. 'The photographic picture never existed, either for Jesus Himself or His apostles. The original picture which existed from the beginning, was of a numinous and interpreted character, and it was this which proved to have the power to conquer existence.'[2] The original picture cannot be confirmed by conservative criticism nor can it be destroyed by radical criticism.

Thirdly, for Tillich, the quest of historical criticism for the historical Jesus yields, like all historical enquiry, only a high degree of probability. The historical method asks how trustworthy the records are in every particular case, how dependent they are on older sources, how much they might be influenced by the credulity of a period. All these questions can be answered in an 'objective' way without necessary interference of negative or positive prejudices. 'The historian can never reach certainty

[1] *Systematic Theology* II, p. 133.
[2] *Church Quarterly Review* 147 (Jan. 1959), p. 145.

in this way, but he can reach high degrees of probability.'[1] This is not enough for religious faith, however, and its certainty cannot rest upon such a probability. So Tillich speaks of the historicity of the divine revelation as a matter of 'the immediate certainty of faith' in contradistinction to the historicity of the biblical report which is a matter of degrees of probability attaching to the results of historical research. He then distinguishes between the 'biblical historical Jesus' and the 'historical Jesus' of the historical critic, and he therefore distinguishes between two concepts of the 'historical'. In the context of the Bible 'historical' means 'the continuous process of the divine self-revelation in a series of events, combined with the interpretation of these revelatory events'. Whereas for the historian, 'historical' means what can be verified by means of historical research.

Fourthly, the 'historicity' of the revelation portrayed in the New Testament 'Jesus who is the Christ', means not only that a human being did exist, but also that he was such as to support the biblical picture. He has already admitted that no particular item of information concerning Jesus can be verified. But the power of the picture to transform 'existence' implies that there is an *analogia imaginis*, namely an analogy between the picture and the actual personal life from which it has arisen. One can compare the *analogia imaginis* suggested here with the *analogia entis*—not as a method of knowing God, but as a way (actually the only way) of speaking of God. In both cases it is impossible to push behind the analogy and to state directly what can be stated only indirectly.[2]

Finally, the certainty given by faith comes to the Christian in an experience which has two aspects. It is his as a member of the Church which is the actual continuation of the history of revelation, and secondly it is his as an individual grasped by the revealing event. As St Paul says, 'in Christ' means both incorporation into the Body of Christ, the fellowship of the Holy Spirit, the *ecclesia*, and my being 'hid with Christ in God'. Certainty of the biblical historical Jesus comes only in this way, and it is independent of the 'historical Jesus of critical

[1] *Systematic Theology* II, p. 120.   [2] *Ibid.*, p. 132.

research'. 'With Adolph Schlatter we can say that we know nobody as well as Jesus. In contrast to all other persons, the participation in him takes place not in the realm of contingent human individuality . . . but in the realm of his own participation in God, a participation which has a universality in which everyone can participate.'[1] The event is certain but not the biography which made the event possible. Thus Tillich sharply distinguishes the dimension of faith (the existential) from that of history (the theoretical).[2]

Before we go on to see how Tillich understands the contribution of historical research to theology, we must pause to examine this interpretation of what we can mean by 'the historical Jesus'. We must be grateful to Tillich for calling attention to the semantic confusion in the theological discussion of this problem, but I venture to suggest that he is no less guilty than some of his opponents of exploiting the ambiguities of the term 'history' in order to resolve the dilemma which faces theology here. However, there can be no doubt that Tillich is right in saying that the critical attempts to recover the biography of Jesus by divesting the reports of any theological accretions or legendary embellishments proved without exception to be failures.

The liberal concept of the 'historical' Jesus, produced by the work of Harnack and Loisy amongst others, was shattered by Schweitzer's demonstration that the Gospels were mutilated, not restored, by removing the eschatological references. There are two questions which need then to be asked. First, does this failure of historical research mean that the methodological question of how we are to know anything about Jesus of Nazareth must be answered without reference to historical research? That is, does the failure in fact mean that there is a quest where success is logically impossible?

Secondly, do we improve matters at all when we distinguish the dimension of faith from that of history so sharply that there can be no connection? It will be helpful to start with the second

[1] *Ibid.*, pp. 133-4.
[2] *Ibid.*, p. 134 cf. *Systematic Theology* I, p. 144, and *Dynamics of Faith*, New York, Harper Torchbooks, 1958, p. 88.

question since it will contribute to answering of the first. If this distinction between faith and history is absolute then it is difficult to understand Tillich's argument concerning the historical Jesus. For though we may grant that there is great point in making the distinction it is wrong to claim that this has solved the problem of historicity. The crucial assertions are the first and the fourth of the five points in which his position concerning the historical Jesus was summarized: namely, that the Incarnation was a fact and that the life of the historical person would verify the portrait. But let us start by examining the way which Tillich understands the epistemological status of history. He says that any historical enquiry yields only a high degree of probability and that the historian can never reach certainty.[1] This is highly perplexing and we can only assume that Tillich has confused a perfectly true statement concerning the epistemological status of any statement concerning facts of history with a misleading description of the *historian's* statements. For it is obvious that of any historical or empirical statement we must admit that it is in one sense probable, namely that it is not necessarily true. But the opposition is not between certainty and probability; it is between two kinds of truths, the truths of fact and the truths of logic. We can indeed describe the former as contingent, but this in no way removes from them the possibility of verification. All we can mean if we say they are probable is that when they are verified they are not verified in the same way as the propositions, which are necessarily true. Similarly, if we describe the historian's statements as probable all that can properly be meant by this is that they are not necessarily true statements. To describe them as probable, however, is to suggest that they do not possess a certainty which in the nature of the case they cannot ever possess. His distinction between the two uses of the word 'historical' in connection with the problem of the historical Jesus is therefore produced by his refusal to allow that historical knowledge can ever properly be described as certain. Moreover, here Tillich is trying to get the best of both worlds by insisting on the historical character of

[1] *Systematic Theology* II, p. 120.

these events and yet refusing to make them possible objects of historical investigation. That is, he accepts the normal use of 'historical' as meaning something that happened whilst also saying that the result of the historian's investigations is only probable knowledge—i.e., 'This might be what happened.' Let us return to the distinction between the existential and the historical. It seems to me that Tillich here made a straightforward distinction out of Kierkegaard's paradoxical way of calling attention to the fact that statements about Jesus Christ are logically complex. The distinction between what Kierkegaard called objectivity and subjectivity is a useful one in trying to understand the use of history in Christian theology. It will not, however, bear the weight laid upon it by Tillich here. For it leads us to gloss over the very complexity that Kierkegaard wanted to bring out by its use, and so we are told by Tillich that the risk of faith is existential and not at all historical, and the historical picture is then the picture of Jesus. What we must know, and what Tillich never tells us, is the evidence on which he can make his assertion that there would be perfect correspondence between a photograph of Jesus and the picture of him in the New Testament. Bearing in mind the point raised already about the status of historical statements, we must point out that this assertion of Tillich's is rather a hopeful guess or a fallacy due to the confusion of what is logically true, for if this is not a tautology produced by the redefinition of the concept 'historical' we must be told in what way there is any possible *justification* of this assertion, and justification means appeal to an independent standard. And it is this independent standard that Tillich admits is lacking. Again it seems to me that Tillich has not distinguished the various 'relations' one can have with an historical figure—that is, the ways in which we can talk of someone who has existed in the past. King Arthur, for example, is in all probability an historical figure at the fifth and sixth centuries who really lived in Britain and fought battles. We may be concerned to discover more hard facts about this figure to establish the historical pattern of British fortunes, but on the other hand all Welshmen know that King Arthur sleeps until the day when he will triumphantly lead his fellow-countrymen to establish a glorious future. In the latter case 'Arthur' is a mythical symbol of Welsh expectations and aspirations, and here it is not the historical core of the myth that is important. However, in the case of Jesus, unless the history is emphasized, the doctrine of Jesus as the Christ cannot be fully maintained. Tillich sees this and has himself said so, but what he does not see is that the difference between the two ways of looking at Arthur meant that what was needed in the case of the political myth was not enough for the first case. 'Jesus must have been such as to warrant the claim that he was the Christ.' What kind of statement is this? It is not like the statement that Benjamin Jowett must have been a person of considerable stature before Sir Geoffrey Faber could describe him as one of the key figures of Victorian England. We can bring out the difference between them by imagining another biography of Jowett which would remove any possible evidence for Sir Geoffrey's judgment. Then would we not agree with Professor Willey that Jowett was, after all, but 'sanctified shrewdness'? I cannot do better than quote a story plot which Mr Somerset Maugham has outlined:

'He was a philanthropist. His work was important and its value is enduring. He was hard-working and and disinterested. He was in his small way a great man. He looked upon drink as a curse and, busy as he was, yet found time to go up and down the country giving temperance lectures. He would not allow any member of his family to touch alcohol. There was one room in his house which he kept locked and would permit no one to enter. He died suddenly, and soon after the funeral his family broke into the room which had always excited their curiosity. They found it full of empty bottles, bottles of brandy, whisky, gin, bottles of char-treuse, benedictine and kümmel. It was only too plain that he had brought the bottles in with him one by one, and having drunk their contents had not known how to get rid of them. I would give a great deal to know what passed through his mind when he came home after delivering a temperance lecture and behind locked doors sipped green chartreuse.'[1]

[1] Somerset Maugham, *A Writer's Notebook*, London, Heinemann, 1949, p. 85.

Now here is a portrait which seemed at all points to correspond with the photograph. But the truth of the portrait depended on there being no contradictory evidence. When such evidence is forthcoming we are forced to abandon the portrait. Now this is always true of an historical situation—it can be different. How then does Tillich say that there *must* be a correspondence? I think his confusion here brings out the non-historical or metaphysical character of Christological assertions. What is unfortunate is that he imagines that this statement is homogeneous with the historical statement he also makes concerning Jesus. Are we then to say that historical criticism cannot shake the conviction that Jesus is the Christ? I find it impossible to answer this question with a straightforward 'Yes' or 'No'. Tillich is surely right when he says that the biblical assertion that Jesus is the Christ is not regarded as an assertion made on the evidence which historical criticism yields. As Kierkegaard puts it, 'from history one can learn nothing about Christ'. However, though it is true that it is not on this evidence that the assertion is made, it does not follow that certain facts need not be known to be true in order to support the claim that Jesus is the Christ. The way we come to know something is not necessarily the way our knowledge is justified. At the very least we must surely admit that it is necessary for us to have grounds for accepting as true the historical assertion that there was such a person as Jesus of Nazareth. It is true that not all the history possible will add up to the assertion of faith that Jesus is the Christ, but this does not mean that the history is irrelevant. Just as the facts of the case are not all that are needed in order to obtain the legal judgment pronounced by a jury as they pronounce their verdict but are nevertheless the necessary preliminary desideratum, so the historical analysis is not all we have to do to the New Testament whilst still being something relevant to our verdict or commitment.

We return now to our first question. Does the failure to produce a biography of Jesus mean that we can never penetrate the barrier between New Testament Christianity and the historical Jesus? If it is thus impossible to obtain any purely historical evidence, Tillich's own position is not as safe as he thinks. But quite apart from that it seems to me that the methodological situation is not as hopeless as Tillich has suggested. The fact that we have to depend on the New Testament picture for our general view of the subject does not mean that there cannot be any historical verification. Indeed, is the assumption that the New Testament records are in general quite reliable not a reasonable hypothesis? It can hardly be called a mere assumption and its trustworthiness can be approximately gauged from the comparison of it with other records.

Let us now see how Tillich understands the relevance of historical criticism to Christological doctrine. The rise of historical criticism was, he says, an expression of Protestant courage, and is an element of which Protestantism can be proud. There are three ways in which historical criticism is relevant to theology. First, by revealing the difference between historical, legendary and mythical elements in the Gospel records, historical criticism can help the theologian understand the Christological symbols of the Bible. Tillich distinguishes four steps in their development. First they appear and grow in their own religious culture and language. Then they are used as living expressions of people's self-interpretation and answers to the questions implied in their own existential predicament. Next they undergo a transformation of meaning as they are used to interpret the event on which Christianity is based. Finally, they are distorted by popular superstition which is supported in this by 'theological literalism and supernaturalism'. If these symbols are stripped of their literalistic connotations they can be used again by theology. In other words, historical criticism can help the theologian 'demythologize' the Bible. Secondly, historical research shows how the biblical authors developed the implications of their sharing in the revelation and indirectly contributes to the same development in the critic. Finally, if we examine the Bible we shall find that its writers took up contemporary notions and symbols and transformed them. What was thus done naturally, as it were, the theologian will then attempt to do deliberately—that is, he will attempt a new correlation of faith and the whole of culture.

IV

THE MEANING OF THE INCARNATION

WE must now seek to understand what Tillich means when he talks of Christ as the bringer of the New Being. In other words, how does he understand the 'meaning' of the Incarnation? To call Jesus the Christ meant for the disciples, says Tillich, that with him the new aeon would come about, that he would bring about a new state of things.[1] This expectation was not fulfilled in accordance with the hopes and aspirations of the disciples. This meant that they had either to abandon their hopes or radically change their content. This change of content was effected by identifying the New Being with the sacrificed Jesus. This identification had been made earlier by Jesus himself, but had been resisted by the disciples. Their faith in the paradoxical Messianic claim was created by the experiences of Easter and Pentecost. The theological interpretation and justification of this paradox was the contribution of Paul.

The New Being in Jesus as the Christ is expressed in his whole being, and neither his words nor his deeds nor his sufferings nor yet his 'inner life' make him the Christ. These are all expressions of the New Being which is the quality of his being. The first expression of this is his words, and Tillich emphasizes the supreme importance for New Testament religion of the spoken word. However, as the Word, he is more than all the words he has spoken. And this, for Tillich, is the concrete point which must be grasped; for otherwise we shall relapse into a legalistic view of salvation and so replace Jesus as the Christ by 'the religious and moral teacher called Jesus of Nazareth'. The second expression of the New Being in Jesus as the Christ is his deeds. These too, have been reported of and made into

[1] Cf. *Systematic Theology* II, pp. 112, 135f.

examples to be imitated so that he becomes not a new lawgiver indeed but himself the new law. Tillich admits that in a sense this is true, for the fact that Jesus as the Christ represents the essential unity between God and man makes it incumbent on every human being to take on 'the form of the Christ'. He does not understand this, however, to mean that we are commanded to imitate the Christ. Indeed he says that if the word 'imitation' is used at all in this context 'it should indicate that we, *in* our concreteness, are asked to participate in the New Being and to be transformed by it, not beyond, but within, the contingencies of our life'.[1] The third expression of the New Being in Jesus as the Christ is his suffering. 'Only by taking suffering and death upon himself could Jesus be the Christ, because only in this way could he participate completely in existence and conquer every force of estrangement which tried to dissolve his unity with God.'[2] The significance of the Cross in the New Testament picture of Jesus as the Christ led to the orthodox separation of his suffering and death from his being. But the suffering on the Cross is not something additional which can be separated from the appearance of the God-Man under the conditions of existence. The suffering of Jesus as the Christ is an expression of the New Being in him.

Tillich says that his use of the term 'New Being' in relation to Jesus is analogous to his use of the term being in his doctrine of God. When applied to Jesus as the Christ, the term 'New Being' points to the power in him which conquers existential estrangement, or, negatively expressed, to the power of resisting the forces of estrangement. 'The biblical picture of him confirms his character as the bearer of the New Being or as the one in whom the conflict between the essential unity of God and man and man's existential estrangement is overcome.'[3] The paradox revealed by this picture is that although he has only a finite freedom yet he is not estranged from the ground of his being. This conquest of estrangement by the New Being should not be called 'the sinlessness of Jesus', says Tillich,[4] because this is a negative term used in the New Testament merely to show

---

[1] Cf. *Systematic Theology* II, p. 141.   [2] *Ibid.*
[3] *Ibid.*, p. 144.   [4] *Ibid.*, pp. 145-6.

his victory over the Messianic temptation. Tillich, in fact, calls this term a rationalization of the biblical picture which is always positive. Three things are emphasized in the picture: the complete fortitude of the Christ, the reality of the temptations arising out of it, and finally, the victory over these temptations.[1] The reality of the temptations must be admitted since it is the corollary of the real fortitude of Christ. 'The Church was right, though never fully successful in resisting the monophysitic distortion of the picture of Jesus as the Christ.' If one accepts the temptations as real and not simply appearances then one must first face the problem of the evaluation of desire. For the temptation is serious only if there is an actual desire towards that which has the power to tempt, and this would suggest that there is estrangement prior to the decision either to succumb or to resist the temptation. Tillich resolves this difficulty by making three points.[2] First, temptation presupposes desire but is not constituted by it since the temptation is that the desire should be changed into concupiscence which Tillich defines as 'the inhibited desire to draw the whole of reality into one's self'.[3] His second point is that unity with God does not mean the negation of desire, but only that the finite is desired within this unity rather than alongside it. Finally, resistance to the temptation was not a matter of contingency but as much a matter of destiny as of freedom. The New Testament takes very seriously this matter of destiny and portrays his appearance as the Christ always as both a decision by himself and the result of a divine destiny. The picture of the New Being in Jesus as the Christ is not therefore a picture of a divine automaton, for none of life's ambiguities is removed in his existence and he faces serious temptation, real struggles. The picture we have is that of a personal life in which all the ambiguities of life are transcended in permanent unity with God.

Such, then, is the picture. What now of the dogma? First it must be realized, says Tillich,[4] that dogmas do not arise for speculative reasons—they are, as Luther said, 'protective'

[1] *Ibid.*, p. 146.   [2] *Ibid.*, pp. 148-9.   [3] *Ibid.*, p. 159.
[4] *Ibid.*, p. 161.

doctrines intended to preserve the substance of the Christian message against distortion from outside or inside the Church. Two questions can be asked concerning the dogma—(1) What measure of success did it have in the task of preserving the Christian message against distortion? (2) How successful was the conceptualization of the symbols expressing the Christian message? Tillich's answer is that the Christological dogma saved the Church, but with very inadequate tools.[1] The inadequacy of the tools is due not only to the inevitable inadequacy of any concept to express the message of the New Being in Jesus as the Christ, but also to the dependence of the Greek concepts upon a concrete religion 'determined by the divine figures of Apollo and Dionysus'. The dangers that beset the conceptual interpretation of the assertion that Jesus is the Christ are twofold—that of denying the Christhood of Jesus and that of denying that the Christ is indeed Jesus, the carpenter's son. Reviewing the two great decisions of the early Church on Christological dogma (Nicaea and Chalcedon) Tillich says that 'both the Christian character and the Jesus character of the event of Jesus as the Christ were preserved', despite the inadequacy of the conceptual tools. This means that Protestant theology must accept the 'Catholic' tradition in so far as it is based on the substance of the two great decisions of the early Church and, on the other hand, try to find new ways of expressing the Christological substance of the past. Neither orthodox nor liberal Protestant theology can do just this. The doctrine of the two natures leads to absurd conclusions, as liberalism revealed, and so Tillich thinks it should be replaced by the 'dynamic-relational concepts' of 'eternal God-man-unity' or 'Eternal God-Manhood'.[2]

Before proceeding to Tillich's interpretation of the Cross and the Resurrection it may be useful to raise one or two questions with regard to his general Christological position. The first question that must surely cry out for an answer is—What kind of concept is that of the New Being? When I attended his lectures in 1953 I asked him about this and explained that it seemed to me that if one spoke of it as a class concept then one

[1] Cf. *Systematic Theology* II, p. 167.   [2] *Ibid.*, p. 171.

would have to say that it was a class which had only one member. There is nothing wrong in this because one can in the same way speak of 'God' as a one-member class. However, Tillich's reply was that he was more Platonic than I was and did not accept this Aristotelian logic. Therefore he would describe the New Being as neither genus nor species but a power. This suggests to me that Tillich is not clear about the logical status of his key Christological concept. Moreover, if the 'New Being' is 'the power of Jesus Christ which conquers estrangement' are we to understand that for Tillich the assertion that Jesus is the Christ is nothing more than an explanatory hypothesis? This cannot be the case; for Tillich regards the 'New Being' as almost synonymous with 'Christ'. In the context of this discussion mentioned above the assertion 'Jesus is the Christ because he is the bearer of the New Being' could properly be described as a tautology. It seems difficult to resist the conclusion that in this translation of the classical Christology, Tillich has achieved a rendering which can also only be understood by reading the original. For if one tries to understand it from within the system one meets hopeless confusion in the use of the term 'being' to denote the essential existence of God (if not indeed to 'name' God) and also to denote reality. What Tillich means to say about Jesus when he talks about the New Being, the New Testament says with just as much clarity by means of its proclamation that the Kingdom of God has come, for God was in Christ reconciling the world unto himself. When we come to his evaluation of the Christological dogma, however, one cannot but applaud the fine historical feeling and sense he displays. The first thing which needs to be noted about the dogma is indeed the fact that, however adequate or inadequate its concepts may be, it did protect the Catholic faith of the Church from being distorted. Tillich goes on to say that it is quite clear that the concepts are in fact woefully inadequate and the main reason he evinces, we have seen, is that the concepts are dependent on Hellenistic religion. What exactly he is referring to here is not at all evident, but he does mention a little later the concept of the Logos. It is impossible for us here to enter upon a detailed discussion of the history of the

95

Logos-doctrine, but we can point out that after Clement of Alexandria the doctrine of the Person of Christ came to be set out more and more in terms of the idea of Sonship rather than the Logos-idea. Further, one of the crucial uses of the term is that of the Fourth Gospel, and it would surely be wrong to say that the origins of the Logos-doctrine in the Fourth Gospel are to be found in the Hellenistic cults of Apollo and Dionysus. Dodd has shown that there are enough parallels between passages referring to the Logos in Philo and the propositions of the Prologue to the Fourth Gospel to justify the assumption that Philo's doctrine influenced the Fourth Evangelist's use of the term.

> 'While therefore the statements of the Prologue *might* be understood all through on the assumption that λόγος is the Word of the Lord in the Old Testament sense, yet it seems certain that any reader influenced by the thought of Hellenistic Judaism, directly or at a remove, would inevitably find here a conception of the creative and revealing λόγος in many respects similar to that of Philo; and it is difficult not to think that the author intended this.'[1]

However, as Dodd has pointed out, the Logos-doctrine of the Prologue 'can in great part at least be interpreted without much difficulty upon Old Testament presuppositions.'[2] He concludes that 'the author started from the Jewish idea of the Torah as being at once the Word of God and the divine Wisdom manifested in creation, and found, under the guidance of Hellenistic Jewish thought similar to that of Philo an appropriate Greek expression which fittingly combined both ideas.'[3]

This factual error does not mean that Tillich is wrong when he says that historical criticism is largely responsible for our understanding of the development of Christological symbols. Moreover, one can agree that the conceptual tools which we have inherited from traditional theology are inadequate, but it is far from clear in what way they are inadequate. 'Neither

[1] C. H. Dodd, *The Interpretation of the Fourth Gospel*, Cambridge, 1953, p. 277.
[2] *Ibid.*, p. 272.   [3] *Ibid.*, p. 278.

the orthodox nor the liberal methods of Protestant theology', says Tillich, 'are adequate for the Christological task which the Protestant Church must now fulfil.' But once again the nature of the inadequacy is important, and the crucial question is— What exactly is the present Christological task of the Church? According to Tillich it is that of finding 'new forms in which the Christological substance of the past can be expressed'. There is a sense in which there must be continuous reflection on the puzzles of theological doctrine in order to put the traditional statements in a new way, but we must be careful lest we think of this enterprise as an attempt at translation. It is more like the attempts at solving traditional metaphysical problems such as our knowledge of the external world and our knowledge of other persons. Here we are concerned to remove the bands that keep us tied to the paradoxes of the old metaphysics and we shall ultimately be satisfied only by a new metaphysics. The new metaphysics, however, is in no sense a translation of the old. The reasons which Tillich brings forward to support his rejection of the two-natures theory are strange and in the end, as far as I can see, only verbal. Perhaps they exemplify the general tendency which we have noticed before to regard meanings as things and the meaning of words as something fixed. Here again perhaps, then, is the fallacy that words are bearers of something mysterious which is their meaning. What we are to understand by the word 'nature' in the context of the doctrine is revealed only by the context. True, if we are to understand the doctrine in any philosophical sense we shall need to see more than its domestic logic—but that is another matter. The crucial question with regard to Tillich's Christ-ology is whether the substitution of his dynamic-relational concepts for the two-natures theory does not involve him in an adoptionist Christology. Tillich raises and faces this question himself and makes two points by way of an answer. First, an adoptionist Christology has biblical roots just as much as an incarnational Christology has. Secondly, neither of them can be fully stated without implying the other. It is the second point which is the more interesting, for the first can only be answered by a detailed examination of the New Testament evidence. In what way does an adoptionist Christology involve an incarnational view? Tillich's reply is as follows:

> 'Adoptionism, the idea that God through his Spirit adopted the man Jesus as his Messiah, leads to the question: Why just him? And this question leads back to the polarity of freedom and destiny which created the uninterrupted unity between him and God. . . . The symbol of his pre-existence gives the eternal dimension, and the doctrine of the Logos, which became historical reality (flesh), points to what has been called "Incarnation".'[1]

Equally, incarnation implies adoption. The use of the term 'incarnation' in Christian theology points, says Tillich, to the paradox 'that he who transcends the universe appears in it and under its conditions'.[2] But if we press the language, we get not Christian doctrine but pagan transmutation myths and the corollary problem of how what 'becomes something else yet remains itself'. So Tillich concludes that incarnation means 'manifestation in a personal life' in which is 'a dynamic process involving tensions, risks, dangers, and determination by freedom as well as by destiny. This is the adoption side, without which the Incarnation accent would make unreal the living picture of the Christ.' It is very difficult to resist the conclusion that here again the argument depends on the fallacy we mentioned above—namely, that words are repositories of hypostatic meanings. How do the connotations of 'incarnation' imply transmission? Only if we think of statements about God as being peculiar material statements—that is, if we regard 'incarnation' as meaning what it means in pagan mythology. But there is no reason for doing so unless we believe that since the word has been used thus then this must be part of its meaning. As for adoptionism, we can make a perfectly good story of that without involving ourselves in incarnation. To the question 'Why this man?' we can answer 'Because he was extraordinarily virtuous' and to ask 'Why was he thus?' is to ask a meaningless question, if it is the causal question Tillich has in mind. It seems to me that he has to resort to some rather desperate dialectics in order to save his Christology from being

[1] *Systematic Theology* II, p. 171.   [2] *Ibid.*, p. 172.

in the end inadequate. This is not to say that he has achieved nothing valuable in the process; for his strictures on both orthodoxy and liberalism make us see that the solution of the Christological puzzle must be sought beyond the confines of party theology.

The natural consequence of this discussion of the problem of Christology is a discussion of the doctrine of Atonement; for Christology, says Tillich, is a function of soteriology. Therefore, when the New Testament relates the story of Christ it is not concerned to take the story of an unusually interesting man, but it seeks to give the picture of one who was the Christ and who, therefore, has universal significance. Consequently the individual traits in the picture are not covered over, but 'in every expression of his individuality appears his universal significance.'[1] The universal meaning of Jesus as the Christ is expressed by two central symbols which correspond to his subjection to existence and his conquest of its estrangement—the 'Cross of the Christ' and the 'Resurrection of the Christ'. These are interdependent symbols, and if separated they lose their meaning. For the Cross is the Cross of him who has 'conquered the death of existential estrangement' and the Resurrection is the Resurrection of him who 'as the Christ, subjected himself to the death of existential estrangement'. If the Cross and the Resurrection are interdependent then, says Tillich, 'they must be both reality and symbol'. In both cases there is a factual element or else it cannot be said that the Christ has entered existence and conquered it. 'But there is a qualitative difference. While the stories of the Cross probably point to an event that took place in the full light of historical observation, the stories of the Resurrection spread a veil of deep mystery over the event.'[2] 'The historical objectivity of the Cross is easy to appreciate, and it will be agreed that the Cross is therefore an event.' But it is also a symbol for it is understood as possessing universal significance. Tillich goes so far as to say that 'as the Cross of the Jesus who is the Christ, it is a symbol and a part of a myth'.[3] Whatever the historical circumstances may have been then the Cross is a symbol based on fact. But the same is true of the

[1] *Ibid.*, p. 175. [2] *Ibid.*, p. 177. [3] *Ibid.*

99

Resurrection. It, too, is a familiar mythological symbol, and it was unavoidable that the idea of Resurrection should be applied to the Christ. However, the disciples' assertion that the symbol had become an event transcended the mythological symbolism of the mystery cult. 'The character of this event remains in darkness, even in the poetic rationalization of the Easter story.'[1] Resurrection was the acid-test for deciding whether Jesus was the Christ, and a real experience made it possible for the disciples to apply the symbol of resurrection to Jesus and so to acknowledge him definitely as the Christ.

Three theories have been put forward as attempts to make the historical fact of Resurrection probable. The first is the primitive physical theory told in the story of the tomb which the women found empty on Easter morning. The sources of this story are late and questionable, says Tillich, and there is no trace of it in the earliest tradition we have concerning the Resurrection, namely I Corinthians 15. This is a rationalization of the idea of resurrection making it identical with the absence of the body. 'Then the absurd question arises as to what happened to the molecules which comprise the corpse of Jesus of Nazareth. Then absurdity becomes compounded into blasphemy.'[2]

The second theory is the spiritual one. Taking the Pauline records of manifestations, it understands them as records of manifestations of the 'soul' of the man Jesus to his followers analogous to the soul-manifestations in spiritualistic experience. To this Tillich rightly replies that it is not the Resurrection of the Christ but a matter of general immortality and the claim that souls which have survived death can manifest themselves in the world.[3] But the Resurrection as a fact was more than this since it is described in the story as the reappearance of the total personality.

The third theory is the psychological theory, according to which the Resurrection is an event which took place in the minds of Jesus's disciples. Tillich does not describe this theory in any detail, nor does he tell us how far it takes the

[1] *Systematic Theology* II, p. 178.　　[2] *Ibid.*, p. 180.　　[3] *Ibid.*

psychological interpretation of the story. It is sufficiently clear however, that 'the psychological theory misses the reality of the event presupposed in the symbol.'[1]

After this brief discussion of traditional theories, Tillich puts forward his own theory concerning the Resurrection. To understand what it is, he says, we must see what is overcome by it. 'The negativity which is overcome in the Resurrection is that of the disappearance of him whose being was the New Being.'[2] The disciples had been convinced that the power of his being was that of the New Being; and on the other hand, they felt that Jesus' disappearance was inconsistent with the character of the bearer of the New Being. 'In this tension something unique happened. In an ecstatic experience the concrete picture of Jesus of Nazareth became indissolubly united with the reality of the New Being.'[3] He is present wherever the New Being is present. He 'is the spirit' and 'we know him now' only because he is in the Spirit. 'This event happened first to some of his followers who had fled to Galilee in the hours of his execution; then to many others; then to Paul; then to all those who in every period experience his living presence here and now.'[4] This is the event which was so readily interpreted by means of the symbol 'Resurrection'. The combination of the event and the symbol is the central Christian symbol, the Resurrection of the Christ.

This 'restitution theory' which he has propounded concerning the event of the Resurrection is, Tillich thinks, most adequate to the facts. However it 'remains in the realm of probability and does not have the certainty of faith'.[5] As a historical conjecture it seems to me most inadequate inasmuch as its description of facts is abstract and vague, and therefore the actual historical claim is at a minimum. Also, it does not conduce to clarity to oppose this to the statements of faith as probability to certainty. If it is adequate to the facts then it is a piece of accredited history. But it is not clear how its adequacy to the facts can be judged. Moreover, we can also raise the question of how the factual character of the Cross and the Resurrection is apprehended according to Tillich. We recall

[1] *Ibid.* [2] *Ibid.*, p. 181. [3] *Ibid.* [4] *Ibid.* [5] *Ibid.*, p. 182.

the statement which he makes more than once that, since the Cross and the Resurrection are interdependent symbols, they must be both reality and symbol.[1] Nowhere does he make any attempt to show this is so, and it can hardly be regarded as self-evident. Indeed it is not difficult to conceive of two symbols which are interdependent and yet do not make any historical claims. In early Brahmanism, for example the Brahmanaspati, Agni, and Soma, are interdependent, and yet not in any sense historical. Similarly, in the following lines from Dylan Thomas we have a non-historical interdependence of symbols:

'Abaddon in the hangnail cracked from Adam,
And from his fork, a dog among the fairies,
The atlas-eater with a flair for news,
Bit out the mandrake with to-morrow's scream.'[2]

Discussing the symbols which corroborate the symbol 'Cross of Christ' and the symbol 'Resurrection of the Christ', Tillich emphasises that neither story is a story of an isolated event. The story of the Cross is a story of 'that event towards which the story of his life is directed and in which the others receive their meaning'[3]—i.e., he who is the Christ subjects himself to the 'ultimate negativities of existence' and they are not able to separate him from God. Similarly, the story of the Resurrection reports 'the event which is anticipated in a large number of other events and which is, at the same time, their confirmation'.[4] It shows the New Being in Jesus as the Christ victorious over the existential estrangement to which he has subjected himself.

The point of these symbols, namely the universal significance of Jesus as the Christ, can also be expressed in the term 'salvation'. The term salvation has as many uses as there are things from which we can be saved, but its distinctively theological use is to express salvation from 'ultimate negativity' or eternal death. However, this too has been variously conceived in the

---

[1] Cf. *Systematic Theology* II, p. 177.
[2] Dylan Thomas, *Collected Poems*, London, Dent, 1952, p. 71.
[3] *Systematic Theology* II, p. 182.   [4] *Ibid.*, p. 183.

history of Christianity so that salvation in the Roman Catholic Church is from guilt and its consequences and in classical Protestantism it is salvation from the law.[1] Tillich, however, understands it as meaning essentially 'healing', 'reuniting that which is estranged, giving a centre to what is split, overcoming the split between God and man, and man and his world, man and himself'.[2] Just as there is a history of revelation, the centre of which is the event Jesus as the Christ, so the appearance of salvation through Christ is not separated from the processes of salvation, which occur throughout all history. Indeed where there is revelation there too is salvation; for revelatory events are saving events in which the power of the New Being is present. Understood thus salvation cannot develop into the problem of what happens to those people for whom encounter with Jesus as the Christ is impossible. To describe these as in any sense doomed to exclusion for eternal life is for Tillich an absurd and demonic idea. But if this is the case, then one may ask what Tillich can mean by saying that Jesus is the Saviour. This does not, he says, mean that there is no saving power apart from him, but rather means that he is the ultimate criterion of

[1] A full discussion of this subject is clearly impossible here, but the distinction—for all its attractive neatness—can hardly be said to be accurate. Its only possible application is with reference to the debates carried on by Matthias Flacius Illyricus (1520-75) who maintained that good works lead to condemnation (see Wilhelm Preger, *Matthias Flacius Illyricus und seine Zeit*, Erlangen, 1859-60, vol. 2, pp. 310-412, *et passim*). As a general characterization of the Protestant and Catholic positions, however, the distinction is misleading. It over-simplifies Protestantism; for surely in Luther's theology salvation was as much from sin as from law. To be saved, says Luther, 'is to be released from sin, death and the devil and to be brought into Christ's kingdom and to live with him there for ever' (*Primary Works*, London, 1896, p. 133—cf. *A Commentary on St Paul's Epistle to the Galatians*, London, 1807, pp. 185-95, 255ff.). Similarly, it misleadingly reduces the complexity of the Catholic doctrine. The Council of Trent defines justification as being 'not only the remission of sins but also the sanctification and the renewal of the inner man by the voluntary reception of grace and its gifts by which man becomes just from unjust and friend from enemy' (see also canons 10 and 11 of the Council). The doctrine of the Church, says Professor J. Rivière, is entirely established by the synthesis 'of the religious element and the moral element of the profession of faith and the practice of works which is its consequence' (*Dictionnaire de Théologie Catholique*, Tôme VIII, 2,216; cf. 2,212).
[2] *Systematic Theology* II, p. 192.

every saving process. In him the healing quality is complete and unlimited. Moreover, there can be no distinction between his person and his work. 'Jesus as the Christ is the Saviour through the universal significance of his being as the New Being.'[1] Other terms used to describe him as the saving power are Mediator and Redeemer. Both have semantic difficulties— 'Mediator' suggesting a third reality between God and men, and 'Redeemer' suggesting the idea of someone from whom men must be ransomed. These dangerous connotations need not, however, prevent the use of these terms to express a doctrine of atonement.

The doctrine of the atonement, says Tillich, is 'the description of the effect of the New Being on those who are grasped by it in their state of estrangement'.[2] Thus he regards the atonement as being both a divine act and a human reaction; or, to put the matter differently, when we talk of atonement we are describing two quite different processes, one of which is by definition transcendent, whereas the other is psychological. Atonement means the removal of human guilt as the factor responsible for man's separation from God. This act of God, however, is effective only in so far as man reacts and accepts the divine offer of reconciliation. Therefore, for Tillich, atonement necessarily has a subjective as well as an objective element. Because of this subjective element 'a moment of indefiniteness is introduced into the doctrine of atonement'.[3] This is why, Tillich thinks, the Church has refused to develop a dogma of Atonement similar to the dogma concerning the Person of Christ. And since there has been no dogma, different types of Atonement doctrine have been put forward, each of which has some particular strength as well as its characteristic weakness. Two main types can be distinguished—the objective and the subjective; and besides these main types there is the third class of what we may call mediating theories. Thus Origen's theory of the Atonement is radically objective—man was released from the bondage of guilt and self-destruction by means of a deal between God, Satan and Christ in which Satan was fooled. Satan received power over Christ, but as he had no

[1] *Systematic Theology* II, p. 195.   [2] *Ibid.*, p. 196.   [3] *Ibid.*, p. 197.

right to exercise power over someone who was innocent his power over Christ and those who are with Christ is broken. Tillich criticises this class of Atonement doctrine (which, he says, includes Aulén's view in *Christus Victor*) as being essentially a cosmic drama which has no relation at all to man. It happens above man's head but is the source of his certainty that he is liberated from the demonic power. This, however, says Tillich, is not what the biblical objectivism means. 'In Paul's triumphant verses about the victory of the love of God in Christ over all the demonic powers, it is the experience of the love of God which precedes the application of this experience to a symbolism involving demonic powers—consequently, the symbol of the victory of Christ over the demons.'[1] Turning his attention to the concrete symbols, Tillich comments first on the metaphysical significance of Satan's betrayal, namely, that 'the negative lives from the positive, which it distorts'. The message of Christianity to the age in which it appeared was a message of liberation from its fear of the demonic powers. The process of atonement is that of liberation. However, this is possible only 'if something happens, not only objectively, but also subjectively'.

The subjective type of Atonement theory was developed by Abélard. This theory concerns itself with the liberating impression made upon men by the picture of Christ the Crucified. This impression is that of his self-surrendering love which awakens in man an answering love which is convinced that God is ultimately love and not wrath. This theory does not satisfy Christian theology, says Tillich, because it ignores the need for justice in love. 'The violated justice cannot be re-established by the message of divine love alone.... The message of a divine love which neglects the message of divine justice cannot give man a good conscience.'[2] Tillich takes an analogy from the psycho-analytic teachings of inducing abreaction in order to gain a catharsis. The outstanding greatness of the Anselmian theory for Tillich is that it does adequately express this psychological situation, though formally it is an objective type of theory. The point of the theory is that the work of

[1] *Ibid.*, p. 198.   [2] *Ibid.*, p. 199.

105

Christ makes it possible for God to execute mercy without violating the demands of justice, mercy and justice constituting a tension in the divine. This work alone is sufficient for that since, as man, the God-Man could suffer and, as God, he did not need to suffer his own sins. The believer's guilt is thus fully recognized, but his punishment has been taken over by the suffering of the Christ. Despite its legalism and its quantitative notion of sin the Anselmian theory thus makes a valuable point. There are other weaknesses in the theory which have been mentioned in connection with the terms 'Mediator' and 'Redeemer', and again there is the fundamental criticism that the subjective side of the atoning process is not present at all.[1]

On the basis of this discussion of the types of Atonement theory Tillich then offers six principles 'which should determine the further development of the doctrine of atonement or what may even replace it in future theology'.[2]

1. 'The atoning processes are created by God and by God alone. This means that God is not dependent on the Christ in the process of removing guilt. Rather the Christ as the bearer of the New Being mediates the reconciling act of God to man.'[3]

2. There are no conflicts between God's reconciling love and his retributive justice. The justice of God is 'the act through which he lets the self-destructive consequences of existential estrangement go their way'.[4] Moreover the execution of justice is itself an operation of love since justice is 'the structural form of love without which it would be sheer sentimentality'.

3. The divine removal of guilt and punishment is not an act of overlooking the reality and depth of existential estrangement. For herein lies the difference between human forgiveness and God's—that human forgiveness must

---

[1] *Ibid.*, p. 200. A full discussion of Anselm's doctrine of Atonement is impossible here and we must content ourselves with pointing out that Tillich is wrong when he says that the subjective element is completely absent from Anselm's doctrine. See J. McIntyre, *St Anselm and his Critics*, Edinburgh, Oliver and Boyd, 1954.

[2] *Systematic Theology* II, pp. 200-3.   [3] *Ibid.*, p. 200.   [4] *Ibid.*, p. 201.

always be mutual since both parties are guilty. 'But God represents the order of being which is violated by separation from God; his forgiveness is no private matter.'[1]

4. God's atoning activity must be understood as his participation in existential estrangement and its self-destructive consequences. This is the core of the doctrine of Atonement, and here we have to face the problem of what it means to say that God takes the suffering of the world upon himself by participating in existential estrangement. Tillich's answer to that, of course, is that the expression is symbolic and points to the eternal conquering of non-being in the divine life whilst not contradicting God's eternal blessedness and his eternal 'aseity'.[2]

5. In the Cross of Christ the divine participation in existential estrangement becomes manifest. Tillich insists that this interpretation means more than 'becomes known'. 'Manifestations are effective expressions not only communications.'[3] The Cross of the Christ is a manifestation 'by being actualization'—not the only one but the central one. 'The Cross is not the cause but the effective manifestation of God's taking the consequences of human guilt upon himself. And, since the atoning process includes the subjective side, namely, the experience of man that God is eternally reconciled, one can say that atonement is actualised through the Cross of the Christ. This partly justifies a theology which makes God's atoning act dependent on the "merit" of the Christ.'[4]

6. Through participation in the New Being, which is the being of Jesus as the Christ, men also participate in the manifestation of the atoning act of God. They participate in the suffering of Christ, accept it and are transformed by it. This is the threefold character of the state of salvation —in classical terminology, Regeneration, Justification and Sanctification.

[1] *Ibid.*
[2] *Ibid.*, p. 202. On existential estrangement see following chapter.
[3] *Ibid.*   [4] *Ibid.*, p. 203.

Regeneration is the classical term for the relation of the New Being to those who are grasped by it. In its biblical usage this term does not mean only something subjective but also 'a state of things universally'. It is the new state of things which the Christ brought, into which the individual enters and so is 'reborn'. The message of conversion is twofold—first, a message of a new reality to which we are asked to turn, and secondly, a message that we should turn away from the old reality. Regeneration if it is thus understood, has little to do with the creation of emotional states and reactions but is the state of having been drawn into the new reality manifest in Jesus as the Christ.

The priority of Justification or Regeneration is the issue between a Lutheran theology and a pietistic one. The Lutheran emphasis is on Justification, whereas, the pietistic is upon Regeneration. 'A decision between them', says Tillich, 'is dependent partly on the way one defines the terms but partly also on different religious experiences.' If, however, Regeneration is understood as participation in the New Being, it precedes Justification; for Justification presupposes faith. As with Regeneration, we can distinguish the two elements of Justification—the objective event and the subjective reception. 'Justification in the objective sense is the eternal act of God by which he accepts as not estranged those who are indeed estranged from him by guilt and the act by which he takes them into the unity with him which is manifest in the New Being in Christ.'[1] Justification is an act of God which is in no way dependent on man; but for man there is the task of accepting that he is accepted though he is unacceptable. Justification must never be understood as something merited by faith. 'The cause is God alone (by grace), but the faith that one is accepted is the channel through which grace is mediated to man (through faith).'[2] As an act of God Regeneration and Justification are one, but Sanctification is distinguished from both 'as a process is distinguished from an event in which it is initiated'.[3] Sanctification is the process in which the power of the New Being transforms personality and community both within and without

[1] *Systematic Theology* II, p. 205.   [2] *Ibid.*, p. 206.   [3] *Ibid.*, p. 207.

the Church. The sharp distinction which has been drawn in the history of doctrine between Sanctification and Justification reveals historical exigencies rather than any difference in the meaning of the terms.

Our exposition of Tillich's interpretation of atonement concludes our discussion of his Christology, and before we leave it we must attempt some sort of criticism. There can be no doubt that this is a most courageous answer to the question, What does it benefit me now in this modern age that I should believe all this about Christ? Tillich's use of the analogy between the situation of divine forgiveness and that of psychological therapy is illuminating, and one can agree that it is here that we can hope to find the language which will provide effective analogies by which to proclaim the gospel of God's redeeming love. Even so, there seems to me to be something highly suspect in Tillich's insistence that there is a subjective element in atonement so that the doctrine of atonement is at once a statement about God and a statement concerning man. It seems to me that if we understand doctrinal statements in this way we are in danger of distorting their character. At least it must be emphasised that the doctrine of Atonement is not capable of interpretation as a description of certain psychological processes. For there is all the difference in the world between saying 'God has reconciled us to himself through Christ' and 'Today I feel much happier than I did yesterday about my religious obligations.' This crude example brings out the fact that however the first statement is to be interpreted it must always be a statement about God and so is not a description of a state of affairs capable of exhaustive empirical verification. In so far as the doctrine of Atonement makes reference to God at all it is a description of transcendent actions and so incapable of reduction to any set of statements which contain merely empirical language. The assertion that God was uniquely present in the passion and death of Jesus making Atonement, 'reconciling the world unto himself', is the very core of this doctrine. Brunner says very well that the Atonement is not history. 'The Atonement', he continues, 'the expiation of human guilt, the covering of sin through his sacrifice, is not anything which can be conceived from the point of view of history. This event does not belong to the historical plane. It is super-history, it lies in the dimension which no historian knows in so far as he is a mere historian.'[1] Since we are not talking of an event which, besides being an actual past occurrence is also a present reality it seems unnecessary to regard the death of Christ as initiating a process which is continued in the believer's personal history. Tillich's remarks about the subjective element of atonement that it makes atonement partly dependent on man's possibilities of reaction and introduces a moment of indefiniteness into the doctrine[2]—seem to lessen the once-for-allness of atonement. When we acknowledge the mercy of God who gave his only son to suffer death on the Cross for our redemption we say that Christ 'made there (by his one oblation of himself once offered) a full, perfect, and sufficient sacrifice, oblation, and satisfaction, for the sins of the whole world'. And if it is *one* oblation *once* offered and a perfect sacrifice and satisfaction there can be no other part of atonement. The difficulty which faces Tillich here is apparent if we recall the devices he resorts to in his attempt to bridge the gap between the language about God and the language about what goes on in us. The fifth principle he lays down says that in the Cross the divine participation in existential estrangement was manifest and further that manifestation here means effective expression—that is, a disclosure which somehow transforms. But this is the very issue he has previously avoided in his efforts to understand atonement as referring to psychology. Indeed one cannot help feeling that there is a tension between the language of Tillich's objective moments and the more psychological language, a tension that is not resolved even by the description of Justification as the work of grace channelled by faith.

In conclusion we may say that the tendency to reduce theological statements to empirical language is seen in the brief discussion of Sanctification[3] where there are some hints that Tillich would understand it as something belonging to the

---

[1] E. Brunner, *The Mediator*, London, Lutterworth Press, 1937, p. 504.
[2] *Systematic Theology* II, p. 197.   [3] *Ibid.*, p. 207.

language of morality. But if 'being sanctified' is logically synonymous with 'being good' then we must ask why we are neither wholly bad nor good when we yet believe that God has sanctified us in Christ. To ask whether we can do wrong after we have been sanctified is like asking whether we can play the piano after you have been confirmed. That is to say, the relation between ethical language and Christian doctrine is not that of translation or implication. Hobbes' remark about holiness is relevant here—it belongs to God, he says, by special and not by general right.[1] If then we speak of X being sanctified we make claims not so much about X but about God. This may well lead us to wonder whether it is at all useful to distinguish between the three terms: Regeneration, Justification and Sanctification. Is it not because we confuse three models for speaking of God's merciful action with the names of some three mental acts like my conversion to the Communist Party's point of view, my pledging myself to the Communist Party, and my increasing knowledge and understanding of the Communist Party line? Once again we need to point out that words do not always have meaning as names.

[1] Hobbes, *Leviathan*, ch. 35 (Everyman edition, p. 221).

V

THE DOCTRINE OF MAN

WE have seen the importance for Tillich's system of his Christological doctrine; and since the New Being serves as a criterion of what constitutes saving revelation we might with justice say that this is the central doctrine in Tillich's system. However, the system is so interrelated that we could with equal justice maintain that the central doctrine is the doctrine of man. For, according to the method of correlation, such fundamental affirmations of faith as God, Christ, and the Kingdom of God are the answers to the existential questions of human finitude, human sin, and human destiny. Thus his doctrine of man in a sense underlies Tillich's view of these affirmations. It is certainly the basis of his ethical and political theories.

Tillich does not understand man's selfhood to be something completely independent of the world. Man is directly aware of the structures which make cognition possible because he lives in them and acts through them. If we are to develop a doctrine of man, then, says Tillich, we must start with man's self-relatedness which is the characteristic of all his experience, and, therefore, the presupposition of any question concerning this experience. To be a self means that man is both over against the world (he is a subject) and also in the world (he can be an object). Because of his self-consciousness man transcends his spatio-temporal environment, and yet he is also continuous with nature. These statements concerning man are not generalizations from empirical observations but are *a priori* truths like Kant's doctrine of the Categories as the *a priori* forms of the understanding. The reciprocal relationship between 'personal' and 'communal' is a structural characteristic of being. Similarly freedom goes hand in hand with destiny.

The structure of man's essential nature is the structure of finite freedom. Tillich does not put the problem of freedom as the question of determinism versus indeterminism. Neither of these positions does justice to man's understanding of his own ontological structure.[1] For in both theories the question is understood as the question of whether a thing has a certain quality or not. Moreover, says Tillich, when the question is put in this way, there can be no doubt that the determinist is right, since a thing is by definition completely determined. Thus indeterminism postulates decision without an attempt to defend the freedom of man's cognitive and ethical action; and if this is the indeterminist's justification of freedom he is really identifying it with unintelligible accident. Further, neither of the two theories can be spoken of as true, for truth involves an intelligible decision for the true against the false as a possibility. Mechanistic determinism cannot make room for decision, and indeterminism cannot make room for intelligibility.

The question of freedom should not then be raised as the question of a quality of a faculty but as that of an element in man's ontological structure.[2] Whatever goes to make man personal is, therefore, related to his freedom. The fact that determinacy is characteristic of broken segments of personality does not mean that the personality as a whole is not free. Whereas mechanical action may be illuminatingly described in terms of the freedom of the self the converse is never the case. And if we say that there is no difference between personal behaviour and mechanical action inasmuch as it is the stronger motive that prevails in the former just as the stronger force prevails in mechanical action, this is only to beg the question of what we mean by a 'stronger' motive. A motive may be selfish or otherwise, but what would it be to have a strong motive? Tillich concludes that the self is responsible in so far as its acts are determined not by something external but 'by the centred totality of the person's being'.[3] And when it is thus understood there is nothing about freedom to conflict

---

[1] See Chapter I (p. 33f.) for discussion of Husserl.
[2] Cf. *Systematic Theology* I, pp. 202-3.   [3] *Ibid.*, p. 204.

with destiny. The self which decides is self which has been formed by nature and history; the self includes 'bodily structures, psychic strivings, moral and spiritual character, communal relations, past experiences, and the total impact of the environment'. Having a destiny is compatible with freedom because persons can realise their destinies.

It is the polarity of freedom and destiny which distinguishes human existence from other levels of existence for Tillich. For the structure of man's essential nature is the structure of finite freedom. The concept of finitude is the core of Tillich's doctrine of man, and it is one of the most difficult to understand and explain. Part of the difficulty is due to his connection of this concept with the dogma of *creatio ex nihilo*. As we have seen in our discussion of his doctrine of creation,[1] Tillich understands the *nihilo* to describe the source of human nature. We come out of non-being. The source of this idea of an existent nonbeing is perhaps Heidegger who insists that the logical act of negating presupposes an ontological basis. The very fact of logical denial presupposes a type of being 'which can transcend the immediately given situation by means of expectations which may be disappointed'.[2] This being is man and Tillich goes on to say that 'unless man participates in nonbeing, no negative judgments are possible, in fact, no judgments of any kind are possible'. Ontologically as well as logically, it is wrong, says Tillich, to place being and nothingness in absolute contrast. 'There can be no world unless there is a dialectical participation of nonbeing in being.'[3] Though Christianity talked of creation as *ex ouk on* (undialectical nothing) rather than *ex me on* (the dialectical nothing), there are three points, says Tillich, at which the theologian must face the dialectical problem of nonbeing. They are the doctrine of sin, of man's creatureliness, and of God. First, when Augustine and others called sin 'nonbeing' they did not mean that sin has no reality but rather that sin has no positive ontological standing, while at the same time they understood 'nonbeing' as 'resistance to being' or 'perversion of being'. Secondly, man is created out of nothing and to nothing he must return. This is why neither the Arian

[1] See above, p. 68.   [2] *Systematic Theology* I, p. 208.   [3] *Ibid.*

doctrine of the Logos as the highest of the creatures nor the Platonic doctrine of natural immortality can be accepted by Christian theology. Finally, 'if God is called the living God, if he is the ground of the creative processes of life, if history has significance for him, if there is no negative principle in addition to him which could account for evil and sin, how can we avoid positing a dialectical negativity in God himself?' Böhme, Schelling and others after them have, therefore, related non-being dialectically to God. Being, limited by non-being, is finitude. To be something is to be finite. Finitude is experienced only by man.

> 'The finite self faces a world; the finite individual has the power of universal participation; man's vitality is united with an essentially unlimited intentionality; as finite freedom he is involved in an embracing destiny. All the structures of finitude force finite being to transcend itself and, just for this reason, to become aware of itself as finite.'[1]

In his explanation of the opposition of 'infinite' and 'finite', Tillich calls infinity a directing and not a constituting concept. This seems to be the same distinction as Kant drew between regulative and constitutive principles.[2] The former are necessary for thought, contributing to the unification of our conceptual knowledge but are not directly related to objects. Tillich can describe infinity in this way because he does not identify infinitude with being-itself. Being-itself 'precedes the finite, and it precedes the infinite negation of the finite.'

On the level of awareness finitude appears as anxiety, for finitude is the ontological basis of anxiety or *urangst*. Like finitude, anxiety is an ontological quality and 'can only be seen and described'. It must be distinguished, on the one hand, from fear, which has a definite object and can be effaced by action, and, on the other hand, from neurotic anxiety resulting from inner conflicts the resolution of which by psychotherapy removes the neurosis.

[1] *Systematic Theology* I, p. 211.
[2] See *Critique of Pure Reason* B 537, 671-96.

Following Heidegger once more Tillich regards anxiety as directed towards 'nothingness'. The recovery of the meaning of anxiety he regards as one of the achievements of the twentieth century. Anxiety is the self-awareness of the finite as finite, and as such has revealing power. Its strongly emotional character 'indicates that the totality of the finite being participates in finitude and faces the threat of nothingness'. As ontological, finitude characterizes both the outward and the inner forms of experience. So Tillich proceeds to discuss the categories, 'the forms in which the mind grasps and shapes reality'. Both the conception of category and the method of Tillich's discussion are more or less Kantian. What is not Kantian is the existentialist interpretation of the categories as objectively the union of being and nothing and subjectively the union of anxiety and courage. Both the subjective and the objective side of this analysis are, Tillich insists, ontological and not psychological in character. Like Kant, Tillich makes each category yield an antinomy where a decision concerning the meaning of the category cannot be based on an analysis of the category itself.[1] Therefore, he concludes that since metaphysics cannot solve the problem an existential attitude must be adopted.

Time, the central category of finitude, has always fascinated philosophers by its mysterious character, and some have emphasised its negative element while others have called attention to the positive element. The former argue that the present is an illusion, that it is nothing more than a point moving from a non-existent past to a non-existent future. Those philosophers who have emphasised the positive element of time have regarded time as creative, having an irreversible direction and ever producing something new. Yet neither analysis is satisfactory. Time cannot be illusory because being means to be present, and if the present is illusory then being is conquered by nonbeing. On the other hand, it will not do simply to say that time is creative, for time also drives towards destruction and 'swallows' what it has created. Corresponding to this objective antinomy there is an inward polarity between anxiety and courage. The onward march of time towards nonbeing

[1] *Systematic Theology* I, pp. 213ff.

comes home to man in his anticipation of his own death in his anxiety about *having* to die. This anxiety is potentially present in every moment and belongs to the created character of being quite apart from estrangement and sin. 'It is actual in "Adam" (i.e. man's essential nature) as well as in "Christ" (i.e. man's new reality).'[1] Now this natural anxiety is balanced by a courage which affirms temporality. And this courage, effective in all beings, is consciously effective only in man. Indeed man is the most courageous of all beings because he has to conquer the deepest anxiety. The present implies space, says Tillich, because 'the present always involves man's presence in it, and presence means having something present to one's self over against one's self'.[2] Like time, space unites being with non-being and anxiety with courage. Again as with time any discussion of space leads us to contradiction. Positively, we may say that every being strives to maintain a 'place' for itself. To be means to have space socially as well as physically—that is, a vocation, a sphere of influence, a place in remembrance and anticipation. These needs are natural and innocent. On the other hand, 'no finite being possesses a space which is definitely its own'[3] and ultimately every place must be lost and with it being itself. This means ultimate insecurity and so anxiety. But this anxiety is balanced by the courage with which man affirms the present, and with it, space.[4]

Causality, like time and space, is ambiguous, expressing both being and non-being.[5] Interpreted affirmatively, causality points to the power from which things proceed, the power which can produce and maintain realities despite the resistance of non-being. On the other hand, however, finite things cannot be said to possess their own power of coming into being; they are 'thrown' into existence. The contingency of the world points to the fact that finite existence can lapse into non-being. The category of causality has its subjective counterpart in the polarity of human anxiety, at our lack of self-sufficiency and the courage which achieves self-reliance despite the inescapable facts of contingency and dependence.

[1] *Systematic Theology* I, p. 215.   [2] *Ibid.*, p. 216.   [3] *Ibid.*
[4] *Ibid.*, p. 217.   [5] *Ibid.*

'The anxiety in which causality is experienced is that of nonbeing in, of, and by, one's self, of not having the "anxiety" which theology traditionally attributes to God. . . . Courage ignores the causal dependence of everything finite.'[1]

The fourth category which describes the union of being and nonbeing in everything finite is substance.[2] Substance points to something underlying the flux of appearances. The concepts of substance and accidents are both logically and ontologically interdependent and so 'in both substance and accidents the positive element is balanced by the negative element'. As far as man is concerned the concept of substance is related to the question of self-identity. Questions about an immortal soul express our anxiety at the anticipation of complete loss of identity with one's self in death. We can solve the problem only by trying to attribute permanence to a creative work, a love relation, a concrete situation, himself, and in this way displaying the courage of affirming the finite.

This discussion of the categories concludes our discussion of Tillich's doctrine of the finite, and before we proceed to his related doctrines of the Fall and Sin we must examine what he has said about the nature of finitude. It will be as well to start with the criticism of detail and then to make our criticism of the general concept of the finite. Tillich begins with the self-world correlation and so avoids the epistemological confusion of either rationalism or idealism. What is more difficult to understand is his conception of 'individualization' and 'participation' as ontological elements which are *a priori* in some such way as Space and Time and the Categories are *a priori* for Kant. What does it mean to say that the knower participates in what is knowable? To say that this polarity of individualization and participation solves the problem of nominalism and realism is to make a purely empty claim. For the category of individualization seems to mean only that if anything exists it is an individual, which is a harmless enough tautology. However, the concept of participation is ambiguous and, therefore, capable of producing confusion. 'Without participation the category of relation would have no basis in reality.

[1] *Sytematic Theology* I, p. 218.   [2] *Ibid.*, p. 219.

Every relation includes a kind of participation.' 'Participation' is thus understood in the widest possible sense as including even such relations as exclusion, hostility, and indifference. Thus once more we have a tautology, and whenever there is relation we find participation. But this is to use a blanket term to cover far too many and too diverse relations so that we gain nothing by using it. Indeed there is the danger of making a particular relation such as knowledge a matter of participation (in the ordinary sense of the term) simply because it must conform to our definition.

Equally baffling is Tillich's discussion of freedom. We may readily agree that the problem of freedom has been posed far too often in an unsatisfactory way. But it is surely trivial to say that thus determinism always wins because 'by definition *a thing*—lacks freedom'.[1] Nor is it the case that both determinism and indeterminism are formally fallacious inasmuch as they deny by implication their claim to express truth. The determinist position is quite simply that the two stories which can be told about voluntary action—the scientific and the personal—seem to conflict, and whilst we deliberate by design the response leading to action comes by nature when the proper forces have been brought to bear. This cannot imply anything about the general possibility of truth. Tillich complicates the problem further by his discussion of the experience of freedom as deliberation, decision and responsibility, and his insistence that destiny is the basis of any freedom.

One final point of detail must be mentioned. Tillich's conception of the nature of finitude depends upon the validity of his interpretation of the phrase *creatio ex nihilo*. As we have said earlier,[2] Tillich interprets this as meaning that the human creature carries within him the heritage of non-being. We have also pointed out the error of this as an interpretation of the Christian doctrine of Creation in so far as it makes for dualism and also misinterprets the expression *ex nihilo*, giving the phrase a descriptive function which it does not have and hypostatizing the *nihil*. It is clear that if we reject this we have in principle rejected the description of anxiety and the categories as well.

[1] *Ibid.*, p. 202.   [2] See p. 68.

This is not to deny that there is some valuable psychological insight in the discussion of the significance of the categories for man.

This criticism of the concept of finitude brings us to the general criticism. Tillich's use of the term 'finite' seems rather ambiguous, for though he says quite clearly that the term 'infinite' is only a directing and not a constituting concept he seems to regard 'finite' as essentially a constituting concept. This, however, is to do the impossible. For consider what we mean by saying that anything is finite. 'Finite' only has meaning in relation to 'infinite'. There is no sense in saying that X is finite unless I can somehow say that Y is infinite. According to Tillich I can perfectly well talk of the infinite, but any statement of the form 'Y is infinite' will not have a literal meaning and can in no sense predicate something of Y. Of 'X is finite', Tillich would want to say that it is a statement in which we attribute a certain property to X. But if the use of 'X is finite' can only be fully elucidated by showing the use of 'Y is infinite', we cannot agree that this is the proper use of 'X is finite'. In brief, if 'finite' and 'infinite' are polar concepts can the one be a regulative and the other a constitutive concept? Secondly, in what sense is man's experience of finitude revelatory? Tillich seems to suggest that this experience is some sort of argument for God, though one must admit that his terms 'question' and 'answer' need not be interpreted in this way. However, if this is in any way regarded as an argument for God, then it is surely mistaken. For if only because of the polar character of the concept 'the finite', to say that the world is finite or the structure of man is finite freedom is already to assert the conclusion of this argument. If man is described as finite then we are in fact saying that God exists (or as Tillich might say, is). Let us consider our statements 'X is finite' and 'Y is infinite'. We said that the first at least is understood as attributing a certain property to X. But what kind of property is finitude? In other words, when we say of man's freedom that it is finite, do we mean to specify something in the freedom as we specify the colour of a wine when we say 'Claret is red'? Or consider the term 'infinite'. If I say that God is infinitely powerful I do not mean to say that just as Mr Krushchev governs the destiny of a very large population so God—only much more. What I mean to say is that no comparison between Mr Krushchev's power and God's can be ultimately satisfactory. As describing a particular attribute then the word 'infinite' does not relate directly to objects, does not seem to be itself an attribute. But this brings us once more to the point we made earlier, that talking of finitude is only possible on the basis of a knowledge of God and his attributes.

The doctrine of man's 'existential' nature is not a description of man's actual being but is the analysis of those qualities of man's nature which express the contrast between what he actually is and what he essentially is. Tillich's contrast is expressed in the doctrine of the Fall which is described by Tillich as the transition from essence to existence.[1] He favours this phrase because it is a 'half-way demythologization' of the myth of the Fall. However, even such a phrase as this is partly mythological since the term 'transition' contains a temporal element just as much as the term 'fall'. It is impossible completely to avoid mythical terms, says Tillich, because 'existence is not a matter of essential necessity'.[2] For both idealism and naturalism the doctrine of the Fall is false. Idealism reduces the doctrine to an assertion of the difference between ideality and reality with reality pointing toward the ideal. Naturalism, on the other hand, 'takes existence for granted, without asking about the source of its negativity'.[3] We can take the myth of Genesis 1-3 as a guide to the task of describing the transition from essential to existential being. The myth points to four things: (1) the possibility of the Fall, (2) its motives, (3) the event itself, (4) its consequences.

How the Fall (or the transition from essence to existence) is possible has in part been answered, according to Tillich, by his discussion of the polarity of freedom and destiny and by the discussion of man's awareness of his own finitude and of finitude universally. The transition is possible because of freedom which is in 'polar unity with destiny', and because man's freedom is finite. Man is free not only in so far as he is capable of moral

---

[1] *Systematic Theology* II, pp. 33, 35f.   [2] *Ibid.*, p. 33.   [3] *Ibid.*, p. 34.

action and generally creative but also because he has the power of contradicting himself and his essential nature. It is this final quality of man's freedom that gives Tillich a further step toward answering the question of how the transition from essence to existence is possible. Finally, he says, we must realise that the transition from essence to existence is possible because finite freedom works within the frame of a universal destiny—that is the final step toward the answer. Traditional theology was mistaken in its assertion that the Fall was possible because of Adam's freedom to sin. 'The possibility of the Fall is dependent on all the qualities of human freedom taken in their unity.'[1]

Before we can say what the motives of the Fall are we must, says Tillich, understand the state of essential being in which these motives are found. This has been metaphorically described in both myth and dogma as a state of history prior to history, but it can be described psychologically as a state of 'dreaming innocence'. These terms are chosen carefully, and each is interpreted as pointing to something that precedes actual existence, to non-actualized potentiality. The state of dreaming innocence pushes forward, is driven on by man's awareness of himself as finite.

This awareness is 'anxiety', and so in man freedom is united with anxiety. Tillich indeed suggests that one 'could call man's freedom "freedom in anxiety" or "anxious freedom" '. This leads Tillich to his psychological analysis of the Genesis story in order to reveal 'the motifs of the transition from essence to existence'. He finds two interrelated elements: the divine prohibition and the anxious dilemma of man. 'The divine prohibition presupposes a kind of split between creator and creature, a split which makes a command necessary, even if it is given only in order to test the obedience of the creature.'[2] The cleavage itself in turn presupposes the desire to sin, a state Tillich describes as 'aroused freedom'. 'Man is caught between the desire to actualize his freedom and the demand to preserve his dreaming innocence. In the power of his finite freedom he decides for actualization.' Subjectively the dilemma is

[1] *Systematic Theology* II, p. 37.   [2] *Ibid.*, p. 40.

experienced as a double anxiety—the anxiety of losing himself by not actualizing himself and his potentialities and the anxiety of losing himself by actualizing himself and his potentialities. Thus man 'stands between the preservation of his dreaming innocence without experiencing the actuality of being and the loss of his innocence through knowledge, power and guilt'.[1] Man's decision for self-actualization produces the end of dreaming innocence.

This transition from essence to existence, says Tillich is the 'original fact' which 'gives validity to every fact'. In other words Tillich makes this transition 'a universal quality of finite being', part of what we mean when we speak of anything as finite being. It is not surprising, therefore, that in his interpretation of the Fall Tillich talks of the cosmic dimensions of the doctrine. The transition must be expressed by two forms of myth—the myth of the transcendent fall and that of the immanent fall. Both are necessary because the individual act of estrangement is not an isolated phenomenon but part of the universal tragedy of human existence. The myth of the transcendent Fall has its source in pagan religious philosophy and received a Christian form with Origen. Always it expresses the universal dimension of existence. On the other hand existence is rooted in ethical freedom, and we distort its character if we deny this in affirming its tragic destiny. The unity of freedom and tragic destiny 'is the great problem of the doctrine of man'.[2] There are two reasons why the doctrine of 'original sin' has been so violently rejected by the modern mind. First, its mythical expression was taken literally by its attackers and defenders and so was unacceptable to the modern mind with its emphasis on the critical function of historiography. Secondly, the doctrine seemed to imply a negative evaluation of man, which was in sharp contradiction to 'the new feeling for life and the world, and the impulse of modern man to transform world and society'. For Tillich it is the duty of theology to support the historical-critical attitude toward both the biblical and the ecclesiastical myth and also to emphasise the positive valuation of man's essential nature.

[1] *Ibid.*, p. 41.   [2] *Ibid.*, p. 43.

'Theology must join—and in most cases has joined—the historical-critical attitude towards the biblical and ecclesiastical myth. Theology further must emphasise the positive valuation of man in his essential nature. It must join classical humanism in protecting man's created goodness against naturalistic and existentialistic denials of his greatness and dignity. At the same time, theology should reinterpret the doctrine of original sin by showing man's existential self-estrangement and by using the helpful existentialist analyses of the human predicament. In doing so, it must develop a realistic doctrine of man, in which the ethical and tragic element in his self-estrangement are balanced. It may well be that such a task demands the definite removal from the theological vocabulary of terms like "original sin" or "hereditary sin" and their replacement by a description of the interpenetration of the moral and the tragic elements in the human situation.'[1]

Tillich holds that the empirical evidence which makes such a description appropriate is extensive, since both analytic psychology and analytic sociology have shown how destiny and freedom are interwoven in every human being and all social and political groups. Creation and the Fall coincide 'in so far as there is no point in time and space in which created goodness was actualized and had existence'. This coincidence is not, however, a logical one; though it is universally true that essence moves on to existence, the latter cannot be deduced from the former.[2]

This interpretation of the doctrine of the Fall must be admitted to be both subtle and attractive. There can indeed be few doctrines more difficult to expound convincingly to the contemporary student of theology. Yet though we must applaud our author's attempts to make theological statements about the Fall and Original Sin intelligible we must beware lest our quest for understanding makes us read these as if they were Dr Samuel Johnson's latest deliverances of Common-Sense. Is the doctrine of the Fall in any sense an empirical statement? Are we really saying with Dylan Thomas merely that 'we are not wholly bad or good'? It is true that the doctrine of Original Sin does at least mean that as a matter of fact men

[1] *Systematic Theology* II, p. 44.   [2] Cf. *ibid.*, pp. 4, 50.

do not succeed in living up to their highest ideals. That is to say, we must admit that the doctrine is robbed of some meaning if we so interpret it as to empty it of any empirical claims by making it say only something about the relation of all men to God. Thus I could say that when I assert the doctrine of the Fall I do not mean to say that X, Y, or Z are guilty of crimes which we may or may not know but only that in God's sight they are as men who have been found guilty of some crime. Here the empirical claims of the doctrine is at minimum whilst its distinctive universalism is preserved. It is this universalism which is at once the fascinating and the baffling thing about the doctrine. If this is said to be true universally, then do we mean to say that we have always found it to be the case in the past that men are failures in the great moral test or do we mean to say something more? Now if we do want to say more, what exactly is it? It seems to me that Tillich wavers between understanding this more-than-empirical character of the doctrine as a logical statement and on the other hand making the necessity a matter of contingent truth. Niebuhr's justly famous aphorism that sin is inevitable but not necessary brings out the paradox of the doctrine more clearly. To say that sin is inevitable is then like saying that inevitably we shall be over-drawn at the bank again this year. But it is not quite on all fours with this. It is more like saying that it is inevitable that the roads to Aberdeen will be icy for the greater part of the months of December and January or that it is inevitable that when we have temperatures of only ten to twenty degrees Fahrenheit the water in the horse-trough will be frozen. The point is that this kind of empirical statement has almost the force of a definition. Similarly the doctrine of Original Sin does not make a straight-forward empirical generalization about what one finds to be the case with regard to men's moral behaviour. In his analysis of original sin Kierkegaard says:

'There is no question of any relation to the whole world or to anything that is past. It is a question only of a man being guilty, and yet he must become guilty by fate, by that therefore of which there was no question. . . . This contradiction, interpreted in a

125

mistaken way, gives the mistaken concept of original sin; rightly understood, its gives the correct concept. . . . So guilt comes neither as a necessity nor by chance.'[1]

This contradiction that Kierkegaard speaks of is what constitutes the core of the doctrine, that one should be accounted guilty for something which is not strictly imputable to the individual. But to say this is a contradiction is once more to read the doctrine as an empirical statement (this time a moral one). If we want to say that the doctrine of Original Sin makes use of ethical categories then we must admit too that the transcendental element of the doctrine (its reference to what we are in God's sight) removes it from the realm of ordinary moral discourse. So though my acts may be very relevant to my confession that I have sinned and have gone astray with all my fellows, yet saying I have stolen my neighbour's wife or his ox will not be identical with saying I am a sinner. We may say in conclusion then that what the elucidation of this doctrine needs is neither retranslation nor an empirical justification but a careful description of the way in which any such evidence is relevant to it. Once more Tillich's apologetic emphasis makes him conflate the two different tasks of the theologian—logical description and apology.

When he interprets the Genesis myth, Tillich certainly talks in a non-empirical way about the individual act of sin as an act of freedom imbedded in the universal destiny of existence.[2] This kind of metaphorical description of the human situation is surely the borderline of religion and metaphysics. And indeed it seems at times that Tillich is in danger of making his religious category a purely metaphysical one. The distinctive character of the Christian conception of sin is that it is regarded as both inevitable and volitional. What perplexes us about Tillich's discussion of sin is that he seems to understand this inevitability of sin in terms of a connexion between sin and finitude. 'The disruption of the essential unity with God is the innermost character of sin.' Sin is 'a universal fact before it becomes an

---

[1] Kierkegaard, *The Concept of Dread*, p. 88.
[2] *Systematic Theology* II, p. 43.

individual act, or more precisely, sin as an individual act actualizes the fact of estrangement'.[1] All this could be a very healthy protest against the excessive moralism which has threatened to distort the essentially Protestant doctrine of sin which, as Tillich again rightly says, views sin qualitatively and not quantitatively. But when he introduces his mysterious concept of 'structure of destruction'[2] we begin to feel that matters are not quite as satisfactory. The original fact, he says, is the transition from essence to existence, and the universality of the transition makes its fateful necessity. This brings to mind Luther's remark that necessity belongs to physics and not to theology and that if this concept is to be used in theology it must be bathed and washed. What Luther had in mind was the preservation of the volitional character of sin as an act of the individual despite the fact that it might be described as inevitable in relation to the natural man. Tillich does not, it is true, want to affirm that sin and finitude are synonymous; but it is also true that he does not succeed in preserving the distinction intact. For it seems to me that he makes it necessary for man if he is to become man to become sinner also, since he says that individuality involved separation from the ground of being, and sin is defined as the rupture of the original essential unity of Creator and creature. And once more this is due to the ambiguity of the terms he employs—such as 'estrangement' and 'the loss of unity', which can be interpreted both conceptually and dramatically. The difficulty one meets here as elsewhere in Tillich is that he does not distinguish between his interpretative concept and the myth he seeks to interpret. Thus when he says that the meaning of the myth is that the very constitution of existence implies the transition from essence to existence he is talking both theory and myth. And if he can talk of implication it is not surprising that he talks also of necessity. But whatever the doctrine of Original Sin means, the myth of the Fall clearly points to the fact that we need not have sinned. Then in our endeavour to understand the proneness to wander which we own in our confession, we may bid the muse sing of man's first disobedience. This is to insist that it will not do to

[1] *Systematic Theology* II, p. 64. [2] *Ibid.*, pp. 69-70.

regard sin as a mere accident. Tillich's intellectualization of the myth seems to me to endanger the myth's power. For the myth does not absolve us; but Tillich's peculiar myth might well become a matter of saying: 'Sin is necessarily bound up with finitude. And if it is implied by the order in which we find ourselves, it is no longer our responsibility.' Tillich's doctrine of Original Sin is a curious mixture of Neo-Platonism and Existentialism.

Christian theology has always distinguished between original and actual sin, and though Tillich insists that sin is 'a universal fact before it becomes an individual act' he does not reject the distinction. Indeed one may question whether he does not in fact understand sin so much in terms of ontology that the historical dimension is not emphasized. There is nothing to be gained from following his discussion of the relation of the term 'estrangement' to the term 'sin',[1] for it only reveals Tillich's peculiar understanding of the nature of language. However, it is significant that he wants to emphasise man's personal responsibility for sin. He distinguishes three elements in sin[2]— unbelief, concupiscence, and *hubris* ($\H{v}\beta\rho\iota\varsigma$) in this way supplementing the Augsburg Confession's definition of Sin as a state '*sine fide erga deum et cum concupiscentia*'. Unbelief is what the Reformers understood by the term 'sin', and they defined 'unbelief' as 'an act of the total personality, including practical, theoretical and emotional elements'. For Protestant Christianity therefore the term means 'the act or state in which man in the totality of his being turns away from God'.[3] It is the separation of man's will from the will of God. Tillich rejects the concepts of disobedience and denial because he argues that these terms presuppose a separation from God. Questions and answers, whether positive or negative, already presuppose a loss of a cognitive union with God.

> 'He who asks for God is already estranged from God. . . . He who needs a law which tells him how to act or how not to act is already estranged from the source of the law which demands obedience.'[4]

[1] *Systematic Theology* II, pp. 51-3. [2] *Ibid.*, pp. 53-4.
[3] *Ibid.*, p. 54. [4] *Ibid.*

Here we see the tension between Tillich's ontological understanding of sin and the historical understanding of sin. He does not want to use any model for the description of sin which does not imply a deliberate act or historical choice which in fact is the story form used by the Bible. Why our statements about our relation to God seem most suitable when they are put in terms of contingency is difficult to understand, but that this is the case is indubitable. No Plotinian concept of man as a sinner *qua* natural object will do justice to the Christian doctrine of sin. It is not that we are not identical with God but that we have turned our backs on him—this is sin. And because Tillich is aware of this he is anxious to stress the historical character of the model. Yet it was precisely this which he denied in connection with the myth of Adam's fall,[1] and similarly the description of estrangement has been completely ontological. This definition of sin as unbelief need not, thinks Tillich, conflict with the Augustinian interpretation of sin as love turned away from God to self. Both emphasise the religious character of sin as indicating a relation between us and God and the possibility of a reunion of what is estranged. However, as against the Augustinian theory we must emphasise that sin is a matter of our relation to God and not to ecclesiastical, moral or social authorities.

Tillich uses the Greek tragic concept of *hubris* to define further what he means by sin. '*Hubris* is the self-elevation of man into the sphere of the divine.'[2] As in the Greek tragedy so in Hebrew religion, thinks Tillich, it is the great who are driven toward *hubris*. Man's greatness lies in his being 'infinite', and so universally it is true that he falls into the temptation of *hubris*. This is not one form of sin—as the word 'pride' in English suggests. 'It is sin in its total form, namely, the other side of unbelief or man's turning away from the divine centre to which he belongs. It is turning toward one's self as the centre of one's self and one's world.'[3] Self-elevation characterizes all human history, and all men have the hidden desire to be like God.

[1] Cf. *Systematic Theology* I, p. 288. [2] *Systematic Theology* II, p. 57.
[3] *Ibid.*, p. 58.

'No one is willing to acknowledge, in concrete terms, his finitude, weakness and his errors, his ignorance and his insecurity, his loneliness and his anxiety. And if he is ready to acknowledge them, he makes another instrument of *hubris* out of his readiness. A demonic structure drives man to confuse natural self-affirmation with destructive self-elevation.'[1]

Why should man be tempted to become centred in himself? 'The answer is that it places him in the position of drawing the whole of his world into himself.' This is the temptation that man meets in his peculiar position as neither God nor beast: lower than God—higher than beast.

'Every individual, since he is separated from the whole, desires reunion with the whole. His "poverty" makes him seek for abundance. This is the root of love in all its forms. The possibility of reaching unlimited abundance is the temptation of man who is a self and has a world. The classical name for this desire is *concupiscentia*, "concupiscence"—the unlimited desire to draw the whole of reality into one's self.'[2]

It is important to understand the 'unlimited' character of this desire. It is not, as Bishop Butler would say, a particular passion but a general principle, referring to all aspects of man's relation to himself and to his world. Thus Tillich rejects the particularizing of this 'desire' whereby 'concupiscence' is made synonymous with sexual desire. This tendency is seen even in Augustine and Luther, and whereas it was understandable in Augustine 'who never overcame the Hellenistic and especially Neo-Platonic devaluation of sex' it is difficult to understand how the Reformers could consistently maintain this identity. Its only justification is the un-Protestant doctrine that 'hereditary' sin is rooted in sexual pleasure in the act of propagation. This ambiguity in the use of the word 'concupiscence' has created an unfortunate ambiguity in the Christian attitude towards sex. 'The Church has never been able to deal adequately with this central ethical and religious problem', says Tillich, and he offers his restatement as a contribution to its solution. He finds support for the doctrine in existentialist

---

[1] *Systematic Theology* II, pp. 58-9. [2] *Ibid.*, p. 59.

literature, art and philosophy and also in psychology, but he insists that neither Nietzsche's 'will to power' nor Freud's '*libido*' is an adequate interpretation of concupiscence.

The peculiar characteristic of sin is that it is a 'universal fact before it becomes an individual act'. It is impossible to separate sin as fact from sin as act. 'They are interwoven, and their unity is an immediate experience of everyone, who feels himself to be guilty.'

> 'Estrangement as fact has been explained in deterministic terms: physically, by a mechanistic determinism; biologically, by theories of the decadence of the biological power of life; psychologically, as the compulsory force of the unconscious; sociologically, as the result of class domination; culturally, as the lack of educational adjustment. None of these explanations accounts for the feeling of personal responsibility that man has for his acts in the state of estrangement. But each of these theories contributes to an understanding of the element of destiny in the human predicament. In this sense Christian theology must accept each of them; but it must add that no description of the element of destiny in the state of estrangement can remove the experience of finite freedom and, consequently, the responsibility for every act in which estrangement is actualised.'[1]

Tillich denies that there is such a thing as collective guilt but believes that individual guilt helps to create the universal destiny of mankind and in particular the special destiny of the social group to which a person belongs. In this indirect sense whole nations and even mankind as a whole are guilty of whatever crimes are committed in their history.

In his state of estrangement man is under the domination of death and suffers the anxiety of having to die. Coming from nothing he returns to nothing. There is no suggestion in the Bible that man is naturally immortal—his nature is mortal. According to the Genesis story, argues Tillich, man has come from dust and will return to dust. He has immortality only as long as he is allowed to eat the fruit of the tree of life, the divine food. This Tillich interprets as a symbolical assertion of the fact that 'participation in the eternal makes man eternal;

[1] *Ibid.*, pp. 64-5.

separation from the eternal leaves man in his natural finitude.'
Sin is not the cause of death but what gives death the power
which is conquered only by participation in the eternal. If a
man is left to the domination of death the essential anxiety
about non-being is transformed into the horror of death. Sin
transforms the anxious awareness of one's having to die into
the painful realization of a lost eternity.

This concludes our exposition of Tillich's doctrine of man. In
the course of our exposition we had occasion to refer to the
tension between the idea of sin as voluntary and the idea of sin
as ontological estrangement, and to this we must return. For
the central difficulty in Tillich's doctrine of man is the ambiguous status of finite freedom. From one point of view it is man's
end, the *telos* of creation, but from another point of view this is
man's shame. It is true that Tillich repeatedly declares that
finitude and sin are not synonymous, but I very much doubt
whether the two terms are consistently distinguished. It seems
to me that Tillich's use of the idea of necessity in connection
with the doctrine of sin makes nonsense of the voluntariness of
sin as act. If man is to be man then he must actualize his
freedom, but this is precisely what makes him a sinner, according to Tillich. In this way the concept of sin is emptied of the
very significance that Tillich's analysis of its threefold character
ascribes to it, though even here the same shifting of emphasis
from voluntariness to ontology is to be seen. It is unfortunate
that in his discussion of sin Tillich never distinguishes between
the myth itself and his interpretative concept. The result is
that we can never tell when he is expounding a theory and when
he is relating the myth. His choice of interpretative concept—
the transition from essence to existence—is characteristically
intellectual, and this is frankly said to be chosen because it is
'a half-way demythologization'. Thus the language in which
the concept of Sin is expounded seems a strange intellectualization of the myth, and its employment of the concepts of
implication makes the necessity of sin suspiciously like logical
necessity. If this is the case then there is no further possibility
of retaining the distinction between finitude and sin.

The discussion of man's essential mortality shows Tillich's

own anxiety to preserve the distinction between finitude and sin intact. He quite rightly points out that any doctrine of immortality has little biblical basis, that the Bible always regards man as essentially mortal—man born of woman hath but little time to live. Whether his interpretation of the Genesis myth as emphasizing the fact that man's eternality is dependent on his eating of the tree of life is correct or not is not our concern here. What is of interest is that it displays an ambiguous use of the word 'eternal'—meaning by it both that which is above time and an endless time. With regard to the problem of survival, then, we can accept what Tillich says; for the Christian hope is that death has been conquered by God in Christ and that the resurrected Christ is 'the first fruits of them that sleep'. What is not so clear is the way in which sin transforms the anxiety of essential finitude into an existential evil, 'a structure of destruction'. What is 'the painful realization of a lost eternity'? The picture is that of Marlowe's Faustus having at last to pay the wages of sin—'I will fly up to my God, who pulls me down.' An ontological loss of eternity we could understand as the change effected by sin, but a painful realization is a matter of psychology. Once again Tillich's failure to keep different things separate results in obscurity.

VI

THE DOCTRINE OF THE CHURCH[1]

THE Church is a subject of both systematic and practical theology, but the systematic doctrine of the Church is 'the immediate basis of all practical theology'. The systematic theologian is concerned to understand the nature and function of the Church while the practical theologian asks how a function has been performed and how it should be performed.

The question of the Church's nature divides itself into three questions:

(a) How are we to understand the foundation of the Church?
(b) What is its nature?
(c) What are its attributes?

The foundation of the Church can only be understood in correlation with the Christ. In our discussion of Tillich's Christology we emphasized how, for him, the Christ is the Christ in so far as he is thus received—that is, not in a vacuum but in correlation with those who receive him as the Christ. The community in which Jesus is received as the Christ is the Church. This Church—'literally the "assembly of God" or "of the Christ" '—is the historical continuation of the 'people of God' or the 'chosen race' of the Old Testament.

Jesus' calling the Twelve Apostles indicates his Messianic purpose of collecting the true people of God. The Church, therefore, is the community of those who are called out of all nations (*ekklesia*) by the good news preached by Jesus' 'messengers', the apostles. What is distinctive about this community, however, is its foundation in its reception of Jesus as the Christ.

---

[1] Unless otherwise stated the quotations in this chapter will be from Part IV of the Preliminary Draft of *Systematic Theology* which was distributed by Tillich for the private use of his students (*Propositions*).

134

Not only is it true to say that he is not the Christ without the Church but the converse also is true, that the Church is not the Church without Christ. The foundation of the Church cannot, therefore, be a matter of history but the work of the divine Spirit. In this connection Tillich does not hesitate to say that Simon Peter has lasting significance for the Church not because of any questionable theory concerning his initiation of the Roman episcopate but simply because he was the first to recognize Jesus as the Christ. The common assertion that the Church began at Pentecost Tillich interprets as a mythical assertion of the spiritual foundation of the Church. 'The story of Pentecost points in legendary terms to the spiritual foundation of the Church: it describes its ecstatic beginning, the new certainty of Jesus as the Christ, the communion of love and the power of the message to conquer people in all nations.'[1] This spiritual foundation is not to be understood deistically. It is the New Being in Jesus as the Christ being actualized as community by the creative power of the divine Spirit through word and sacrament.

The word is the main instrument in the foundation of the Church. When the divine Spirit works through the human word this word becomes the 'word of God'.[2] The content of this word must always be the New Being in Jesus as the Christ since he is eternally the Word of God. What makes the word, then, the Word of God is both its content and its being word of God, for somebody. Even the biblical word is 'Word of God' only in so far as the Spirit bears witness to it. This does not exclude anything from becoming the 'word of God', for someone. 'Every word can become the vehicle of the divine spirit in a special situation.' The criterion, however, is always the Word become flesh, the New Being in Jesus as the Christ. 'The message of him *is* the "Word of God" as the objective standard of everything that might become "Word of God".'

The Church is founded by sacrament as well as word because of the 'unity of man's spirituality with his vitality'. This makes sensuous instruments necessary in the Church's foundation, and the divine Spirit, working through sensuous objects, makes

[1] *Ibid.*, p. 23.   [2] *Ibid.*, p. 24.

them 'sacramental' objects. We call a religion sacramental when it emphasises the presence of the divine in sacred objects or ritual acts over against its ethical character. It is the spiritual effect of the act which makes sacraments significant in the life of the Church. How does such an effect come about? It concerns both the conscious and the subconscious side of man's spiritual life. Catholicism has misinterpreted the spiritual effect of a sacramental act on man's subconscious spirituality so as to make the effect magical. Humanism, on the other hand, has seized on the conscious effect and so over-intellectualized the spiritual efficaciousness of sacraments. Lutheranism and Calvinism have worked for a synthesis, the former stressing the unconscious side and the latter the conscious. Consequently the temptations they face are different—Lutheranism always faces the danger of understanding sacraments as magical operations and Calvinism is always in danger of relapsing into intellectualism. Dealing with the sacramental materials Tillich describes them as symbols rather than signs—they are not 'signs pointing to a spiritual meaning strange to them, but they are symbols, representing a power in themselves and, therefore, irreplaceable.' Tillich has distinguished between sign and symbol in *Systematic Theology* vol. I[1] where he says that symbols, unlike signs, participate in the reality to which they refer. However, this distinction is never justified, and it is difficult to see how it can be justified. It is clearly a very useful distinction in this context, for it will enable us to say that the sacramental elements must, as symbols, participate in the uniqueness of that which they represent. The selection of special sacramental activities as sacraments in the technical sense has no biblical foundation any more than it has foundation in systematic theology. The reasons for such selection are those of tradition, practical evaluation and criticism of abuses. Also they arise either in connection with main events in the personal life of the individual or in his life within the Church—baptism and marriage are examples of the first while confirmation and ordination are examples of the second type.

These two instruments of the Church's foundation cannot be

[1] *Op. cit.*, pp. 264-8.

separated, 'since the word has sacramental potentialities and the sacrament presupposes the Word'. Tillich distinguishes between the logical meaning of words and their expressive power, and presumably he has in mind the now familiar distinction between descriptive meaning and emotive meaning. It is the latter kind of meaning which gives religious words sacramental qualities as when, for example, the archaic language of the Authorized Version of the Bible is used in church services. Sacraments presuppose the word because the sacrament appeals to man's conscious mind and will therefore be interpreted in words whether these are uttered or not. Finally, Christ as the Word of God is both word and sacrament, and their unity in him means that they should also be united in his Church. A rediscovery of the value of the word produces a new realization of the value of the sacrament.

The Church is the New Being as community—the community of faith and love. As the community of faith the Church receives the New Being in Christ as its foundation and its life-principle. Therefore, should anyone reject this foundation and deny that Jesus is the Christ he automatically effects his own spiritual exclusion from the community of the Church, and if he makes his denial 'a matter of teaching or propaganda' he is to be excluded formally. 'Everybody who accepts the Church with its foundation as the community to which he spiritually belongs can be a member of the Church even if he is, temporarily or permanently, unable to share actively its faith.'[1] It is clear, then, that its nature as the community of faith is one of the greatest responsibilities laid upon the Church. From this it follows that it is responsible for judging whether a doctrine implies the negation of its faith, and it must reject such a doctrine as an attack on its very foundation. The denunciation of heresy is thus an essential characteristic of the Church, and if it ceased to denounce heresy it would cease to be the Church, the community of faith. In its defence of the faith against heretical distortion the Church must refrain from invoking the support of social or legal coercion; for such support would rob the defence of its spiritual character.

[1] *Propositions*, Part V, p. 26.

As the community of love the Church reveals the New Being in concrete actuality 'in the relation between its members, between itself and all men, between man and nature'.[1] Since it is the community of love the Church is the place of equality, of equality, that is, before God. This does not necessarily imply social or political equality, even within the Church itself, but it does necessarily imply the rejection of any form of inequality the practical consequence of which is that a real community of faith and love is impossible. Moreover, as the community of love the Church is the agent of charity towards everybody in need both inside and outside its fold. Once more this has an indirect sociological result rather than a direct one. It does not necessarily involve something like the 'welfare state' but it does reject any individualism which uses charity as a means of maintaining the evils of a *status quo*. The exercise of love involves discipline, and the Church is perfectly consistent if it excludes from its fold those who act against love. Its love toward these is expressed in its discipline, and were discipline absent the character of the love would be gravely weakened. This in turn does not involve arbitrary restrictions on the entry or re-entry of persons into the Church's communion. 'The Church receives without discrimination, without limits in its readiness to forgive, without imposing conditions except the acknowledgement of its foundation.'[2]

The nature of the Church is paradoxical inasmuch as it is both theological and sociological. Considered as a theological phenomenon the Church is 'the assembly of God' or 'the body of Christ'. Considered sociologically, the Church is a social group having a religious basis and a religious purpose. Therefore the principles of social behaviour such as the laws concerning the rise of *élites* are as evident here as anywhere else. There is no special society with a different sociological pattern created by the religious basis or the religious purpose. However, it is quite wrong to imagine that either the one or the other interpretation is the whole story. The error of Roman Catholicism and of some forms of Protestantism, says Tillich, is that the double nature of the Church is denied by a one-sided theory.

---

[1] *Propositions*, Part V, p. 26.   [2] *Ibid.*, p. 27.

'The Roman Catholic way of resolving the sociological nature of the Church into its theological nature creates a sacred sociological structure above the general sociological laws while the Protestant way of resolving the theological nature of the Church into its sociological nature denies implicitly the New Being in Christ.'[1] Both negate the paradox that the theological nature of the Church is actual in and through its sociological nature. Holding this paradoxical view of the Church Tillich rejects the distinction between the visible and invisible the Church. At least, he rejects any suggestion that there are two 'Churches'. 'The visible and the invisible Church are two aspects of the same Church.'[2] The Church as a theological object, the actuality of the New Being in a community, is 'invisible' 'because it is an object of faith'. However, the Church as a historical community is a 'visible' empirical object. If we misunderstand this traditional distinction between the Church as visible and the Church as invisible, says Tillich, we will devalue the empirical Church over against the spiritual Church. As visible the Church is open to the same ambiguities of life as any other empirical phenomenon—'its destructiveness, its fragmentary, tragic and demonic character'. The Church as invisible represents the overcoming of these ambiguities of life in spiritual creativity and greatness. We must, however, guard against the temptation to transfer the characteristics of the Kingdom of God to the Church by speaking of the Church as triumphant or by including within it the realm of essential being, that is to say, the realm of angels. This would be to forget that the Church is both visible and invisible at the same time. By making the Church as visible an object of faith Roman Catholicism creates a historical group which is, by definition, above the ambiguities of life. Equally contradictory, however, in the opposite way is the tendency in humanist Protestantism to deny the invisible Church and so reduce the Church to the status of one historical group alongside others. The former method seeks to affirm historical reality while denying the inevitable relativity and the latter seeks to give the Church concrete reality to the detriment of its theological character.

[1] *Ibid.*   [2] *Ibid.*

As against both these descriptions the Christian doctrine of the Church which is derived from the Christological paradox holds that the invisible Church is paradoxically actual in and through the visible Church.

Tillich here introduces his distinction between the Church manifest and the Church latent. The main difference between this distinction and the customary opposition of invisible and visible Church is that both the latent and the manifest Church are historical phenomena. 'The Church, as the actuality of the New Being, is manifest in history. The Church as prepared by history is latent in history.'[1] Both are present in all periods of history and are at once theological and sociological, invisible and visible. The advent of Jesus, however, does make a further distinction within the manifest Church necessary. The Church is manifest before the appearance of Jesus as the Christ only by anticipation whereas after his appearance it is manifest also by reception. The manifest Church is a definite historical group within which the New Being receives concrete historical expression. In other words, by the 'manifest Church' Tillich means the historical communities which have called themselves Christian and in which the living Christ has been revealed. The latent Church, on the other hand, is not such a specifiable or identifiable historical group, and is made up of those groups within paganism, Judaism or humanism which also reveal or actualize the New Being. The relation between the two is hard to describe. Tillich says: 'The latent Church stands always under the quest to become manifest, while the manifest Church is always exposed to criticism by the latent Church. The latent Church within the Christian civilization is a negative as well as positive challenge for the manifest Church.'[2] If we understand this aright what it means is that those non-Christian groups which seem to manifest the work of the Spirit may become affiliated with the organized Christian Church; but whether they do so or not their criticism of the Church can have either a beneficial or adverse effect on the life of the organized Church. To recognize that there can be a latent Church precludes the possibility of ecclesiastical

[1] *Propositions*, Part V, p. 28.   [2] *Ibid.*

arrogance, but Tillich insists that this does not mean that the Church is not the community in which the New Being in Christ is actual.

When we ask what the attributes of the Church are we find the answer in the description of it as 'one, holy, catholic Church'. The attributes of the Church, then, for Tillich, are: holiness, universality and unity. These point, he says, to 'the victory of the New Being in Christ over existential separation and its demonic-polytheistic expression'.[1] This is ambiguous, and it is not clear in what sense these attributes 'point to' the victory of the New Being. It may mean that the attributes of the Church are the work of the Spirit or again it may mean that the *raison d'être* of the Church with just these attributes is the fact that in Christ the separation between men and God was brought to an end. When he speaks of the attributes of the Church as emphasizing the paradoxical character of the Church Tillich seems to have the first sense in mind. So he says that the description of the Church in terms of these attributes is neither realism nor idealism. 'The attributes of the Church negate a "realistic" interpretation of the Church which shows the permanent contrast between its meaning and its reality. And they negate an "idealistic" interpretation of the Church which asserts a permanent approximation of its reality to its meaning.'[2] This seems to mean that in so far as we describe the Church as one, holy and catholic we are neither merely describing the real state of affairs, the empirical facts concerning the sociological groups which make up the Church, nor the ideal state of affairs, the Church of our dreams which has no relation to the facts. It is the other meaning which seems to lie behind Tillich's assertion that 'the Church is holy because of the holiness of its foundation: the New Being in Christ'.[3] However, he moves back to the first meaning in what he says further about the holiness of the Church. The Church is holy, he says, as a community in which the separation of man from God which we have seen to be a tragic fact of existence is overcome and in which God is present through his Spirit. This could be affirmed by the use of the Reformation term 'regeneration'

[1] *Ibid.*   [2] *Ibid.*   [3] *Ibid.*, p. 29.

in our description of the Church—'the "holy" Church is the community of *regeneration*'. Similarly the use of the term justification will serve to point out that the 'existential unholiness' of the Church does not render its claim to be holy false. 'Even the corrupted Church is holy Church. The "holy" Church is the community of justification.' The judgement of justification is not only pronounced by the Church but serves as a judgement of the Church. The Church is holy, says Tillich, because it judges itself in the power of the prophetic Spirit. It thus carries within itself the principle of its reformation and so we can describe the holy Church as the community of sanctification. Neither Roman Catholicism nor humanist Protestantism does justice to the paradoxical character of the Church since the former would reject the prophetic judgement of the Church against itself and the latter interprets the holiness of the Church as the aggregate holiness of the individual members. Similarly, neither has a proper understanding of reformation. Catholicism wrongly regards it as an accident in the history of the Church instead of recognizing that it is a principle which is implied by the very conception of the Church as holy. Humanist Protestantism, on the other hand, makes it a matter of continuous transformation instead of a return to 'the Church's one foundation, the source of its holiness'.

The ambiguity which we distinguished in Tillich's understanding of the way in which the attributes of the Church 'point to' the New Being is revealed again in the discussion of the Church's universality. He begins by saying that the Church is universal because of the universality of its foundation, the New Being in Christ. This would seem to mean that the Church is universal because it has its foundation in the universal Christ, the One who is for all mankind. However, this is in itself ambiguous since the universality of the Church now could either be a matter of analogy or obedience to the founder's rules. That is, we can either say that the Church must be universal if it is to resemble its foundation or we can say that the Church must be universal if it is to carry out the commands of its founder. The discussion, however, soon moves away from the subject of foundation and we are told that the universality of the Church has to do with the limits of particular claims. 'The Church is universal as the community in which every particular claim is valid in the limits of its finitude and rejected if it trespasses these limits and aspires to infinite validity.'[1] The universality of the Church must further be understood both 'intensively and extensively'. That is to say, it is its power of receiving all that is good so that it is the re-established unity of those elements of being which in existence contradict each other, and also it is power of uniting every particular group. To say that the Church is universal is so far from denying its inevitable particularity that we can say of every particular Church that it is the universal Church. The universality of the Church is again a paradox that neither Roman Catholicism nor Humanist Protestantism properly understands. The former refuses to acknowledge its own historical particularity and the latter makes its particularity a matter of historical relativism. The universality of the Church, however, is actual only in and through its particularity.

Finally, the Church is one. It is one because its foundation is one, namely the New Being in Christ. When he proceeds to give this assertion concrete significance Tillich speaks of the unity of the Church over and above and even in its confessional divisions. 'The one Church transcends its own inescapable splits.' The divisions of the Church he regards as resulting from 'an existential dissent about the one foundation of the Church and therefore, insuperable as long as the dissent exists'. What the 'existential dissent' is we are not told, and so it is not clear in what sense we can say that the division is insuperable whilst also maintaining that the Church is one despite its confessional divisions. Tillich's theology has been called a 'theology for the ecumenical movement',[2] and he himself says that the ecumenical movement 'is a powerful expression of the one Church and its one foundation'. Even so, what can be achieved by the movement is, he thinks, limited.

[1] *Propositions*, Part V, p. 29.
[2] Walter M. Horton, 'Tillich's Rôle in Contemporary Theology', *The Theology of Paul Tillich*, p. 43.

'It is able to remove divisions which have become historically obsolete, to create a new consciousness of the unity of the Church and to replace confessional fanaticism by interconfessional co-operation, especially towards those outside the Church. But the ecumenical movement cannot remove genuine divisions, not even by an eventual creation of the "United Churches of the World".'[1]

This limitation of what the ecumenical movement can hope to achieve does not mean that for Tillich the unity of the Church is any less real since paradoxically this is actual only in and through its divisions.

This final point is rather difficult to understand since it is not clear what the relation is between the two statements: 'The Church of Christ is One' and 'The unity of the Church ... is actual only in and through its divisions'. As enunciated by Tillich the former is fairly clear since we are referred to the unity of the foundation. It is then clear that this is no plain description of what we are likely to find in the history books or if we start looking for the Christian Church. It is primarily a statement about the New Being in Christ. But does it then make sense to say that the Church is one in spite of its confessional divisions? And if it does, will this not mean to say that the Church is one leads us to regard an actual unity as being the real condition of the Church? This makes the final point concerning the Church's unity less significant than it appears. For since the fact of unity implies that this unity ought to be realised, then to say that the unity of the Church is actual only in and through its divisions can only mean that there is no other Church of which the divided Churches are shadows.

We come now to the questions of the functions and the institutions of the Church. In the final volume of *Systematic Theology* Tillich will discuss these questions in some detail, but since this detailed discussion is not yet available there is no purpose in giving more than a bare outline of what he has said on these questions in the past. The functions of the Church he regards as related to its spiritual foundation, to its historical existence, to its life and the world outside itself. There are thus

[1] *Propositions*, Part IV, p. 30.

four principles which determine the functions of the Church. The first is the principle of spirituality—that in every function of the Church the spiritual foundation of the Church must be expressed. If the Church acts it must be clear that it is the *Church* which is acting and not some other agent. The second principle is that of adequacy. In every function of the Church the material in which it acts must be treated with respect and must not be distorted. That is to say, any use of the Church's authority which does violence to the material in which the Church is acting is a misuse of that authority. The third principle is that of tradition. Every function of the Church must express 'the reality of the total Church from its foundation to the present moment'. For the Church to remain the community of the New Being in Jesus as the Christ it must preserve some link with the tradition. Finally, the fourth principle is the principle of reformation. Every function of the Church must be tested and re-fashioned by the ultimate criterion, the manifestation of the New Being in Jesus as the Christ. It is noticeable that Tillich does not appeal to a principle of 'biblical foundation'. He argues that there is no need of such a principle since in so far as the Bible is an element of the historical reality of the Church the idea of biblical foundation is implied in the principle of tradition, and in so far as the Bible is the original document of the manifestation of the New Being the idea of biblical foundation is implied in the principle of reformation. 'Original Protestantism has not turned Bible against tradition but the standard of reformation against a tradition which claimed to be above reformation.'[1]

The functions of the Church are to be distinguished from its institutions, though it is through the institutional as well as through the spontaneous activities of the Church that the functions of the Church are performed. However, the functions of the Church are immediate and necessary expressions of its nature whereas the institutions of the Church are mediated and conditioned. This distinction protects the Church, Tillich thinks, against ritual legalism, since every institution is challengeable and may come to an end without thereby destroying any essential

[1] *Ibid.*, p. 31.

function of the Church. The first function of the Church is worship, and this necessarily contains adoration, prayer, and contemplation, whereby the Church turns to the ground of its being and its ultimate concern. Any one of these forms of worship, if used exclusively, can have disastrous results—for example, contemplation, exclusively used, 'removes the living intercourse between God and man'.[1] Secondly, like every organism the Church lives by extensive and intensive expansion. This expansion of the Church 'in space, time, substance and effect' is a part of the 'faith in Jesus Christ' and cannot be cut off from it. Thirdly, the Church has constructive functions in which 'it builds its life with the materials of man's spiritual functions and transcends them'. The Church is necessarily always constructing in the aesthetic, cognitive, social and political realms 'a Christian sector expressing the foundation and serving the life of the Church'. Finally, the Church has transforming functions in which it influences the life outside itself in the same spheres in which it performs its constructive self-expression and self-realization. Thus 'Christian philosophy is a philosophy which is of a Christian cultural substance'.

The institutions of the Church comprise its institutionalized activities, its offices, its organization, its legal status. All the Church's institutions are determined in three ways—by the religious and theological understanding of the nature and functions of the Church, by the traditions in so far as they have proved their power to express and to construct, and finally by the new demands arising in every new historical situation. In any conflict the first determination is decisive. The theological criteria by which all institutions of the Church must be judged are given by systematic theology, but questions concerning the structure and the adequacy of special institutions are treated by practical theology. We conclude this chapter, then, with a brief summary of these criteria. The institutionalized activities must be performed as activities of *the Church*, and though they must be performed by bearers of the organized Church they need not be performed by central representatives. All functions of the Church are the right and duty of every member. There

[1] *Propositions*, Part IV, p. 33.

146

must, however, be differentiation of offices for three reasons: (i) orderly performance of all activities is desirable; (ii) a division of labour is necessary; (iii) personal and professional adequacy. But this does not establish a sacramental difference between church members. 'There is no priest in the Christian Church in the sense of a necessary and exclusive mediator between God and man.'[1] Further, there is no theological principle determining a certain number and structure of church offices. As a social group the Church is an organized political body which is able to act as a whole towards itself and towards other social groups. Its organization, therefore, needs a central authority through which it is able to act. The establishment of such a central authority must unite 'a sacramental-objective and a voluntary-subjective element'. The legal status of the Church within the whole of the social life is determined by its relation to the State, the ultimate bearer of power and law. Church and State are united if the social and cultural forms and their political control are an expression of the spiritual substance of the Church. Even in such a unity, however, the transforming function of the Church must be indirect and must not be an imposition of its own cultural forms on the social group as a whole.

In conclusion, I want to make one or two criticisms of Tillich's doctrine of the Church. The general criticism which must be made is that the discussion tends to run along very rigid lines so that one feels that the points made about the Church had to be made because of the pattern of the discussion rather than because of the nature of the Church itself. For instance, all that was said of the Church as one was repeated of the Church as universal. It is not at all clear from the outline of the argument what impels Tillich to proceed in this way. The reference to the foundation is in a way easy to understand, and it will be readily agreed that the Christian doctrine of the Church is more obviously Christo-centric than any other Christian doctrine. Where the Christian Church is, we are obviously connected, in some way or other, with Jesus Christ. There is unanimous testimony in the New Testament to the

[1] *Ibid.*, p. 39.

fact that the Church is constituted not by anything that man has done or can do but by what God has done in Christ.[1] 'Calvin', says Barth, 'liked to apply to the Church a military conception, that of *la campagnie des fideles*. A company comes together on the basis of a command and not on that of a free agreement.'[2] However, though it will always be necessary for us to refer to the King, whose calling the Church obeys, in our endeavour to understand the nature of the Church this does not mean that we must repeat, as Tillich does, the pattern of conceptual analysis. His constant use of paradox is likewise unhelpful, and the absence of any explanation of how we are to understand the various paradoxes makes them almost empty of meaning. The method which Tillich has adopted here is thus very unfortunate.

With regard to the content of the discussion, the first point I wish to raise concerns the distinction between the Church manifest and the Church latent. This distinction seems to me an unnecessary distinction because it seems to say nothing about the Church as such, and also because no indication is given of the way in which it is applied. If what Tillich has in mind is his favourite emphasis on the relation of all history and culture to the proclamation of the Gospel, the *praeparatio evangelica* in short, then why does he think it necessary to speak of a latent *Church*? Furthermore, is it not the use of the word 'Church' here which leads to the assertion of the double character of the latent Church, an assertion which would otherwise have nothing to commend it? Indeed there seems to be nothing more achieved by this distinction than is done by the distinction between the Church visible and the Church invisible. 'The acknowledgement of the latent Church', says Tillich, 'undercuts ecclesiastical and hierarchical arrogance.'[3] But does not the other distinction do this equally well? Talking of the Church invisible does not necessarily imply the folly of abandoning one's concrete congregation—warts and all. My

[1] R. N. Flew, *Jesus and His Church*, London, Epworth Press, 1938, p. 254 *et passim*.

[2] Barth, *Dogmatics in Outline*, London, SCM Press, 1949, p. 142.

[3] *Propositions*, Part V, p. 28.

final criticism is of Tillich's rejection of any principle of Scriptural authority in the Church. We can agree that the Bible has authority in the Church because the Christ is *Rex et Dominus Scripturae*, for the Catholic Church is not only derived from him but also ruled by him. Precisely for this reason, however, we are committed to the position that in the Church the Scripture is the final court of appeal. This is not because we wish to maintain that the Bible is a final authority but rather because we are convinced that the Bible can be made the Word of God by the Holy Spirit. It is said that Gladstone once attended the City Temple to hear Dr Parker preach, and, on coming out, he was heard to say, 'I cannot understand these Congregationalists—they seem to have nothing to lean on except the Holy Spirit.' But to lean on the Holy Spirit is not synonymous with saying that the manifestation of the New Being can be known without the Scriptures which are the record of the revelation. Tillich would not indeed want to say this, but is he not led to such a position when he talks about the Bible being implied in the principle of reformation? Surely the uniqueness of the Bible is that in it the Word of God has been written so that it can be a living testimony to the Word Incarnate. Whilst we can agree with Tillich's insistence on the importance of tradition, we must insist that it is dangerous to do this at the expense of the Scriptures; for tradition has developed by feeding on the Scriptures.

VII

HISTORY AND THE KINGDOM OF GOD

TILLICH distinguishes two senses in which the word 'history' is used—the subjective and the objective. 'History means firstly the account of past events, secondly the events themselves.'[1] The subjective meaning of history Tillich regards as its primary meaning because of the 'special relation of history to man'. What distinguishes historical accounts from annals and chronicles is their interpretative character and what distinguishes them from epics is their empirical character. That is to say, an account is historical only if it reports facts and also in the report gives some sort of interpretation of these facts. Therefore, not every event that occurs is historical in this sense. Historical events have four characteristics. They are events in which (i) human freedom is a determining factor, (ii) human purposes are pursued, (iii) values are realised, (iv) something unique and individually significant occurs.

Some at least of these characteristics of history are discussed in Tillich's earlier book, *The Interpretation of History*. Thus the first of the four characteristics listed above is presumably what he has in mind when he maintains that history exists only where there is decision.

'History exists where there is decision, namely a decision which is concrete, on the one hand, and which is rooted in the depth of the Unconditioned on the other hand. Decisions in the conditioned sphere mean nothing in themselves. As long as they do not contribute to the meaning of history. The critical school of German philosophy had the merit of emphasising that individual events are the subject of historical research, while in natural sciences the general laws are sought. This distinction is meaningful only if individuals are more than samples of something universal,

[1] *Propositions*, Part V, p. 1.

either some being or some value. If individuality is to have unconditioned meaning it must be interpreted as the appearance of a
concrete genuine decision which transcends itself. That such
individualism is possible nowhere else but in the personal sphere,
that is, where there is freedom and where there is fate, requires
no proof.'[1]

It is clear from this quotation too that Tillich wants to insist
on the uniqueness of historical data in the sense that history is
concerned with particulars rather than laws. In this connexion
also it is worth noting that the concept of meaning is also made
dependent on the presence of indeterminacy resulting from
human freedom. The all-important characteristic of history
then is that it deals with individual events, for everywhere else
the individual is interpreted in terms of the universal. With
regard to history, however, the logic of essence is inadequate.[2]
Towards the end of the book he returns to the idea of history
as producing novelty when he contrasts the ideas of reality as
nature and as history. The first is symbolized by a circle but the
second by the line of time. 'The line of time has always one
and the same direction. It has the characteristic of going
toward something—more exactly toward something new.'
'The definite direction of time is an expression of its meaningful
character.'[3]

This concept of history obviously limits history by excluding
nature—at least in one sense. 'As far as nature is neither
dependent upon freedom nor connected with purpose and value
nor significant in its individual products, it has no history.'
There are, however, two ways in which nature is historical.
First, in so far as it shows spontaneous creativity, evolutionary
progress, unique and significant constellations, it contains
within it historical elements. Secondly, it participates in history
as the permanent base of history. The subject of history is
human individuals and groups, though human individuals are
subjects of history only in so far as they represent a special
historical group or mankind as a whole. 'The actual subjects

[1] *The Interpretation of History*, New York and London, Scribner, 1936,
p. 138.
[2] *Ibid.*, p. 214.   [3] *Ibid.*, pp. 245-6.

of history are social groups which have the power to exist and which represents a special system of values.' Since the power of an historical group to exist depends on its possibility of acting with a united will, history is the history of the states. As we saw above, not every event that occurs is historical. 'The history of an historical group includes those events which are important for the establishment, development, and maintenance of its power and vocation. All other events have the character of mere becoming, not of history.'[1] Tillich does a little later distinguish between the logical and the empirical subject of history and says that mankind is the logical subject, but he does not tell us what the empirical subject is. This distinction between the logical and empirical subject of history might be thought to be analogous to the distinction in logic between the logical and the grammatical subject.[2] The subject of the grammatical sentence need not be identical with the subject of the proposition expressed by that sentence. In the sentence, 'Socrates is mortal' the grammatical and logical subjects are identical, but in the sentence, 'The author of *Waverley* was Scott', 'the author of *Waverley*' which is the grammatical subject does not stand for the logical subject. Here the logical subject of predication is 'Scott'; for 'having written *Waverley*' is predicated of 'Scott'. In view of the incompleteness of Tillich's discussion of history it may be dangerous to say any more on the matter, but one cannot leave the matter in mid-air. Our reference to the logical distinction between the grammatical subject and the logical subject would suggest that what Tillich here means is that, though we speak of history as being about events it is really predicated of mankind. This does not seem particularly illuminating, but it might be argued that to talk of events as the subject of history blinds us to the fact that history is concerned with what has happened to men rather than some development of the world. That is, the aim of the historian is to explain what has happened; and this kind of explanation, inasmuch as it differs from scientific explanation of certain

[1] *Propositions*, Part V, p. 2.
[2] See A. N. Prior, *Formal Logic*, Oxford, Clarendon Press, 1955, pp. 178ff.

'events' (e.g. 'The water was displaced'), refers to or is about certain individuals. Moreover, it might be said that the logical subject of history is mankind because the criteria of historical importance, the basis on which events are selected for recording, is 'the concerns of man and society'. This is to assume that what we are talking of here is the logical subject of subjective history. If we are talking of objective history then the point of the distinction is the trivial truth that history is events for which men are responsible.

It must be said at the outset that this description of history is extremely vague; for, though a distinction was made between subjective and objective history it has not been made clear which sense of the term we are discussing when we are talking of historical events. There are also some respects in which this description of history seems to be actually false. We shall consider but one such point—the suggestion that an event must be unique to be historical. Professor R. H. Tawney definitely rejects the view that the subject-matter of history precludes generalization and claims that the notion that history is concerned with a string of unique and disconnected events does violence to the actual procedure of historians. This view is particularly inapplicable to economic history which Tillich recognizes as part of what he means by 'history'.[1] 'Nothing could be less appropriately described as unique and self-contained', says Professor Tawney, 'than the stages in the economic development of European countries'; and he adds, 'It is not only within the limits of Western economic civilization that comparison is instructive. A student is not likely to make much of the sharply contrasted Industrial Revolutions now taking place in China and Russia if unacquainted with the conditions which produced different versions of the corresponding movement in England, Germany and the United States, and retarded it in France.' Similarly, Professor Toynbee is by no means impressed with the difficulties arising out of the alleged unique character of historical events. 'We shall merely ask our critics to agree with us', he says, 'that a given phenomenon may be unique and therefore incomparable in some

[1] *Propositions*, Part V, p. 2.

153

respects, while at the same time in other respects it is a member of a class, and therefore comparable with other members of that class in so far as it is covered by the classification.'[1] The important qualification in Toynbee's description is that there may be respects in which historical facts are indeed unique. Thus presumably he would not wish to argue that all historical explanation takes the form of propounding and proving general laws. As Professor Ryle has pointed out, we make law-like statements (which he calls 'dispositional statements') which are neither themselves laws nor deductions from laws.

> 'The suggestion has been made that dispositional statements about mentioned individuals, while not themselves laws, are deductions from laws, so that we have to learn some perhaps crude and vague laws before we can make such dispositional statements. But in general the learning process goes the other way. We learn to make a number of dispositional statements about individuals before we learn laws stating general correlations between such statements.'[2]

It is the question of the interpretation of history, however, that most concerns Tillich, and he begins his discussion of this by making clear that here he is not concerned with historiography but with the theological questions concerning history. 'The question of the meaning of history is the question of the significance of history for the ultimate meaning of existence.'[3] The question of the meaning of history divides into five questions: (i) Does history have a meaning of its own? (ii) Where and in what form does the meaning of history manifest itself? (iii) How is the meaning of history visible in the historical process? (iv) In which symbol is the meaning of history as a whole expressed? (v) Which symbols concerning the beginning and the end of history are adequate?[4] Interpretation means for Tillich 'the creative union of the interpreter and the interpreted in a third beyond both of them', and so he says that history

[1] A. Toynbee, *A Study of History*, vol. I, p. 178.
[2] G. Ryle, *The Concept of Mind*, London, 1949, p. 124. For an interesting refutation of the view that historical explanation is an application of general laws see Dray, *Laws and Explanation in History*, Oxford Univ. Press, 1957.
[3] *Propositions*, Part V, p. 5.   [4] *Ibid.*

will never be understood by the person who tries to stand outside it. 'The meaning of history can only be discovered in meaningful historical activity. The key to history is historical action, not a point of view above history. Historical activity is the active participation in the life of a historical group. The meaning of history manifests itself in the self-understanding of a historical group.'[1] The point of view for the interpretation of history as a whole must then be some historical group in which the meaning of the whole becomes manifest. The question of the meaning of history is identical with the quest for this group. History presupposes the actualization of human freedom and spirit and therefore participates in the creative and the self-destructive character of life. The contrast between creativity and frustration in the historical process is the question implied in history which cannot be answered out of history itself. Tillich concludes that all attempts to interpret history on the basis of unconquered existence must of necessity miss its meaning.

'History can only be interpreted in connection with the manifestation of the New Being in which existence is overcome, and the manifestation of which constitutes the centre of history. The question of the meaning of history is identical with the quest for the Christ.'[2]

In some respects this interpretation of history owes a great deal to the Bible. Tillich conceives history, as did the Old Testament prophets, as always crisis in the sense of being under judgment and at the same time as having an aim toward which it is moving. The main content of history as it moves towards its end is the struggle between good and evil, a struggle which has a social as well as an individual dimension. This eschatology is given a centre in the New Testament teaching concerning the final revelation in Christ. It has been pointed out by J. L. Adams in his paper on Tillich's interpretation of history, that it expresses 'motifs central in the Protestant-Christian interpretation of time and history', and among these are the Pauline doctrine of justification by faith and the

[1] *Ibid.*, p. 6.   [2] *Ibid.*, p. 7.

doctrine of the kingdom of God.[1] The first points to the victory of the New Being over estrangement in the very experience of the doubts and contradictions of existence. The doctrine of the kingdom affirms likewise that the divine power has already broken through into history and promises a fulfilment to come. It might be argued too that the strong practical emphasis in Tillich's interpretation is biblical. Certainly, it is one of the most interesting points in his theory, and it is unfortunate that we do not have the benefit of a fuller discussion than that of the *Propositions*. When we are told that we shall only discover the meaning of history in historical activity this can be understood either as some kind of prediction about our success in doing history or as a commendation of a principle of action. Acceptance of the principle does not guarantee the truth of the theory of historiography or interpretation of history, and as such a theory it does not seem to be true. Indeed, I find it hard to resist the feeling that when we have finally discovered how Tillich is using the term 'meaning of history' here we shall find that it is not any historiographical concept at all. For he later says that the quest for the meaning of history is the quest for the group in which the meaning of the whole is manifest. It may yet be true that if we come to the point at which we are prepared to say that we believe the meaning of the whole has been thus revealed this knowledge is as much a practical as it is a theoretical affair. When we turn to the discussion in his earlier work, *The Interpretation of History*, we do get some illumination. There Tillich talks of the realization of meaning as the essential content of history. But what is meant by 'the realization of meaning' is far from clear. Meaning, we are told, is realized only by freedom. 'History has meaning only in so far as the threat of meaninglessness is overcome in concrete decision.'[2] It seems clear that the term 'meaning' here refers to the meaning an agent creates when he fulfils an intention or acts purposively. This brings us back to the remark in the *Propositions* that one can discover the meaning of history only

---

[1] J. L. Adams, 'Tillich's Interpretation of History', *The Theology of Paul Tillich*, p. 302.

[2] *The Interpretation of History*, p. 255.

from the viewpoint of historical action. This can mean that the only successful attempt at writing world history will be that of the man whose standpoint is that of an actor rather than a spectator. If this is what is meant then it will be to the point to ask whether the 'Histories' that have been written are therefore unsuccessful and how they are unsuccessful. We need bother ourselves no more with this question for it is clearly false to claim this, and so we can assume that our author does not mean this. Secondly, it can mean that anyone who asks the question, What is the meaning of history? will never discover the answer to his question except as an historical agent. What lends this view plausibility is the notion that history consists in the discovery of the thought which is the inner side of the event to be explained. But this could only be the case with certain kinds of history such as diplomatic history which is often concerned with specific acts of individuals. However, history is concerned with other data as well as the mental factors in social phenomena. All this does nothing to explain the term 'the meaning of history', and we may begin by noting that the term is not part of the historian's language. It is more likely to be used by the philosopher and as a philosophical question it is at least initially a linguistic question. We may compare 'the meaning of history' with 'the meaning of a painting'. When we look at something by Picasso we are very likely to be perplexed and we may feel that we do not know what the artist 'means'. If we can relate the painting to Picasso's intentions we shall then say that we understand what Picasso *means*. In this way we can speak of the meaning of the painting. But it is well known that a work of art can have meanings beyond anything that can properly be called the expression of the artist's personality. If we ask then for *the* meaning of the painting the only answer that will not be misleading is that it is the painting itself. In the same way it may well be true that the meaning of history is not something external to it. If we say this then we could also say that the meaning of history is discovered in historical activity. It thus becomes clear that Tillich is concerned with metaphysical questions and more particularly with the commendation of a faith which is one element of the metaphysical

157

answer. This seems to be the only way in which the remarks about the interpretation of the meaning of history can be justified. One minor point of criticism may be mentioned in conclusion before we once more follow Tillich's exposition of his view of history. The way in which the term 'meaning of history' has finally been understood here is very different from Tillich's use of it in the discussion in *The Interpretation of History* to which we have referred, where it describes the teleological concept used to explain the forward movement of historical time.

Tillich's interpretation of time as the decisive category of historical existence follows that of Schelling and Bergson. He defines historical time in terms of a contrast between space and time, nature and history. Time and space are, he says, neither things nor qualities of things but 'forms in which the finiteness of things appears'.[1]

> 'The fundamental difference in the character of time is the difference between historical and natural time. Man participates in both of them although he is man because he has historical time. Natural time is time under predominance of space and therefore under the law of endless repetition and circular motion. Historical time overcomes the predominance of space, has a direction and runs toward something new. Natural time is reversible; historical time is irreversible.'[2]

In the inorganic realm of nature time is physical, the quantitative time of pure motion; in the organic realm time is biological, the time of genesis and decay. This natural time is bound to space, whereas historical time breaks free of the circle of repetition. Man as a social creature is not bound to his spatial environment but is able to remember his past, interpret his present and anticipate his future intention.

The central idea in Tillich's interpretation of history is that of *kairos*. This doctrine was conceived in a situation in which, Tillich says, 'it was necessary to find a way between socialist utopianism and Lutheran transcendentalism.'[3] It was an

[1] *Propositions*, Part V, p. 3.
[2] *Ibid.* Cf. *The Interpretation of History*, pp. 243ff.
[3] *The Theology of Paul Tillich*, p. 345.

attempt to capture the sense of promise in utopianism and at the same time to offer warning against its dangers. The word itself is the New Testament equivalent for the Old Testament 'time' or 'season' and is commonly translated as 'fulfilled time' or 'the time of fulfilment' since fulfilment here is the arrival of the time foretold. Tillich describes the Pauline use of *kairos* referring to the time of the coming of Christ as the unique and universal sense of the word, but says that the word has also a general sense. So he describes as 'kairotic' those moments at every turning point in history in which the eternal judges and transforms the temporal. Tillich emphasizes the uniqueness of each moment in history. The number of possibilities open to me in any historical situation is limited and the situation demands of me a free decision. This does not dismay the Protestant. 'The fundamental Protestant attitude is to stand in nature, taking upon oneself the inevitable reality; not to flee from it, either into the world of ideal forms or into the related world of supra-nature, but to make decisions in concrete reality.'[1] The decision must, however, unite individuality and universality or it has no meaning. 'The relation between *kairos* and *Logos*', says Professor J. L. Adams of Tillich's interpretation of history, 'is not one of disjunction; it is dialectical; *kairos* points to the limits set for the realization of *Logos* in a particular historical situation and yet it opens up a new, unique way for the realization of *Logos*.'[2]

The symbol of the Kingdom of God indicates the fulfilment of history.

'The Kingdom of God is the fulfillment intended in history and implied in the ultimate. The Kingdom of God is the transcendent fulfillment, the name for the ultimate from the point of view of fulfillment. The Kingdom of God therefore embraces everything in the course of history as its transcendent meaning.'[3]

The Kingdom of God does not belong entirely to another world but points to history itself in so far as it points to the struggle between the divine and the demonic kingdom which has human history as its battlefield. There are static and dynamic elements

[1] *The Interpretation of History*, p. 134.
[2] *The Theology of Paul Tillich*, pp. 306-7.
[3] *The Interpretation of History*, p. 280.

in this symbol. It expresses first the ultimate fulfilment in which the contrast between essence and existence is overcome universally and completely. The symbol has a sociological and political character, indicating the significance of justice and of personality and personal relationships for the ultimate fulfilment. The symbol does not exclude the use of other symbols such as 'eternal life' so long as these symbols are not interpreted anti-socially or anti-personally. The dynamic elements in the idea are three-fold—its historical character, its critical function, and its indication of the final victory. The symbol points to the struggle between the divine and the demonic kingdom within human history. It reveals the demonic elements in existence and judges them. Finally, it points to the final victory of the divine over the demonic kingdom and to the exclusion of the demonic elements from the ultimate fulfilment. The symbol of the Kingdom of God therefore expresses the relationship of the unconditioned meaning of existence to actual existence, and so answers the question of the meaning of history. It interprets history as directed towards the ultimate fulfilment above the cleavage of essence and existence, and from this point of view answers the questions of the centre, the end, the beginning and the course of history. Every realization of meaning, however, is only fragmentary; and so the symbol of the Kingdom of God points beyond the struggle and the transformations of history to a fulfilment in a dimension that transcends history. 'The symbol of the Kingdom of God points to a supra-historical unity, totality and clarity of the contradictory, fragmentary, and ambiguous meaning actualized in the historical process.' The symbol thus unites an historical and a supra-historical element since the meaning of history both transcends history and appears in it. Every attempt to express the fulfilment in terms merely of time will distort its meaning, making it a history after history, a time after time.

The symbol of the Kingdom of God affirms the independent meaning of history in three ways: (i) by excluding the ultimate significance of the spatial realms and 'their polytheistic expressions', (ii) by excluding the ultimate significance of the non-historical manifestations of the divine and their sacramental expressions, (iii) by excluding the ultimate significance of finite creations and their romantic expressions. Two of these three points are more or less easily understood, but what Tillich means by 'non-historical manifestations of the divine' we cannot say. The exclusion of the ultimate significance of spatial realms guarantees the independent meaning of history since time is the distinctive characteristic of history, and time is related more directly to human concerns than is space. The gods of space being denied, history takes on an independent significance. Again, the meaning of history is not a creation of man's and so the denial of the ultimate worth of such creations also guarantees the independent meaning of history. Further, as the idea affirms the meaning of history so also does it protect it, and this too in three ways. First, it protects it by overcoming the static idea of eternity and its mystical expressions. It is quite clear that the idea, containing as it does dynamic elements, cannot be reconciled with a static conception of the nature of eternity such as one has in Aristotle's doctrine of the unmoved mover. Secondly, the symbol protects the independent meaning of history 'against the utopian idea of the final stage of history by its supra-historical character'. What exactly this means is not clear, but it may be that for Tillich the symbol denies the utopian interpretation of history which would see the meaning of history only in the final stage which as it were sums up all that has gone before. It would do this because the symbol implies that all stages of history are bearers of meaning. Finally, 'the symbol of the Kingdom of God protects the independent meaning of history against the idea of an infinite progress by its definite character'. That is, the idea does imply a definite goal of history, which would deny any suggestion that there is no limit to the progress achieved in history.

The appearance of the New Being in whom the contrast between essential and existential being is overcome constitutes the centre of history, and in Christ as the centre of history the Kingdom of God manifests itself as the ultimate meaning of history. The Church, as the social group whose existence and meaning is based on the New Being in Christ, represents the Kingdom of God in history. Tillich is very emphatic that the Church is not identical with the Kingdom of God. 'This', he says, 'is not even Augustinian (and far less is it Reformation) theology'.[1] The Church can be perverted into a representation of the demonic kingdom. Even so, it cannot be destroyed in its being and meaning since it is founded on the New Being which has overcome existence. The manifestation of the Kingdom of God in history determines the course of world history so that every event, directly or indirectly, serves the purpose of the Kingdom of God. This providential character of history is not a matter of mechanical or logical necessity. 'It works by making every moment of the world historical process, however fragmentary and distorted it may be, contribute to the ultimate meaning of history.' The ultimate meaning of world history and the ultimate meaning of individual life are interdependent. The Kingdom of God as the end of history is the transformation of existence into the New Being which is beyond essential and existential being. This implies the disclosure and isolation of the anti-divine elements in existence and the reunion of the separated elements of existence within the totality of the New Being. This can be further described as universal unity and perfection. The ultimate fulfilment is the universal unity of all beings in the New Being. This means universal peace and harmony. The ultimate fulfilment is also the universal perfection of the qualities of being in the New Being.

The doctrine of the Kingdom of God with its key concept of the *kairos* is what lies behind Tillich's religious socialism. This is a question raised not by the general sense but by the special sense of the word *kairos*. It is the problem of the possibility of Christian ethics and has to do with all of man's relations with other men. The adjective 'religious' is not meant to sugar the pill of socialism, but to express the true character of the social struggle for justice. From the end of the First World War until his exile from Germany Tillich's theology was characterized by a vigorous political conviction and commitment. He gave the German movement of religious socialism its philosophy. As

[1] *The Theology of Paul Tillich*, p. 348.

we have seen, Tillich did not, any more than Marx, believe that theory and practice are separate.[1] It is not surprising, then, that theoretical though his early work was it was also involved in the social and political movements in Germany between the two wars.

The historical interpretation from which the social message is immediately derived is an analysis of modern society. Tillich believed it was characterized by a victory of the Unconditional Demand over the power of the Origin so that society has become unstable, seeking with endless dissatisfaction to find its own end in itself. This is the bourgeois spirit. The power of the Origin is that aspect of being which holds us in the order out of which we have arisen.[2] Over against the Origin stands the Unconditional Demand, that is the demand for justice. Justice, says Tillich, 'is the true power of being'. Therefore 'the actually original is not the truly original'. The truly original is that toward which the Unconditional Demand points, but which the Origin should never fulfil simply by the power of its being. Thus the Demand creates a break with the Origin—it introduces freedom into human life and puts the Origin under criticism in the name of its own fulfilment. Historically the first expression of the Ultimate Demand breaking the power of the Origin is the Old Testament where prophecy stands over against the tendency of the Origin to become mythical, imperialistic and priestly. Christian history, however, poses a different problem because it depends on Christ as the centre of history, the *kairos*. All history can be divided into periods of preparation, which are characterized by expectation, and periods of fulfilment in which culture expresses the meaning revealed in the *kairos*. Christ's coming is the centre and standard of this process so that all history becomes the history of salvation. Within this history the struggle between the divine and the demonic, of course, goes on.

'The only unconditional prospect is the promise and expectation of the supra-historical fulfilment of history, of the Kingdom of

[1] See above, p. 155. Cf. *The Interpretation of History*, p. 18.
[2] See *The Interpretation of History*, pp. 206ff.

God, in which that which has not been decided within history will be decided and that which has not been fulfilled will be fulfilled.'[1]

It was the doctrine of the secondary *kairos*, however, which gave the message of religious socialism in Tillich's earlier writings its urgency. *Kairos* in this secondary or general sense Tillich defines by distinction from other views of history, such as the revolutionary-absolute type which denies the past and affirms the future, the Catholic tendency to make one historical reality absolute at the expense of all others, and the Barthian indifference to the special heights and depths of the historical process according to which the *kairos* is given in every moment of history. As distinct from all these the secondary *kairos* is that moment when a crisis of history, a period of expectation informed by the prophetic demand, condemns a disintegrating social structure and is met by the power of a new creation for which the time is ripe.[2] Thus the interpretation of a *kairos* is always an act of faith and the resultant action *a fortiori* a venture of faith. There is no certainty connected with it. It may not be a correct interpretation, and even if the interpretation is correct the time of the *kairos* may pass without being grasped because the faith of those *en kairo* was not great enough. The meaning of the secondary or general *kairos* is thus left rather vague by Tillich. He says that 'we must conceive of the *kairos* in universal terms', but he does not tell us why we are thus compelled to understand the word as having a general use. Indeed it would seem as if there were reasons for denying that it could have such a use, for this would militate against our understanding of the special *kairos* as unique. Further, Tillich does not seem very clear about the way in which the two uses are related. 'What happened in the unique *kairos*, the appearance of Jesus as the Christ, i.e. as the centre of history, may happen in derived form again and again, thus creating minor centres of importance.'[3] But what is this except to say that as the Word of God dwelt in our midst so the Risen Lord is with his people and under him they effect changes in

[1] Tillich, 'The Kingdom of God and History', *Church, Community and State* (1937 Oxford Conference), London, 1938, vol. 3, p. 141.
[2] Cf. *The Protestant Era*, pp. 47-8.   [3] *Ibid.*, p. xxxiv.

history? In other words, if we are to take seriously the words 'derived form' then what we are talking about is the extension of the Incarnation and not a different kind of *kairos*. Does Tillich's anxiety to extract a political message from the Christian view of history here result in a misrepresentation of the way in which the centre of history, on this view, is related to the rest of history? Tillich does not, of course deny that there are differences in religious significance between the various 'turning-points in history', but he does not introduce any such distinctions into his doctrine of the *kairos*. Thus he says: 'The appearance of the new is the concrete crisis of the old, the historical judgement against it. The new creation may be worse than the old one which is brought into crisis by it. But in the special historical moment it is *en kairo* while the old creation is not.'[1] It is very difficult to see anything in this characterization of the *kairos* that is even remotely derivative from the unique sense of the word.

Two periods of theonomy form the background of the modern era. The earlier one was the culture of the Middle Ages which turned to heteronomy in its reaction against the autonomy of the Renaissance and later against the Reformation. The second theonomous period was the Reformation itself, for Luther was *en kiaro*. He effected a new interpretation of the centre of history so that contemporary man has 'a Christian background that has been qualified by Protestantism'.[2] This is the justification for speaking of the modern age as the Protestant Era. But modern man is the autonomous man who has become insecure in his autonomy. He lacks any world-view, but is prevented from surrendering to some external authority (heteronomy) by his awareness of the ultimate threat to human existence or the human 'boundary-situation'.

Protestantism is thus *en kairo* because modern man is prepared to heed its proclamation of the human boundary-situation. For the Protestant principle drives man to the boundary of his existence, protesting against all attempts to evade it. There every religious expression and every philosophy is confronted

[1] *Ibid.*, p. 44.   [2] *Ibid.*, p. 189.

with the double demand that it 'realize the true, and actualize the good and submit to judgement for its failure to do so'. Man cannot escape from freedom, for even if he attempted to escape this very attempt is the content of a free choice. 'This inevitability of freedom, of having to make decisions, creates the deep restlessness of our existence; through it our existence is threatened.'[1] Protestantism is the proclamation of this boundary-situation—this is its first task. Having insisted on the radical experience of the boundary-situation the Protestant church must also 'proclaim the judgment that brings assurance by depriving us of all security'.[2] Finally, Protestantism must witness to the 'New Being' through which alone it is able to say its word in power, and it must do this without making this witness the basis of a wrong security. Protestantism can be 'open for everything, religious and secular, past and future, individual and social'.[3] It neither devaluates nor idealizes culture but tries to understand its religious substance, its 'theonomous' nature.

The influence of Protestantism is but one side of the historical analysis of modern society of which the other is the development of autonomous humanism. Even non-Christian humanism is, in a sense, a Christian development inasmuch as it is the specifically Christian and complete fulfilment of autonomy. Thus the Enlightenment's belief in reason, freedom and progress is filled with religious fervour and revolutionary power. In the nineteenth century, however, reason was understood in a more narrowly technical sense, being no longer thought of as concerned with the ends and principle of life. It was limited to the service of the existing order, of production and exchange. Man lost control of his historical existence; and so the bourgeois period is an endless procession of man's attempts to fulfil his meaning in the finite and to find in it the rest of unconditioned fulfilment, a rest which is nowhere found.[4] In the capitalist system the transcendent meaning of social ties is destroyed.

'Things become wares—objects whose meaning lies in the production of profits in transactions of buying and selling, not in the

[1] *The Protestant Era*, p. 195.   [2] *Ibid.*, p. 202.   [3] *Ibid.*, p. 203.
[4] Cf. *Religiöse Verwirklichung*, Berlin, Furche, 1929.

enrichment of personal life. They are acquired and disposed of by their masters, not by beings who have some kind of community with them, hence there is no limit in their acquisition. Free economy tends necessarily toward infinite commercial imperialism.'[1]

Though this results in the exaltation of personality above the realm of things it nevertheless makes man the slave of an 'ever-increasing life-consuming activity in the service of unlimited wants'. Life becomes dominated by the economic function and the individual is left alone and in conflict with all others, and so man is threatened with meaninglessness. The point from which Tillich claims to be speaking is 'the situation of that class within the capitalist system whose members are dependent exclusively upon the "free" sale of their physical ability to work and whose social destiny is wholly dependent upon the turn of the market'.[2] This means that the class war is the secret condition of all capitalist society. Thus Tillich incorporates into his analysis of current history what he regards as the basic insights of Marx; for he believes that there is a 'structural analogy' between the prophetic element of biblical religion and Marxism.[3]

Whilst affirming the value of the Marxist analysis of bourgeois society and insisting that there is no religious position beyond the class war, Tillich also regards the radical criticism of socialism as a religious duty. The basis of this criticism is the recognition of the inner conflict within socialism itself, a conflict which arises from the fundamentally religious character of socialism. It may be necessary to remind ourselves at this point that it is Paul Tillich who is speaking and not George Lansbury; for the sense in which Tillich here speaks of the religious character of socialism has nothing to do with the influence of the Free Churches on Socialism in Britain. Socialism, for Tillich, has religious character because religion means life out of the roots of being. Eduard Heimann remarks that this 'use of the word "religious" to the exclusion of the word

---

[1] *The Religious Situation*, New York, Henry Holt, 1932, p. 72.
[2] *The Protestant Era*, p. 241.   [3] See *ibid.*, pp. 278-9.

"Christian" . . . reinforces the liberalizing tendency and the ensuing vulnerability of the doctrine', and he continues:

> 'The problem is not only one of principle—which would always imply far-reaching practical consequences, of course—but of immediate practical importance. The brilliant formula according to which socialism is religious in essence although antireligious in conscious intention is a great help in fighting ecclesiastical legalism and phariseeism, but it leaves us with the question of whether atheism is as good as faith. There are two logical possibilities. Perhaps we are to distinguish an essentially religious atheism from an essentially unreligious one, and subsume modern socialism under the first . . . But can there be anything essentially un-religious? . . . And is not then the real distinction to be made between the different religions in which men believe? Con-cretely, is not Marxism, however profoundly religious, an anti-religion?'[1]

Discussing Tillich's *Principles of Religious Socialism*,[2] Heimann says that the vision of the socialist theonomy he here expounded is 'immaculate' but his understanding of Marxism and its relationship to religious socialism is suspect.

> 'The trouble is not in any principle of his thinking, but simply in a faulty appraisal of the facts of the Marxist doctrine. He rightly sees the barrier between religious socialism and Marxism in the latter's utopianism, but wrongly assumes that Marxism can logically be dissociated from it. He does not see that the conflict is not between the utopianism of Marxism . . . and the realism of religion's socialism, but between the two doctrines of man. Tillich's error is in associating Marxist utopianism with its doctrine of revolution rather than with its doctrine of man, which in an atheistic system, occupies the place of theology.'[3]

For Tillich the Marxist goal is the creative person. He has repeatedly asserted that it is the man in the proletarian worker

---

[1] *The Theology of Paul Tillich*, p. 318.
[2] Heimann does not give a bibliographical reference for these two papers, but says (*op. cit.*, p. 320, n. 11) that regrettably they have 'not been re-published for a larger audience than the original one, and have been overlooked in the list of Tillich's writings' (presumably the one published at the end of the volume, *The Theology of Paul Tillich*).
[3] *Op. cit.*, p. 320.

who reacts to the proletarian situation. Therefore, though the Marxist utopianism must be rejected, Marxism must be retained, in its purified form.[1] So Tillich concludes that Marxism is an essential element in religious socialism. Heimann points out that this is to misunderstand Marx's main scientific message.

> 'All his economic analyses are directed toward the goal of proving that the decline and beginning catastrophe of capitalism is, by the same token, the ascendancy of socialism, in the sense of making socialism the logically necessary effect of that cause. According to Tillich, it is the dehumanization of the proletarian existence under capitalism and the discrediting of capitalism even by its own technical malfunctioning in the economic crisis which becomes intolerable, and which makes socialism a humanly necessary reaction. According to Marx, it is the institutional transformation of industrial life by capitalism which makes a homogenous industrial proletarian society its logical result.'[2]

Though Tillich is right in his rejection of the idea of 'a universal mechanism of incalculable processes' he is wrong in his belief that there can be a combination of Christianity and dialectical materialism, since he ignores the fact that the very mechanism he has rejected is the end sought by Marxism.

Another weakness in Tillich's estimate of Marxism has been his failure to appreciate the fact that it represents a living faith which cannot be accommodated within a rival faith. Communism is indeed for him a religious movement, standing in the socialist *kairos*. Consequently he urged that both the Church authorities and Christian laymen should strive to transform Communism by trying 'to unite Christian principles with the principles of Communism'.[3] This kind of advice was quite unrealistic and doctrinaire, and it is not surprising that by 1949 Tillich was forced to admit that there was no likelihood of the East and West being united in a new religious socialism.[4] However, this does not mean that he has abandoned his

---

[1] *The Protestant Era*, p. 277.
[2] *The Theology of Paul Tillich*, pp. 321-2.
[3] See 'The Churches and Communism', *Religion in Life*, Summer, 1937.
[4] See 'Beyond Religious Socialism', *The Christian Century*, 15th June, 1949.

conviction that religious socialism is the only true social policy. What it does mean is that the concept of *kairos* has been replaced by that of the 'sacred void', the time of waiting for the Christian. This may appear to some of his readers to reveal a 'prophetic caution', but it is not at all clear that it is caution which moves him at this point. Rather is it more likely that he introduces this concept merely to preserve the structure of his theory, and there are at least two reasons why the attempt cannot be said to succeed. The first is that unwittingly Tillich has in effect contradicted his earlier analysis, according to which the powers of being itself were moving in socialism (as a secondary *kairos*) towards fulfilment, and religious socialism thus corresponded to the very meaning of history. It seems as if this earlier estimate of socialism is proved wrong both by the actual movement of events and by the resultant change in Tillich's social theory.

The second reason is the more fundamental consideration that Tillich's whole approach has been doctrinaire. The *a priori* character of his whole social ethic is very well illustrated by his little book, *Love, Power and Justice*. Whereas other works cover the purely metaphysical interest with sociological references this work reveals it as Tillich's paramount and all-consuming interest. The purpose of the book is to show the essential meaning of the three terms—love, power and justice—and also their essential unity. There is no doubt that this little book of 125 pages is a veritable *tour de force* and constitutes one of the most important documents for the student of Tillich's thought. After devoting some space to a description of ontology he gives his ontology of love. Love is the reunion of the estranged, which means that for Tillich self-love is a metaphor.[1] His ontology of power is derived from Nietzsche's idea of 'will to power', which is interpreted as the self-affirmation of life, a concept interestingly developed as both literal and metaphorical.[2] Here Tillich says that 'being is the power of being'. Power is distinguished from compulsion but is said to actualize itself through it. Love is the foundation of power, and creative justice is reuniting love. This leads on to the assertion of the

[1] *Love, Power and Justice*, Oxford, 1954, p. 34.   [2] *Ibid.*, p. 36.

ontological unity of love, power and justice, a unity which is revealed in personal relations, group relations and the ultimate relation to God. The thesis of the book can be summed up very briefly in a sentence which occurs in the final chapter—'Love, power and justice are united in God and they are united in the new creation of God in the world.'[1] Not only has the discussion of concepts which are decisive for both politics and religion become purely theological in the sense that there is no practical interest, but it has become almost entirely formal. It is no coincidence perhaps that Hegel's dialectic also originated as an analysis of love,[2] later to be developed as an analysis of power and justice. This latest discussion of political concepts by Tillich shows that the shade of Hegel still walks in philosophy. The weakness of Tillich's attempt at correlating theology and politics is that the unity he seeks is established by means of definition and deduction, and so is ultimately as empty a thing as the logical form suggests.

One final point can be raised very briefly. If it is true that the Hegelian ontology represents at least one source of Tillich's ontology (and the fact that Schelling is the dominant influence on his philosophical development does not render this any more unlikely than it did in the case of the leader of the Hegelian right, Marheineke), does this not mean that there is in fact an irreconcilable opposition between Tillich's philosophical method and his theological concern? For though Hegel's thought has been generally interpreted as theological and even Christian, it is probably more accurately regarded as radically secular.[3] Therefore the apparent agreement between the theological affirmations Tillich wishes to establish and the philosophical system which is used to support them turns out to be deceptive.

[1] *Love, Power and Justice*, Oxford, 1954, p. 115.
[2] See Hegel, *Early Theological Writings* (trans. Knox and Kroner), ch. 3.
[3] Cf. the discussion of Hegel's attitude to Christianity in my *Subjectivity and Paradox*, Oxford, Blackwell, 1957, ch. 2.

VIII

CONCLUSION

TILLICH has been described as one of the few unquestionably 'great' men of our time, as America's foremost philosopher and most distinguished theologian. It has been said—and this statement of Gorgia Harkness is frequently quoted—that what Whitehead is to American philosophy Tillich is to American theology. The editors of *The Theology of Paul Tillich* have this to say of him:

> 'With Dewey, Whitehead, Russell and Santayana stands a man whom future generations probably will pronounce no whit their inferior either dialectically or in his grasp of the philosophical requirements of our time, but whose feet are planted solidly upon Christian soil, rooted in the Word of God. His name is Paul Tillich.'[1]

Many people who would doubt whether Tillich is as great a theologian as Karl Barth would yet be prepared to say that he is the most significant theologian alive today. If we ask why he is considered so significant there will doubtless be as many different answers as there are readers of his work and it is impossible to give an adequate account of this varied reaction. But some of the main answers would be that his is the most important philosophical work done in theology, that he more than anyone else has spoken to the condition of twentieth-century man, and that he alone amongst theologians has sought to relate theology to the fields of science, art and sociology. In conclusion we shall consider these answers and so gain a fuller picture of Tillich's theology and a deeper appreciation of the theories we have discussed.

[1] C. W. Kegley and R. W. Bretall, 'Introduction', *The Theology of Paul Tillich*, p. x.

172

There can be no doubt that Tillich has dominated the American theological world during the last ten to twenty years. To many Americans (and to some Europeans too) he represents *the* prophet among their theologians. He has furnished a dwelling-place for minds in search of a haven, and there has not been wanting a succession of disciples and devotees who have hailed his system as a modern Protestant *Summa*. Whether his work is regarded as a completed structure which can be modern man's mental home or as a framework within which creative work is yet to be done there is a widespread feeling that he is *par excellence* the *modern* theologian. In the recent volume of essays published in his honour Walter Leibrecht says:

'Paul Tillich has spoken to modern man with a penetration which is perhaps unequalled by any other man of thought. It is the honesty with which he approaches reality and the freshness with which he discusses the perplexities and joys of our individual lives which make his writings fascinating. Concerned as few have been with eternity, he has never turned a deaf ear to time and his fellow men. The prominence in his thought of the notion of *kairos*, the creative act in the moment of the invasion of the finite by the infinite . . . illustrates his insistence on speaking to men in the light of changing circumstances which confront them. With candor he has approached every facet of our tangled lives and has been a true guide to the perplexed in our century.'[1]

Theodore M. Greene has said that one of Tillich's chief contributions is his historically oriented answer to the question, What are the chief anxieties and perplexities of modern man?[2] Tillich has described the historical evolution of Western culture which has now fallen prey to the acids of modernity. This is Tillich's analysis of the contemporary human situation:

'The man of today . . . is aware of the confusion of his inner life, the cleavage of his behaviour, the demonic forces in his psychic and social existence. And he senses that not only his being but also his knowing is thrown into confusion, that he lacks ultimate

[1] W. Leibrecht, *Religion and Culture*, pp. 3-4.
[2] *The Theology of Paul Tillich*, p. 53.

truth, and that he faces especially in the social life of our day, a conscious, almost demonic distortion of truth. In this situation in which most of the traditional values and forms of life are disintegrating, he often is driven to the abyss of complete meaninglessness, which is full of both horror and fascination.'[1]

This kind of analysis is so abstract that one feels it could easily be adapted to describe any situation. I do not wish to deny that Tillich approaches the problems of the modern world with sympathy and real courage. But why is it that when one examines carefully what he writes about this modern situation that one feels almost swamped by the flow of language? I am not suggesting that Tillich's language is completely devoid of content, but I think it is indubitable that the language tends to obscure rather than reveal the picture we are meant to behold. In a word, I very much doubt whether there is anything distinctively *modern* in what Tillich has to say about the human situation. Is not the appearance of modernity due to the fact that Tillich has made great use of the Existentialists' terminology rather than to anything in the content of his writings? Indeed if we consider this Existentialist influence we shall see that in so far as Tillich can be called an Existentialist at all he is certainly not modern. Referring to his university studies Tillich remarks that at this time he came under the influence of Schelling.[2] After mentioning his debt to Martin Kähler for the insight the latter gave him 'into the all-controlling character of the Pauline-Lutheran idea of justification', Tillich goes on to say: 'My Christology and Dogmatics were determined by the interpretation of the Cross of Christ as the event of history in which this divine judgement over the world became concrete and manifest. From this point of view it was easy for me to make a connexion between my own theology and that of Karl Barth and to accept the analysis of human existence as given by Kierkegaard and Heidegger.'[3] A little later in the same chapter he reminds us of the powerful influence of Schelling on him—particularly the work of Schelling's later period: 'I thought that, fundamentally, I had found the union of theology

---

[1] *The Protestant Era*, p. 202. [2] *The Interpretation of History*, p. 31.
[3] *Ibid.*, p. 32.

and philosophy in the philosophical explanation of the Christian doctrine through the older Schelling, in his founding of a Christian philosophy of existence in contrast to Hegel's humanist philosophy of essence and in his interpretation of history as the History of Salvation.'[1] This detailed knowledge of Schelling's later work, together with his knowledge of Kierkegaard and his dependence on the 'philosophy of life' movement had prepared Tillich to accept existential philosophy. This led him to a new understanding of the relation between philosophy and theology.[2] We are not told what this new understanding of the relation is, but on the next page Tillich does say that he regards Heidegger's work as 'theonomous philosophy' which unintentionally establishes a doctrine of man which is both the doctrine of human freedom and human finitude, and which is closely related to the Christian interpretation of human existence. There are two things which must be said about this connection between Tillich and Heidegger. First, it is significant that for Tillich the decisive beginning of existential philosophy is to be found in Schelling's later work, and that the preparation for his acceptance of Heidegger was his acquaintance with Kierkegaard and the *Lebensphilosophie* movement. This, I suggest, makes his brand of Existentialism[3] (which is in any case a very dangerous blanket term) much nearer to the mood of nineteenth-century philosophy than it is to the mood of contemporary philosophy, a mood of iconoclasm and metaphysical seeking which is shared by existentialist and linguistic philosophies. Secondly, however close Tillich may think Heidegger is to the Christian interpretation of human existence, neither Heidegger himself nor his best interpreters have so understood his death-centred evaluation of human existence. So we may repeat that the appearance of modernity in Tillich is like that which a duly edited version of Schelling with a preface by Sartre could be imagined to possess.

There is another respect in which Tillich might be thought to be very much the contemporary theologian. This is his

[1] *The Interpretation of History*, p. 35.   [2] *Ibid.*, p. 39.
[3] Significantly enough Rhein gives no evidence when he says (*op. cit.*, p. 45) that existentialist elements are found in all their fulness in Tillich.

175

emphasis on the apologetic function of theology. In his Introduction to volume one of *Systematic Theology* he insists that the
'situation' cannot be excluded from theological work. Theology,
he says, must answer the questions implied in the situation 'in
the power of the eternal message and with the means provided
by the situation whose questions it answers'.[1] Whether he has
succeeded or not Tillich has attempted to present such a
theology. Not since Schleiermacher has there been such a
full-scale reconstruction or reinterpretation of theology, and
indeed it might even be argued that what Tillich has done is
more extensive and more thorough than was Schleiermacher's
work. Again, one must admit the courage shown by this
venture; but this is not to say that he has succeeded or that such
work is necessary or desirable. That he has not at any rate been
completely successful has been argued in our discussion of the
main themes of his theology. Our further point is that there are
many indications of his being not a modern theologian at all
but rather a nineteenth-century thinker in twentieth-century
dress. It is not without cause that he describes himself as
belonging to the nineteenth century. 'I am', he says, 'one of
those in my generation who, in spite of the radicalism with
which they have criticized the nineteenth century, often feel a
longing for its . . . unbroken cultural traditions.'[2] This longing
explains, for instance, why it is that he should wish to write a
system of theology in an age which has no faith in systems of
thought, and when we shall discuss Tillich's significance as a
philosophical theologian we shall have to return to this. The
longing for the unbroken cultural traditions characteristic of
the nineteenth century has led Tillich to comment on the
unhappy divisions of both the Church and twentieth-century
culture. Thus he is regarded by some as *the* modern ecumenical
theologian or again as *the* contemporary theologian who can
assist cultural reconstruction. Both are in a way aspects of the
appeal which Tillich's apologetic emphasis makes to the
contemporary reader of theology.

We cannot here discuss the whole question of apologetics,

[1] *Systematic Theology* I, p. 6.
[2] *The Theology of Paul Tillich*, p. 3.

and it must suffice to say that the ideal of a new body of theology which has been cast into the contemporary pattern cannot be upheld. The distinction between the form and the content of theology, which is what Tillich expresses as the polarity of situation and *Kerygma*,[1] has one weakness or danger. It suggests that there is a particular entity which can assume various garbs which are successively fashionable and unfashionable. Now it is true that we sometimes borrow language from the philosopher or the poet in order to express something which without such language we had not been able to express. But this is the old story of searching for words to say what we mean with its recurrent cry 'I don't mean quite that, but at the moment I have no other way of putting it.' And thought is no ghostly entity behind the appearance of language. Similarly, the relation of Christian thought to its various expressions is much closer and more complex than this would suggest. The model of translation which is often used in expositions of the apologetic theologian's task is quite inadequate. For, to mention but one crucial defect, in translation there is always an original which can be consulted in order to verify our translation but this is not the case here. Moreover, apologetics savour of the old outworn way of approaching theology from the point of view of philosophy, the method of proof. We call this method outworn because it represents the confidence of the old-fashioned metaphysician in the ability of philosophy to prove what could legitimately be called knowledge. Nowadays we do not think that philosophy can *prove* anything and proof is a word that has gone out of our philosophical vocabulary. In such a philosophical climate there ceases to be any demonstrative apologetics, and indeed the whole business of apologetics is viewed differently.

We must now proceed to consider the two other aspects of Tillich's alleged modernity. Tillich appears to be a theologian capable of resolving the dilemma of the ecumenical movement because he is at once thoroughly Protestant and so open to the appeal of Catholicism. For him neither the 'sacramental' principle of Catholicism nor the 'prophetic' principle of

[1] Cf. *Systematic Theology* I, pp. 3f.

Protestantism can stand on its own. Therefore, however inevitable may be the clash between institutional Catholicism and institutional Protestantism there is, he thinks, no essential conflict between the two principles. They are complementary elements of the true 'theonomous' Christianity, and either, taken on its own, becomes 'demonic'. So Walter M. Horton says:

> 'Should Tillich become active in the ecumenical movement, or should his disciples play some such leading rôle in it as Barth's disciples have played, a doctrine of the true Church might be worked out that would be equally acceptable to Anglo-Catholics and Congregationalists—and perhaps eventually to Roman Catholics and Quakers!'[1]

The basis of Horton's hope is the fact that in Tillich's thought the Catholic principle and the Protestant principle presuppose one another. However, this is far too abstract a thesis to have any concrete implications for the ecumenical situation. Indeed so abstract is Tillich's formulation of his Protestant principle that it is welcomed by a Catholic critic, Father Weigel, as something which lends strength to the Catholic cause. 'Is not', he asks, 'Tillich's half-hearted recognition of the fact that Catholicism has better preserved the substance of Christianity than Protestantism a protest against unlimited protest?'[2] It may well be that Tillich's contribution to the ecclesiological discussion of our time is yet to be made, but it is difficult to resist the suspicion that we shall not hear any startlingly modern message. Is there any greater vision in Tillich's harmonizing of the Catholic and Protestant 'principles' than there was in Matthew Arnold's essay of 1878, 'Irish Catholicism and British Liberalism,' where he says:

> 'I persist in thinking that the prevailing form for the Christianity of the future will be the form of Catholicism but a Catholicism purged . . . freed from its sacerdotal despotism and . . . superannuated dogma.'[3]

[1] *The Theology of Paul Tillich*, pp. 43-4.
[2] Gustave Weigel, 'Contemporaneous Protestantism and Paul Tillich', *Theological Studies* XI, p. 195.
[3] Arnold, *Works*, London, Macmillan, 1905, vol. 10, p. 116.

How naïve these words sound to us now! And it is to be feared that we shall not have a great deal more guidance from Tillich.

By his interest in culture again Tillich reveals his affinity with the nineteenth century. I do not mean to deny that one of the problems facing theologians in the twentieth century is how to relate the claims of the Christian gospel to the urgent need for cultural reconstruction. What makes Tillich so interesting and significant a theologian is that he has always been aware of this function of theology. He has never abandoned the interest in culture which he inherits from Troeltsch and the other Liberals. He has told us how in Berlin his lectures on Philosophy of religion were really a presentation of a 'theology of culture'. It was during this time that he wrote his work 'On the Idea of a Theology of Culture'.[1] One section of *The Protestant Era* is given the title 'Religion and Culture'. Whilst rejecting the medieval authoritarianism and welcoming the revolt of modern man against the dictatorial limitations of his knowledge Tillich seeks a unity of culture which will mirror the unity of the real. We shall see later how deeply Tillich has immersed himself in the various cultural activities of modern man; but for all that, there breathes throughout this interest in modern culture the spirit of an alien age. The simplicity of Tillich's way of relating religion and culture is what reveals this best. The 'central proposition' of his philosophy of religion was: 'Religion is the substance of culture, culture is the expression of religion.'[2] Such a formula could be true of a primitive society where religion is a feature of social activity as such, but it is not at all an accurate description of modern culture. Indeed it is not at once clear what Tillich means by this aphorism. It is not the way in which one naturally describes the cultures of the post-Renaissance period, and this he knows as well as anyone. Does he then mean to say that *really* or *essentially* the relation of culture to religion is that of expression or form to content? In other words what he is doing is offering a

[1] 'Über die Idee einer Theologie der Kultur', *Religionsphilosophie der Kultur*, Berlin, Reuther & Reinhard, 1919.
[2] *The Protestant Era*, p. xxxii.

philosophical analysis of culture. Taken as such it leads us back
to the reduction of the transcendent claims of religion to statements and claims concerning social behaviour which characterized the liberal theology of the last century. If the relation of
culture to religion is that of form to content then what are we
to say about the non-religious cultures which abound in the
modern world? Or to put the question concretely, Is the man
who is devoid of religion also devoid of culture? Thus the
seemingly clear and sound answer to the theological problem
of culture becomes an intolerable paradox. It could only have
seemed sound to one still under the influence of Liberalism.

As a systematic theologian Tillich interprets his task as
partly the correlation of philosophy and theology. We have
examined his conception of philosophy in some detail and all
that now remains is to indicate why it is that as a philosophical
theologian he must be accounted a significant theologian. One
of the refreshing things in Tillich is his keen awareness of the
tradition of philosophical theology. A glance at the pages of
Systematic Theology suffices for us to realise that here is a theologian who does not imagine that philosophy is essentially the
product of the modern world. His language is thoroughly
Hegelian and there are traces of Plato and Aristotle and the
great medieval thinkers. Again and again Tillich has insisted
that it is impossible for the theologian to ignore the work of the
philosopher because the philosopher's work becomes part of
his world. It is abundantly clear from his work that Tillich
himself has been very much aware of his world. He develops a
metaphysics which is in many ways squarely in the Augustinian
tradition but yet owes very much to Schelling and Heidegger.
In his wide knowledge of the traditions of philosophy there is
one serious lack—he knows little or nothing about the kind of
philosophy that has been done in the English-speaking world
during the last thirty years. The result of this is that what he
says about philosophy is very often outmoded. Yet there is
about his philosophical work an air of realism which we must
confess has not characterized the kind of philosophy with which
we are now familiar. Thus one welcomes in Tillich his urgent
concern with the mystery of being, for in the end one has to

admit that unless the philosopher is an ontologist he is not a metaphysician. Though it is true that the primary concern of the philosopher is to criticize and revise concepts, a re-drawing of the map of thought, the ontological concern is the more fundamental characteristic of metaphysics. Mapping out our language is the necessary prelude to the task of bridge-building or system construction which the metaphysicians of the past regarded as their primary purpose. Whether the renewal of metaphysics will take the form of building meta-physical systems or not Tillich's adherence to the traditional method makes him a startling revelation of what has been ignored by contemporary linguistic philosophy. Hence Pro-fessor J. H. Randall, Jun., says of him:

'Paul Tillich seems to me not only the ablest Protestant theologian of the present day, but also by far the most persuasive exponent of the philosophy of existentialism, and, what is more to the point, a real contributor to the present-day revival of metaphysical inquiry. His is a first-rate philosophical mind.'[1]

Confronted as we are by the need to find a new way of doing philosophical theology, we cannot afford not to take seriously the work of one who deliberately takes his stand on the bound-ary between philosophy and theology. Tillich's attempt to define and unravel the epistemological problems involved in theological thinking makes his theology relevant to the philo-sopher. And if what he has to say about the nature of philosophy and even what he regards as the relation of philosophy to theology is woefully deficient, his discussion of the operation of reason in theology does raise the problems of philosophical theology in a fruitful way. Because he recognizes no neat division between philosophy and theology and the need to answer certain philosophical questions before we can proceed to develop our theological problems, Tillich has not only revealed what must be the method of any theology that is truly systematic but has made some contribution to the answering of these problems. 'A help in answering questions'—that is how he regards a system of theology. If many features of the system

---

[1] *The Theology of Paul Tillich*, p. 161.

prove an encumbrance rather than a help, our eagerness to note them must not blind us to the features which prove the success of the system on this criterion.

We come finally to Tillich's significance as the theologian fated to stand on the border-lines of his subject. We have already seen how he has taken his stand on the boundary of philosophy and theology; this, though perhaps unusual in our day, is a not unknown rôle for the theologian. What is really surprising in Tillich's work is that he has with equal deliberation taken his stand on the other border-lines, enriching his theology by analyses of art, the use of scientific insights and discussion of sociological issues. Tillich has described himself as something of a Romantic in his attitude towards Nature, and this—together with biographical circumstances—predisposed him to regard art as material for theological investigation. In *The Protestant Era* he has described the anti-sacramental trend of 'technical reason' in its divorce of architectural forms from their practical meaning. Houses, furniture and all kinds of objects of our daily use are given forms which express neither 'the true nature of the material of which they are made' nor the purpose for which they are produced.

> 'Many of the spiritual leaders in architecture and the applied arts have realized this situation, and they are trying to re-discover the inherent power and beauty of the materials they use and of the products they create. They want to unite themselves with things not in order to exploit them but in an attitude of devotion and in the spirit of *eros* or what the eighteenth century called "natural piety".'[1]

To be significant, however, art must do more than this—it must express man's spiritual insights and aspirations. Thus aestheticism disregards the content and meaning of artistic creation.

> 'Aestheticism deprives art of its existential character by substituting detached judgements of taste and a refined connoisseurship for emotional union. No artistic expression is possible without the creative rational form, but the form, even in its greatest refinement, is empty if it does not express a spiritual substance.'[2]

[1] *The Protestant Era*, p. 123.   [2] *Systematic Theology* I, p. 100.

This high valuation of the spiritual substance of artistic creation lies behind Tillich's appreciation of modern existentialist art which reveals 'the courage to face things as they are, and to express the anxiety of meaninglessness'.

'It is creative courage which appears in the creative expressions of despair. Sartre calls one of his most powerful plays *No Exit*, a classical formula for the situation of despair. But he himself has an exit: he can *say* "no exit", thus taking the situation of meaninglessness upon himself. T. S. Eliot called his first great poem "The Waste Land". He described the decomposition of civilisation, the lack of conviction and direction, the poverty and hysteria of modern consciousness (as one of his critics has analysed it). But it is the beautifully cultivated garden of a great poem which describes the meaninglessness of the Waste Land and expresses the courage of despair.'[1]

Similarly,[2] in Kafka's novels *The Castle* and *The Trial*, we have a classical expression of 'the unapproachable remoteness of the source of meaning and the obscurity of the source of justice and mercy'. Tillich sees in the courage of such creativity a revelation of 'the courage to be as oneself'. Though separated from the sources of courage man is still able to face and accept his separation. Thus Auden's *Age of Anxiety* emphasizes equally both poles of the courage of despair. Sartre's *The Age of Reason* likewise proves his courage of despair. Camus, though he is not existentialist, faces the same problem in the novel *The Stranger* whose hero is a man without subjectivity, without meaning for himself and therefore unable to find meaning in his world. Dramatic art also reveals the same kind of courageous acceptance of meaninglessness. In some plays the revelation of meaninglessness is not mitigated in any way—e.g., Arthur Miller's *Death of a Salesman*—and in others some gleams of light shine in the darkness—e.g., Tennessee Williams' *A Streetcar Named Desire*. Finally, visual art tells the same story.

'The combination of the experience of meaninglessness and of the courage to be as oneself is the key to the development of visual art since the turn of the century. In expressionism and surrealism

---

[1] *The Courage to Be*, p. 136.
[2] For what follows see *The Courage to Be*, pp. 136-40.

the surface structures of reality are disrupted. The categories which constitute ordinary experience have lost their power. The category of substance is lost: solid objects are twisted like ropes; the causal interdependence of things is disregarded: things appear in a complete contingency; temporal sequences are without significance, it does not matter whether an event has happened before or after another event; the spatial dimensions are reduced or dissolved into a horrifying infinity. The organic structures of life are cut into pieces which are arbitrarily (from the biological, not the artistic, point of view) recomposed: limbs are dispersed, colors are separated from their natural carriers.'[1]

All fields of art, then, in expressing man's ultimate concern reveal the meaninglessness of the contemporary situation and the courageous despair of modern man.

Tillich has been unusual too in his interest in science. Characteristically it is science at its most artistic, namely, psycho-analysis, which has captured and retained his interest. Theology, he thinks, has much to learn from the psychological explorations of the inner and unconscious self and also from the therapeutic technique of accepting 'one's own conflicts when looking at them and suffering under their ugliness without an attempt to suppress them and to hide them from one's self'.[2] Psychology, in its turn, has something to learn from the Christian distinction between psychopathic fears, those fears which are morbid and unhealthy and which can be removed by psycho-analytic treatment, and the more fundamental anxiety concerning death and the perpetual threat of meaninglessness of existence. The latter cannot be 'cured'—it can only be removed by a religious 'acceptance of the divine grace which breaks through the realm of law and creates a joyful conscience'.[3] In this way Tillich wants to effect some kind of correlation of Christianity and psychotherapy. Psychiatry and psycho-analysis are invaluable in diagnosing and removing neurotic conditions. Nevertheless, when such therapy is complete a positive social attitude which is the heart of morality is yet to be achieved and equally such therapy is powerless to produce a positive religious orientation. Man's basic disorder

---

[1] *The Courage to Be*, p. 139.   [2] *The Protestant Era*, p. 149.   [3] *Ibid.*

can be remedied then only by a 'theonomous' psychology, a co-operative effort of science and religious ethics. In *Systematic Theology*, too, Tillich uses psychology to develop his theological position on the nature of sin. First, he says that in our attempt at reinterpreting the doctrine of Original Sin in terms of the inter-penetration of the moral and tragic elements in the human situation we have extensive empirical basis for the description in analytical psychology.[1] Later in his discussion of estrangement as concupiscence he considered Freud's *'libido'* which he regards as a conceptual description of concupiscence.[2] Up to a point the theological interpreter of man's estrangement is well advised to follow Freud's analyses, though theology cannot accept Freud's doctrine of *libido* as a sufficient reinterpretation of the concept of concupiscence.

Finally, we must consider Tillich's significant work on the borderline of theology and sociology (for want of a better term to designate the wide field of social questions, ethical and political). Describing the impact of the First World War Tillich says that it was an overwhelming experience of the end of a merely individualistic existence. His sympathy with socialism was of long standing and in these years, he says, 'it broke out ecstatically' and remains an integral part of his outlook today.[3] Shocked by the irrelevance of much that passed as Christian thinking and preaching Tillich conceived his doctrine of *kairos*[4] as an attack on the individualism and other-worldliness of ecclesiastical piety. As we have seen, the doctrine of *kairos*, as Tillich develops it, becomes the problem of whether a Christian ethic is possible. But more explicitly than in the general doctrine of *kairos* Tillich shows his eagerness to find the social dimension of religious truth in *Love, Power and Justice*. This is an ontological study of these concepts which leads to their ethical application. The ontological statements about the nature of love, power and justice are verified by their ability to solve the otherwise insoluble problems of the ethics of love, power and justice. Love is the fulfilment of justice because it is the creative element in justice. In personal encounters and in

---

[1] *Systematic Theology* II, p. 44.   [2] *Ibid.*, pp. 61-2.
[3] *The Theology of Paul Tillich*, p. 12.   [4] *The Protestant Era*, ch. 3.

group relations love and justice are united as also are power and justice. Answering the question of what can be derived from the analysis of love, power and justice Tillich says that 'one of the great powers will develop into a world centre ruling the other nations through liberal methods and in democratic forms'.[1] However, this drives on to the question of the theological character of love, power and justice. In existence they are separated and conflicting and their essential unity can only be re-established through the manifestation of the ground in which they are united. 'Love, power and justice are one in the divine ground, they shall become one in human existence. The holy in which they are united shall become holy reality in time and space.' Love, power and justice are united in God and they are united in the new creation of God in the world. Reuniting love, the power of resisting non-being, and the creative justice are still active in man. Tillich concludes that 'a world without the dynamics of power and the tragedy of life and history is not the Kingdom of God, is not the fulfilment of man and his world.'[2]

We have tried to show the significance Tillich has for contemporary theology and so bring to an end our task of 'introducing' Tillich. It is not perhaps too much to hope that we have succeeded in throwing light on some of the darker places in the System. But one thing I have always strenuously attempted—to be what Tillich once called me, his 'logical critic'.

[1] *Love, Power and Justice*, p. 105.   [2] *Ibid.*, p. 124.

Appendix

CATHOLIC CRITICISM OF TILLICH

ONE of the most interesting features of the progress of theology in our day is the fact that some of the best critics of significant Protestant theology are Roman Catholics. This, as is well-known, is the case with the work of Karl Barth;[1] and I shall try to show that it is also the case with the work of Paul Tillich. Indeed it needs no effort to show this. Not surprisingly Barth only spares him a reference in a footnote or an occasional sentence. However, for the rest of the Protestant world there has been too much glib quotation and praise of Tillich and too little analysis of his work. Even the volume devoted to him in the Library of Living Theology[2] seems to be woefully in-adequate when compared with the meticulous and valuable volumes that make up the series on which it is based, namely the Library of Living Philosophers.[3] Then the *festschrift* volume, *Religion and Culture*,[4] only serves to illustrate my contention, since it is a book occasioned by Tillich rather than one on him. As against the occasional article in Protestant journals there are in Catholic journals nearly a dozen articles on Tillich, all of which are in some way or other critical studies,[5]

---

[1] See *Scottish Journal of Theology* volume 14 No. 2 (June 1961): G. E. Foley, 'The Catholic Critics of Karl Barth in Outline and Analysis'.

[2] *The Theology of Paul Tillich* (ed. Kegley and Bretall), Macmillan, New York, 1952.

[3] See, for example, the supremely useful *Philosophy of G. E. Moore* and the recent excellent *Philosophy of C. D. Broad*.

[4] Ed. W. Leibrecht, New York and London, Harper and SCM Press, 1959.

[5] G. Weigel, S.J., 'Contemporaneous Protestantism and Paul Tillich', *Theological Studies*, Baltimore, 1950, pp. 177-202, 'Recent Protestant Theology', *ibid.*, 1953, pp. 573-85, 'Theological Significance of Paul Tillich', *Gregorianum*, Rome, 1956, pp. 34-54, 'Myth, Symbol and Analogy', *Religion and Culture*, pp. 120-30; G. H. Tavard, 'The Unconditional Concern: The Theology of Paul Tillich', *Thought*, 1953, pp. 234-46, 'Christianity and the Philosophies of Existence', *Theological Studies*, 1957, pp. 1-16,

and more recently we have a monograph on Tillich's Christology by Father Tavard.[1] To attempt a detailed analysis of all
this criticism is obviously impossible here, but I shall try to
indicate what seem to me to be the most important points
raised by these critics.

It will be best perhaps to begin with Father Dulles' discussion
of Tillich and the Bible; for here surely we have a subject on
which we can expect a Catholic critic to have some very
trenchant comments to make. Fr Dulles begins by remarking
that Tillich's views on the Bible are especially interesting for the
Catholic theologian 'since they exhibit some startling approaches toward the Catholic position, and at the same time
some fundamental divergences'.[2] What he welcomes in
Tillich's views on the Bible are the rejection of the supernaturalistic view 'which would depict God as dictating the
Bible or as substituting His own activity for the natural
processes of the human mind'[3] and the strictures Tillich heaps
on biblicism.[4] However, though he agrees with Tillich's
protest against a 'monophysitism' which would ignore the rôle
of the human author, Fr Dulles believes that Tillich is guilty
of a kind of inverse monophysitism since he tends to 'overlook
the divine element in Holy Scriptures and in effect denies that
it is the Word of God'. In this way Tillich 'needlessly repudiates
an article of faith as ancient and sacred as Christianity itself,
and leaves the Christian believer without authoritative guidance'.[5] His second main criticism is that Tillich 'unduly
minimizes the historical elements in the Bible' whilst solemnly
affirming 'that there was a Jesus who lived on earth and spoke

---

'Le thème de la Cité de Dieu dans le protestantisme américain', *Revue des
Études Augustiniennes*, 1959, pp. 207-21; E. O'Connor, 'Paul Tillich: An
Impression', *Thought*, 1955, pp. 507-24; Avery R. Dulles, S.J., 'Paul Tillich
and the Bible', *Theological Studies*, 1956, pp. 345-67; E. Przywara, S.J.,
'Christian Root-terms: *Kerygma, Mysterium, Kairos, Oikonomia*', *Religion and
Culture*, pp. 113-19; Kenelm Foster, O.P., 'Paul Tillich and St Thomas',
Blackfriars, 1960, pp. 306-13.

[1] G. H. Tavard, *Paul Tillich and the Christian Message*, London, Burns &
Oates, 1962.

[2] *Op. cit.*, p. 345.   [3] *Ibid.*, p. 363.   [4] *Ibid.*, p. 364.
[5] *Ibid.* Cf. pp. 360-1.

with His disciples'.[1] Fr Dulles' criticism contains two points: (a) Tillich seems to rely on historical criticism whilst denying that theology implies factual assertions, (b) Either the historicity of Jesus is a theological question and so theology and history overlap or it is not and so Tillich has no right to maintain as a theologian that Jesus was a real person. The final criticism Fr Dulles offers concerns Tillich's use of philosophy—that Tillich 'lets the exigencies of his philosophical system determine in advance what God's revelation can and cannot be. The Biblical message is reduced to the dimensions of an all-too-human philosophy.'[2] It is most refreshing to find a Catholic theologian taking up the cudgels for 'the living God of Abraham and Isaac' against 'the product of philosophical speculation' and to hear him insist on the fact that the Bible is the Word of God. Refreshing though it is, however, this situation may yet only reveal the confusion in our thinking about the Bible and its place in Theology and the Church. It seems to me that Fr Dulles' criticisms of Tillich's use of philosophy and of his views on the place of history in faith's assertions are well-founded and that Tillich has no real answer to them. On the main issue of the interpretation of the Bible, however, I am not so sure that Fr Dulles is entirely right and Tillich entirely wrong. I have no wish to indulge in the favourite game of English theologians and say that the truth lies somewhere in between these two positions. On the contrary let us say boldly that a strong assertion such as Tillich's rejection of supernaturalism is right. Indeed it seems as if Fr Dulles has argued himself into a position which is very difficult for him to maintain, for he will surely have to say that only a guaranteed interpretation based on both Scripture and Tradition preserves for us the divine mysteries of revelation.[3] But, leaving aside such an *argumentum ad hominem*, it seems to me that to deny supernaturalistic interpretations of the Bible does not imply that we have no authoritative guide in matters of faith. The Bible has a normative function in the Church, but the Bible as such is not the final authority in the

[1] *Ibid.*, p. 365. Cf. p. 361.   [2] *Ibid.*, p. 367.
[3] Cf. Fr M. Bévenot, 'Tradition, Church and Dogma', *The Heythrop Journal*, January 1960.

Church. There is only one authority—the living Christ who is the Lord of the Church. The Bible is the Word of God, but the sense in which we here speak of 'word' is not that deceptively clear and definite sense in which it is regarded as something written by God. This much Fr Dulles may accept but what he will not accept is the irresistible conclusion that only by regarding this symbol of 'word' as united with the confession of obedience to the authority of the living Christ can we give it its proper application.

Father Erich Przywara places Tillich quite clearly in the tradition of Boehme and Schelling and characterizes his theology as 'directed to the examination of Christian root-terms', 'the development of a possible "Christian grammar". Such a grammar, for Tillich, culminates in the *kairos*, round which his whole thought moves.'[1] Distinguishing between material and formal root-terms—the former refer to the content of revelation whereas the latter refer to 'the form in which the totality of revelation appears concretely'—Fr Przywara notes that Tillich's philosophy of religion emphasizes the material root-term of justification, but that the root-term which has particular significance for him is the formal root-term, *kairos*. '*Kairos* is "time in the right measure" which is at one and the same time a trans-temporal "measure of real circumstances".' The word *kairos* is particularly applicable to the Christ, but it indicates also the time when 'the Messianic *kairos* in its essential content is set over against Satan as "ruler of this world"... and the "anti-Christ".'[2] This duality of meaning, says Przywara, finds expression in Tillich's concept of the Divine as 'Ground and Abyss', and he goes on to indicate what he regards as highly dubious elements in Tillich's theology—the appearance within it of a clearly Origenistic tradition, the paradoxes that in every theism 'an abyss of atheism is present' and that the Demonic is the Holy which contradicts the Divine. Przywara's essay is not so much a detailed examination of Tillich as the exposition both of a particular type of theological thinking or enterprise—a Christian grammar—and the answer which such a rounded theology contains to the errors arising from its

[1] *Religion and Culture*, p. 113.   [2] *Ibid.*, p. 118.

expression in the tradition of Boehme and Schelling in which, with his customary sure touch, he places Tillich. To my mind the value of his essay, then, is twofold—it is a useful guide to Tillich's philosophical lineage and it draws attention to the fundamental ambiguity in Tillich's doctrine of the *kairos*. It is perhaps an omission on his part that he has concentrated on Tillich's earlier thought where indeed *kairos* is a fundamental concept, and it is always dangerous to single out one such concept from a man's thought and then to argue that his whole work hinges on this. Even so, this earlier work of Tillich's where this argument does hold is not well known to his English readers, and so once more one finds something for which we have to thank Fr Przywara.

Turning to Father Weigel's criticism we shall begin with his paper on 'Myth, Symbol, and Analogy' which contains incidental comments on Tillich's position. Here he is concerned to show the difference between Bultmann's position and that of Barth, Tillich, and Niebuhr. 'Barth, Tillich and Niebuhr seem to see the flaws in the projects of demythologization but, with Bultmann, they feel that there is a *scandalum pusillorum* involved in Biblical rhetoric.'[1] Their solution then is to regard the Bible neither as mythology nor as literal history but as symbolism. Fr Weigel refers to Tillich's distinction between symbol and sign which he rather neatly explains thus:

> '. . . a symbol is a sign but not simply a sign. It is more than a sign because it shares in the reality which it signifies. The green light at the street crossing is a simple sign of an open street because its being is totally alien to the being of the street. Open street and green light are only mythically conjoined. In the phenomenon of fire, however, smoke is a constituent element of the integral phenomenon, and thus smoke is a symbol of fire.'[2]

In this sense the Scriptures are to be understood as symbolic statements. This means that Tillich and others like him have a great advantage over Bultmann because they will not need a programme of demythologizing—the value of the Bible for them is precisely the fact that it contains 'permanently valid

[1] *Op. cit.*, p. 123.   [2] *Ibid.*, p. 124.

symbols'. Even so, says Fr Weigel, they have to face a serious difficulty.

> 'However, the symbolist pays a price for his advantages. The historical concreteness of the Biblical accounts, patent to any reader, is swallowed up into a trans-historical awareness of existence. Christ is risen indeed, but this does not state that Jesus of Nazareth physically rose from the dead. We are only told symbolically that the man of perfect faith rises above death, which then loses its existentially constrictive menace. The man of faith lives "eternally", in dimensions beyond time.'[1]

Though he does not endorse W. F. Albright's criticism of Tillich as 'a modern gnostic', Fr Weigel obviously sympathizes with it and suggests that Tillich's trans-historical symbolism cannot do justice to 'the historical preoccupation of the Christian message'.[2] Elsewhere he has called Tillich's doctrine of theology 'a transformation of the Thomistic *analogia entis*'.[3] 'Tillich from the existentialist point of view reduces Thomistic analogy to the only value it can have in an existentialist scheme. It is the device of symbolic expression where a proposition has no rational content.'[4] So he concludes that Tillich's conception of analogy is inadequate.[5] In his survey of volume I of Tillich's *Systematic Theology*, Fr Weigel had already pointed out that although Tillich rejects natural theology as invalid this is hardly the whole truth and that a Catholic could argue that he has reduced all theology to natural theology.[6] Natural theology, says Fr Weigel, was fathered by Anselm and developed by Aquinas. St Thomas believed that 'the *terminus analogicus* was a valid middle term.'

> 'Tillich does not share the conviction of Thomas. His whole epistemological ontology supposes that the analogical term can have no function in a syllogism. . . . Philosophy offers the question of God, which occasions an insight that is grasped in faith and expressed in symbols. The symbol must never be taken logically,

[1] *Religion and Culture*, p. 125. [2] *Ibid.*, pp. 125-6.
[3] *Gregorianum*, 1956, p. 37. [4] *Ibid.*, p. 43.
[5] *Ibid.*, p. 50. [6] *Theological Studies*, 1953, p. 582.

but only as an existentialist pointer. . . . For a Catholic this concept of analogy is not sufficiently radical.'[1]

Though he regards Tillich's synthesis as better than anything else he knows, Fr Weigel makes some devastating criticisms of both Tillich's philosophy and his theology. Tillich's ontology sounds 'so familiar and yet so strange to Catholic theologians', and ultimately it lacks the fulness of meaning possessed by a Thomistic ontology.[2] His epistemology is 'a *mélange* of Kant, positivism and existentialism'.[3] The ontology in which he believes is existential, and for Fr Weigel is 'not ontology but rather its betrayal'.[4] As for Tillich's theology, Fr Weigel regards it as 'not only a natural theology, but more ominously a naturalistic theology'. The final chapter of *The Courage to Be*, he says, 'seems to equate God with the basic energy at work in the universe but interpreted in terms of human concern'. This book is admittedly phenomenology: but, asks Fr Weigel, is the theology of Tillich only the phenomenology written theologically? One reluctantly feels that the theology does nothing to correct the phenomenology.'[5] Again, Tillich's theological method is unsatisfactory, says Fr Weigel, because it presupposes some kind of nominalism. There is in Tillich's thought, he says, an *a priori* which is above the *a priori* of all theology, namely the revealing God. This principle is that the infinite cannot become the finite. 'This principle is valid only if it is nominalistically understood . . . (and) leaves the Catholic theologian quite cold.'[6] Tillich's doctrine of Jesus Christ as the New Being is for Fr Weigel a great stumbling-block both as it bears on the question of the Person of Christ and as it implies a certain doctrine of revelation. According to Tillich, he says, the Christ and the historical Jesus are not to be identified.

'It is here the Catholic is overwhelmed with misgivings. The faith of the Catholic makes him see only one person in Our Lord. The Catholic accepts joyfully the teaching of the Council of Chalcedon. So did the Protestant Reformers of the sixteenth

[1] *Ibid.*, p. 583. [2] *Gregorianum*, 1956, p. 43. [3] *Ibid..* p. 48.
[4] *Ibid.* [5] *Ibid.*, pp. 47-8. Cf. *Theological Studies*, 1950, p. 200.
[6] *Theological Studies*, 1953, p. 582.

century. So do the fundamentalists of today. For us the Christ is a concrete historical person, one and undivided, and the one Jesus was that one Christ. They cannot be separated. What for Tillich is a patent impossibility is the basic Christian fact according to Catholic belief.'[1]

But the revelation of New Being in Christ came to the world through Jesus. How are we to interpret this? Fr Weigel suggests that the upshot of Tillich's doctrine is that he is a Christian who is saved, and salvation comes from faith alone, and that this is a truism.[2] He concludes,

'Is this an objective explanation of Christianity as it was and as it is, or is it a subjective reconstruction of a historical phenomenon? Does Professor Tillich explain what Christianity is, or does he propose to us what he would like it to be? Subjectivity is a golden word in existentialism, but objectivity has not lost its appeal for the human mind, and more objectivity and less subjectivity is the desideratum of our time.'[3]

So much of Fr Weigel's criticism seems to me not only just but unanswerable—for instance, his strictures on Tillich's epistemology and ontology, and the description of his theology as naturalistic—that I propose to discuss only his interpretation of Tillich's dictum on the nature of symbols. I am not sure that his severe criticism of Tillich's Christology is altogether justified, but we shall refer to that later. As for Tillich's doctrine about symbols, Fr Weigel's interpretation is most interesting, and since Tillich has not repudiated it one may perhaps assume that he accepts it. Whereas all formulations of the doctrine which he has given are vague and have not specified the way in which the phrase 'participate in the reality' (or 'participate in the power') is to be understood, this interpretation of Fr Weigel's is precise. Fr Weigel makes 'participate in the reality of X' synonymous with being a constitutent element of X. Hence smoke is a symbol and not a mere sign of fire. Now it may be thought a matter of no consequence that this is contrary to ordinary usage (though I,

[1] *Theological Studies*, 1953, p. 576.   [2] *Ibid.*, pp. 581-2.
[3] *Ibid.*, p. 582.

for my part, would regard it as very significant inasmuch as it gives a clue to what Tillich is doing here) but it is not a trivial matter that this example is, as it were, tailored to suit the definition and will not hold of other examples. In Jungian theory, for instance, the mandala is said to be a symbol of the self, but it is not a constituent element of the self and cannot be said in any sense to participate in the reality of the self. There is only one religious situation where this definition of symbol seems obviously correct. In the Eucharist the elements are said to be the body and blood of the Lord. So it might be said that here the symbols are indeed constituent elements of the reality symbolized, but in order to say this we should have to maintain some kind of transubstantiation theory which Tillich presumably would not want to maintain.[1] Hence there appears to be no reason for maintaining that symbols participate in the reality of what they symbolize other than our intention to define them in this way. Once more Tillich's profundity turns out to be merely verbal.

This sense of disappointment seems to be shared by Father O'Connor, if we read his 'impression' of Tillich aright. He is filled with admiration for Tillich both as a lecturer and a scholar and, above all, as a person.[2] Father O'Connor formed his impression while listening to some lectures on Schelling Tillich gave at Indiana University in May 1955. One point which became obvious in the course of these lectures was Tillich's 'profound respect for God's transcendence'.

'This constant attitude was perhaps more impressive than the explicit statements to be found in his writings. It is this strong

[1] The authoritative pronouncement of Pope Pius XII in 1947 (in the encyclical *Mediator Dei*) concerning the symbolic way of offering which is found in the Mass is relevant here because it would suggest that the real presence of the Redeemer is just that of the symbols. He says: 'The divine wisdom has devised a way in which our Redeemer's sacrifice is marvellously shown forth by external signs symbolic of death. By the "transubstantiation" . . . both his body and blood are rendered really present; but the eucharistic species under which he is present symbolize the violent separation of his body and blood and so a commemorative showing forth of the death which took place in reality on Calvary is repeated in each Mass, because by distinct representations Christ Jesus is signified and shown forth in his state of victim' (*op. cit.*, para. 74).

[2] E. O'Connor, *op. cit.*, pp. 507-8.

sense of the divine transcendence, we believe, that constitutes the chief speculative basis for Tillich's . . . opposition to the authority claimed by the Church. . . . No doubt there is serious reason to inquire whether Tillich's "reverence" for God is altogether authentic, but it is not necessary to discount it altogether. . . . In our over-eagerness to defend the participation in divine attributes which we maintain that Christian institutions enjoy, and in our familiarity with the visible sacraments by which God permits us to have dealings with Him, we Catholics sometimes lose the humble abasement and reverence for God which these institutions presuppose, and the sense of mystery which is capital in a true appreciation of them. The case of a man like Tillich can usefully recall to us our shortcomings in this regard.'[1]

However, the authority of the Church does not of necessity oppose divine transcendence, but, on the contrary, a true account of it will, says Father O'Connor, show that it is based on this transcendence. For it is 'in virtue of an absolutely free choice by which God assumes her for His use that the Church has divine authority'.[2] Tillich, however, will not admit divine preferences, and the reason, Father O'Connor thinks, may lie in the conception of freedom that he inherits from Schelling. This is that freedom is the possibility of contradicting one's essence. If this is what is meant by freedom then it is clear that we must conclude that it does not exist in God.[3] Father O'Connor admits that this conception of freedom is not that presented by Tillich in his discussion of personality[4] and that Tillich does not deny that God is free. 'Perhaps, however, some of the implications of Schelling's concept influence him in his rejection of the notion of a "divine preference".' If this is so, Tillich 'is denying to God the very autonomy he vindicates for man!'[5] Elsewhere in the Schelling lectures Tillich seemed to follow Schelling in explaining the case of ethical and aesthetic genius as special divine communication to privileged individuals. For Father O'Connor this admission invalidates

[1] E. O'Connor, *op. cit.*, p. 511.   [2] *Ibid.*, p. 512.
[3] *Ibid.*, pp. 512-3.
[4] This is to be found in *Protestant Era*, pp. 129-40—'. . . to be free means to have power over one's self, not to be bound to one's given nature. . . . Freedom is the power of transcending one's own given nature.'
[5] O'Connor, *op. cit.*, p. 513.

Tillich's previous objection to the authoritative Church.[1] But of all Tillich's ideas revealed in these lectures it was his notion of the knowledge of God as a kind of grace which Father O'Connor thinks best illumines the notion of ecclesiastical authority. For, though Tillich's concept of grace is not quite that found in Catholic theology, it does furnish the exact perspective in which the authority of the Church is best understood. If, then, the ideas essential for the acceptance of ecclesiastical authority are already admitted in Tillich's theology we are driven to the conclusion, according to Father O'Connor, that the real ground of Tillich's protest is practical rather than theoretical.[2] This practical source of Tillich's opposition to the authoritative Church Father O'Connor diagnoses as rebelliousness and not entirely a crusade for liberty.[3]

What I find most interesting in this article, however, is its concluding pages. Here Father O'Connor tries to convey his impression of Tillich's theology, and he begins by pointing to one of its most striking characteristics—its 'metaphysical tone'.[4] He recognizes Tillich's concern with metaphysical questions, his tendency to treat all problems in metaphysical language and his extraordinary acquaintance with metaphysical literature. Yet he maintains that 'Tillich is more at home on the phenomenological level of the history of philosophy than in the depths of ontological mystery.'[5] He disregards fundamental distinctions between the orders of being 'while attending only to relatively external resemblances and dissemblances'. The example Father O'Connor gives is Tillich's idea of symbols, quoting from a letter of Tillich's to Father Weigel which the latter had included in his article in *Theological Studies* (1960). There Tillich says that he means by symbolic knowledge what St Thomas means by *analogia entis*. 'But it is patent', writes Father O'Connor, 'from Tillich's writings that he does not mean by *symbol* what St Thomas means by *analogy*, and this is precisely why he has no basis for a natural theology.'[6] Tillich is right in choosing to talk of symbols rather than analogy, 'for

[1] *Ibid.*   [2] *Ibid.*, pp. 514-15.   [3] *Ibid.*, pp. 516-17.
[4] *Ibid.*, p. 519.   [5] *Ibid.*   [6] *Ibid.*, p. 520.

it is symbols that he is dealing with precisely insofar as these are distinct from analogies'—symbols being created by an act of will and analogy having an objective basis for common predication. Tillich's inability to see this difference convinces Father O'Connor that he 'is not thinking on a truly ontological level'.[1] This is confirmed by Tillich's identification of philosophy and the history of philosophy. It is especially the dramatic character of the history of philosophy that Tillich finds interesting. In considering the philosophies of the past he examines not so much their truth as the accidental likenesses between them and the rôle they have played in man's pursuit of wisdom. Father O'Connor puts it very well when he says that Tillich 'has less the attitude of a passionate seeker for truth than that of a spectator engrossed in following the fortunes of other seekers. He is not so much a "philosopher" . . . as a lover of philosophies, or better, a man with a taste for philosophies, like an aesthete's taste for works of art.'[2] I am not prepared to accept this description as entirely correct, but I think that there is not only truth in it but also that it expresses disappointment very like what I came to feel as I looked more carefully at Tillich's apparent profundity. Whether the distinction between symbol and analogy is quite correct or not, it is abundantly clear that this is the way St Thomas would have made this distinction and that therefore Tillich is quite wrong when he says that he means by symbolic knowledge what St Thomas meant by analogy. The only way in which this could be maintained is by comparing the ontological participation of symbol in thing symbolized in Tillich with the doctrine of analogy in St Thomas, and even then it does not work.[3]

Tillich's disagreement with St Thomas is the subject of Father Kenelm Foster's article where he concludes that Tillich is unaware of the all-important distinction within Thomism between *ens* and *ens in se*. The main problem of the article is the difference between Tillich and St Thomas on the proof of

[1] O'Connor, *op. cit.*, p. 520.   [2] *Ibid.*, p. 522.
[3] See E. Gilson, *The Christian Philosophy of St Thomas*, London, Gollancz, 1957, pp. 103ff. and bibliography on pp. 457-8.

God's existence. Father Foster sets out Tillich's views on the proofs of God and the question of God, showing how Tillich denies that one can properly say that God exists. Tillich's use of the term 'existence' as always connoting finitude might lead us, says Father Foster, to think that this difference is a mere matter of terminology.[1] For clearly in this sense of the term God does not exist. 'But the latter is not, it is clear, as simple as that. For one thing, Tillich explicitly and repeatedly rejects any and every argument for establishing the—let us say—"isness" of the infinite being; and for another thing—and here is the more radical disagreement—he appears to reject on principle the judgement *that God is* (as distinct from mere awareness of this reality) whether this judgement be made as the conclusion of an inference or simply as a statement of sheer fact.'[2] Taking up the first of these two points Father Foster suggests that there are two reasons for Tillich's rejection of the accepted theistic arguments: 'because he thinks they are bad arguments and because he thinks that the being whose existence they conclude to falls short of the true, the adequate notion of God'.[3] The first of these receives but slight exposition in Tillich and the criticism he offers is 'quite superficial'.[4] His main objection is to the sort of God whose existence is the conclusion of the arguments. Again and again Tillich insists that 'to argue that God exists is to deny Him'. His three chief reasons for this assertion are, thinks Father Foster, the following: to argue for God's existence is (*a*) to make God a mere object whereas he transcends the subject-object division, (*b*) to make God one finite thing among others, and (*c*) to reduce God to a 'missing part' of the world from which the argument pretends to derive him, and this, too, makes God finite. Essentially, then, the point Tillich makes is that a certain way of thinking about God reduces him to finitude. This way of thinking, says Father Foster, is 'that use of the mind which traditional logic calls *Judgement*'.[5] This is the second operation of the mind, following 'simple apprehension' whereby one forms a concept or cluster

[1] Kenelm Foster, 'Paul Tillich and St Thomas', *Blackfriars*, September 1960, p. 308.
[2] *Ibid.*, p. 309.   [3] *Ibid.*   [4] *Ibid.*   [5] *Ibid.*, p. 310.

of concepts. In view of the evidence given by experience or reasoning one *assents* to the combination or separation of these concepts—e.g. 'Peter is a man.' Two points are noted by Father Foster about the function of the verb 'to be' in judgement— (i) that it is present in every judgement, at least implicitly, (ii) that it has a formal and a material function, the formal function being to express assent to the fact. 'The function of "is" which is proper precisely to its presence in judgement is to express a knowledge that one knows.'[1] Tillich's criticism of St Thomas, argues Father Foster, is based on a misunderstanding of the function of the copula in judgement. He quotes St Thomas' assertion in the *De ente et essentia*, 'The term being (*ens*) is used in two ways: in one way as referring to what is divided into the ten categories (i.e. being as real or existing); in another way as signifying the truth of propositions'.[2] The judgement of existence exhibits the two functions of the copula which have been explained above. As a judgement 'X is an existent' expresses primarily the mind's 'possession of a truth about X—that it is— and not immediately X's actuality of being as this is, so to say, in X'.[3] The question of St Thomas' treatment of God's existence in *De ente et essentia* has been a matter of discussion for scholars.[4] However, Father Foster's remarks are intended as comments on the logical character of judgements of fact or, to use a more familiar term, existential propositions, and it is as such that I wish to treat them. Essentially they seem to me to be quite sound. For the assertion of the judgement, 'The table is', is indeed one function of the copula 'is' inasmuch as the denial of it would entail the use of the form 'is not'. Again, if the verb is made into a noun then it refers to the 'material' of the judgement, the table's own existence. This is clear enough,

[1] Kenelm Foster, 'Paul Tillich and St Thomas', *Blackfriars*, September 1960, p. 308.

[2] *Ibid.*, p. 311, Father Foster does not give any reference for this, but it is clear that he is here quoting *De ente et essentia*, 1 a.

[3] *Ibid.*, p. 312.

[4] See F. Van Steenberghen, 'Le problème philosophique de l'existence de Dieu', *Revue Philosophique de Louvain*, 1947, pp. 301-8, 'Le problème de l'existence de Dieu dans le *De ente et essentia* de Saint Thomas D'Aquin', *Mélanges de Ghellinck* II, 1951, pp. 837-47. Gilson's remarks about *ens* and *esse* are also relevant—see *The Christian Philosophy of St Thomas*, pp. 32ff.

but there would be good reasons for saying that this is bad logic[1]—for instance, it might be argued that this entails regarding existence as a predicate, and this is anathema to modern logicians. Yet it seems to me that Father Foster has a real and valid point, one which I should like to put more simply by saying that there is no other means of asserting the reality of God than the proposition, 'God exists.'

Before we discuss Father Tavard's monograph, it will be as well to mention the criticism he offers in his article on the theme of the City of God and that on the Philosophies of Existence.[2] In the former he begins by noting Tillich's desire to be Augustinian in his Philosophy of Religion.[3] Of those theologians who have discussed the theme of the City of God in relation to the tradition and destiny of the U.S.A., the most important, he says, are the two Niebuhr brothers and Tillich. The article is, then, an examination of this facet of their thought.[4] Whereas Richard Niebuhr's thought could be called analytical and Reinhold Niebuhr's critical Tillich's is eminently constructive and is deliberately pursued in the Augustinian tradition.[5] Father Tavard notes that in a course of lectures on the history of Christian thought Tillich attributes to Augustine several themes which are typical of his own thinking. Thus the ontological perception of the God who is closer to the soul than the soul itself is the counterpart of the Tillichian 'experience of the Unconditioned'. Augustine's reflections on the Trinity correspond to the Tillichian theme of God as the loving ground of all things. Augustine's discussion of time becomes the well-known view of time as καιρός and χρόνος which plays so important a rôle in Tillich's thought. The ease with which one can recognize Tillichian motifs in this presentation of Augustine leads Father Tavard to ask whether 'Tillich has not read Saint Augustine a little too much in the light of his own theology;

[1] See Prior's discussion of singular and existential propositions (*Formal Logic*, pp. 157ff.)
[2] 'Le thème de la Cité de Dieu dans le protestantisme américain', *Revue des études augustiniennes*, 1959, pp. 207-21; 'Christianity and the Philosophies of Existence', *Theological Studies*, 1957, pp. 1-16.
[3] *Revue des études augustiniennes*, p. 207.   [4] *Ibid.*, p. 209.
[5] *Ibid.*, p. 217.

o

whether he has not somewhat monopolized Augustine'.[1] Father Tavard does well to raise this question, and anyone who has heard Tillich lecture on the history of thought will tend to agree that Tillich is guilty of reading his own theology into the thought of the author he is expounding. Father Tavard remarks that he similarly transforms St Thomas Aquinas' doctrine of angelic species into something like his own view of angels as potential qualities of being. Yet, says Father Tavard, the point is that Tillich regards himself as an Augustinian whether his historical interpretations are right or not.[2] In the two volumes of *Systematic Theology* Tillich refers to Augustine in two sorts of context—(i) as the type of anti-Pelagian position which the Reformation should have taken up, (ii) in regard to an ontological cognition of God. But Tillich does not follow Augustine throughout in this matter, for he sees in Augustine a too hasty identification of the *verum ipsum* with the God of the Church. 'The idea of a God of the Church makes it precisely relative to the Church, that is to say conditioned. This God is not God Himself.'[3] These considerations, however, take us far away from the theme of the City of God, and to this Father Tavard now returns.

St Augustine's description of the City of God tends to be what Tillich calls a theonomy.[4] For Tillich man is in search of a theonomy, and the true Church can be nothing other than theonomic, taking her norms from the intimate perception of the divine Being beneath all human experience. This interpretation is Christian because the Christ is the Unconditioned appearing historically in existence. But is this Augustine's City of God? The answer is, No. Tillich thinks that Augustine introduced heteronomic elements into the theonomy developed by Clement and Origen. Augustine's interpretation of history, says Tillich, is of an ecclesiastical or conservative kind.[5] The Church in its hierarchic structure represents the new reality.

---

[1] *Revue des études augustiniennes*, p. 217. The course of lectures referred to is *A History of Christian Thought*, thirty-seven lectures delivered in Union Theological Seminary in 1953, recorded and edited by Peter H. John and multigraphed by the editor.

[2] Tavard, *op. cit.*, p. 218.   [3] *Ibid.*   [4] *Ibid.*, p. 219.

[5] *Protestant Era* pp. xx. Cf. pp. 23, 26.

Hence the City of God as conceived by Augustine is not a true theonomy.[1] It becomes mixed with heteronomy in so far as the divine commandment becomes an external hierarchical authority. This criticism, says Father Tavard, links up with Tillich's criticism of the Augustinian notion of God as a diminution of the *verum ipsum* because it is identified in practice with a particular institution. But God, the true God, ought to be present in the whole universe, in the terrestrial as well as divine city. If the divine City is heteronomy and the terrestrial City autonomy, neither is conceivable except by reference to a theonomy from which they have broken away. Indeed, the ecclesiastical conservatism is an idolatry. The City of God is not then the true divine City which includes the terrestrial City. So Tillich's criticism of St Augustine opposes the Augustinian intuition of God as the ontological ground of all judgement to the vision of the City of God and the interpretation of history as a struggle between the two cities—the divine and the diabolic. The ontological cognition of the Unconditioned should have destroyed all dualism, but the *City of God*, on the contrary, erects a dualism in the interpretation of history and ecclesiology. Augustine had not seen all the implications of a theonomic order.[2] So fundamentally Tillich's criticism of Augustine leads back to his conception of God.

The article on Philosophies of Existence expresses a threefold criticism—(a) that Tillich's apologetic is a loaded argument, (b) that philosophy cannot be a matter of infinite passion, (c) that, even if it could be, 'the only answer to the question of being is to be found in an analysis of being and its characteristics'.[3] The first of these three criticisms I find very interesting indeed. Tillich's existential analysis is guided, says Fr Tavard, 'by the answer he knows he will give'.[4] Either he admits that what he is really doing is giving 'an existential commentary on the coexistence of estrangement from God and justification by faith', in which case the system is not really correlative, or, if he claims that his method is indeed correlative, his apologetical method is 'vitiated by loaded argument'.[5] This criticism is, to

---

[1] Tavard, *op. cit.*, p. 219. [2] *Ibid.*, p. 220.
[3] *Theological Studies*, 1957, p. 12. [4] *Ibid.*, p. 10. [5] *Ibid.*, p. 11.

my mind, both fair and sound, and indeed I have myself argued in several places that Tillich is guilty of a *petitio principii*. The second criticism likewise reminds me of a point I have made[1] in connection with Tillich's discussion of the nature of philosophy, namely, that what leads him to describe philosophy in this way is his anxiety to find in it some element in common with theology. Fr Tavard's point is that the philosophical enterprise is not a matter of concern. The philosophical question, he says, 'cannot be asked with infinite passion. Even when it calls for practical commitment philosophy means detachment. L. Brunschvig was a good witness to this when he remarked that his own death was philosophically irrelevant and moreover uninteresting to himself.'[2] It is not clear how this example was meant to be interpreted, but let us assume that what Fr Tavard wishes to stress is the propriety of the distinction between philosophy and practice whilst admitting the danger of divorcing philosophy from life. Tillich's description of philosophy does tend to blur this distinction. If, however, this interpretation of Fr Tavard is not right and he means to say that philosophy is a rational, dispassionate study where feelings do not count and man's personal destiny is irrelevant then I think his criticism is misguided. Finally, he contends that whether philosophy be existentially involved or not 'the only answer to the question of being is an analysis of being and its characteristics' and that this implies 'a natural theology, describing the characteristics of being, but essentially distinct from a theology of faith and grace'. Consequently, he thinks, Tillich's theology wavers between being an existentialist analysis of Lutheran Christianity and a philosophical meditation on being.[3] One can sympathize with this suspicion of the method of correlation; for one often feels that there are wide tracts of Tillich's theology which have no connection at all with the essentially theological aims of the system.

We come at last to Fr Tavard's book. A remark he makes at the outset is very interesting. The appearance of the second volume of *Systematic Theology*, he says, made it impossible for him to think that 'Tillich's points of view could be reconciled

---

[1] See above, ch. I.   [2] Tavard, *op. cit.*, p. 11.   [3] *Ibid.*

with the faith of the Church as regards the central Christian message, the Christ himself'. And what I find particularly interesting is the comment he makes immediately after this remark—'Yet no major rebuttal came. This could mean either that most theologians found Tillich's Christology unimportant or that they feared to tackle a dominant figure of the contemporary scene in American Protestantism.'[1] It is almost certain that the second hypothesis fits the facts of the American situation, but even there we find some notable exceptions.[2] Fr Tavard, however, offers us study of Tillich's ideas on Christology which is both expository and critical, and which is, nevertheless not purely negative. He begins by discussing very briefly the development of Tillich's thought. He does not attempt any full discussion of the influences on Tillich, but he does indicate the significant periods in his development. His picture of Tillich is that of a 'philosopher of life' whose field of research has been 'the relationship of religion to existence'[3] and who 'has tried to build a prophetic theology for the twentieth century on a Protestant basis'.[4] The norm of Tillich's theology, says Fr Tavard, is best expressed as 'the New Being in Jesus as the Christ as our ultimate concern'.[5] This choice of norm has certain important consequences, not the least of which is that this theology will involve an ontology, though not a philosophical ontology. Also this is a distinctively Christian theology inasmuch as Christ is the bearer of the New Being, but it is not merely biblical. In Tillich's interpretation of the rôle of experience in theology Fr Tavard finds an inconsistency which takes us to the very heart of Tillich's theology. For Tillich experience is the medium through which we receive the sources of theology but it is not itself a source of theology. Its productive power is restricted to the transformation of what is

[1] Tavard, *Paul Tillich and the Christian Message*, p. vii.
[2] One such is E. LaB. Cherbonnier who has, over a period of years, pointed out the dangerous positions to which we are committed if we accept Tillich's system. See *Theology Today*, October 1952, pp. 360-75; *The Journal of Religion*, January 1953, pp. 16-30; *The Anglican Theological Review*, October 1954, pp. 251-71; *The Christian Scholar*, March 1956.
[3] Tavard, *op. cit.*, p. 14.   [4] *Ibid.*, p. 15.
[5] *Ibid.*, p. 22, quoting *Systematic Theology* I, p. 150.

given to it, but this transformation is also described as something required by the message or something that is necessary for its adequate presentation. But how far then, asks Fr Tavard,[1] can we say that experience is not productive? Again, the New Being itself is mediated through the theologian's experience. How far does this mediating experience transform it? Fr Tavard suggests that since at this point the principles of Tillich's theological reflections profess not to be Catholic 'they run the risk of being dependent on one man's experience of the New Being in Christ rather than on the experience of the whole of redeemed mankind'.[2] This seems to me a most unsatisfactory evaluation of the problem, and I cannot help feeling that Fr Tavard is not any clearer than Tillich himself when he talks of 'experience'. The fact that there are snakes in the garden is mediated by Smith's experience, but if it seems to Black and to White also that there are snakes in the garden then they agree that this is true. I am not suggesting that the religious situation is not any more 'subjective' than this situation about snakes in the garden, but I do wish to insist that what makes it so is not simply that here I must appeal to my 'experience'. It is a pity that Fr Tavard's discussion tails off into a mere process of labelling, for I am sure that he is right in thinking that this problem does take us to a central difficulty in Tillich's system. As I have said before, Tillich's phrase 'ultimate concern' is capable of both an objective and a subjective use, and in general he does not distinguish between the two uses. Indeed he assumes that a religious ultimate concern is always a justifiable attitude, saying that only what is ultimate can concern me ultimately. But this is either a purely verbal statement or a pure assumption, and we need to be shown how we can distinguish what is really ultimate from what merely seems to us to be so.

Though Fr Tavard does not think that Tillich altogether avoids asking the question of what we are committed to in our total commitment he seems to think that Tillich too often speaks of commitment, etc., without concerning himself with the objective.[3] But this, he thinks, is precisely Tillich's new path in

[1] *Op. cit.*, p. 25.   [2] *Ibid.*, p. 27.   [3] *Ibid.*, p. 31.

theology—that of reducing the dichotomy between the subject and object. We have faith that we have faith, and if our surrender is not total then our faith is false. 'This', says Fr Tavard bluntly, 'borders on the absurd',[1] but he is prepared to admit that the resources of language are not equal to the demands being made on it and that we can speak of faith only by means of paradox. The paradox is that faith is its own object. Faith is the acceptance of being accepted. But Fr Tavard has a basic criticism—this 'plumbing of existential depth which Tillich places at the core of faith is not a distinctly Christian phenomenon', and if Tillich thinks he is being radical in regarding acceptance of being accepted as faith 'his radicalism can be outdone: faith is our being accepted'.[2] Tillich comes dangerously near to saying that faith is the stuff of all human life, because he has 'ontologized the concept of faith'.[3] 'He studies subjective faith as though it leads an independent existence.'[4] 'He does not indeed deny that faith has a concrete content, but because he does not give it an object he makes its content an ultimate concern about life.' 'From all his analyses he has concluded that faith is the true reading of man's existential estrangement as a relating estrangement, as a healing wound. This means that he has given faith a preliminary content different from its concrete content.'[5] Fr Tavard thinks that this 'methodological distortion' leads Tillich to distort a basic element of Christian belief, namely original sin. He points out that Tillich has himself 'adequately formulated' the objection raised by many critics, 'that sin may become a rational necessity', but 'he does not answer it'.[6] It is, says Fr Tavard, an amazing flaw in Tillich's theological method that he should deny the Fall because of the absence of 'a direct experience of it by mankind today'. To make matters worse, he says Tillich finds that an original Fall 'has no foundation in revelation'. Tillich can treat the entire doctrine of the Fall as mythical only because he overlooks the Pauline doctrine.

'This helps him to ontologize original sin. It has been done at the cost of a clearly scriptural teaching, and by rejecting a whole

[1] *Ibid.*, p. 33.　　[2] *Ibid.*, p. 37.　　[3] *Ibid.*, p. 38.　　[4] *Ibid.*, p. 39.
[5] *Ibid.*, pp. 39-40.　　[6] *Ibid.*, p. 41.

stream of tradition, from the time of the Fathers through the period of the Reformers down to our own time—all for the purpose of bringing the notion of sin in line with Tillich's analysis of estrangement. In classical Christianity faith implies the assumption of man into redemption by Christ, his purification from the stain of sin contracted in the First Man. In Tillichian Christianity, faith remains saving, it saves from estrangement by revealing that estrangement is, after all, not estranging. This estrangement is "sin", incurred by the very fact that we are created. The correlation of faith and sin remains; the classical language may be used, but voided of its substance.'[1]

Fr Tavard is full of admiration for the 'sense of prophetic urgency' that inspires Tillich and is ready to admit that he has made a remarkable effort to define faith in terms that make sense today.[2] Nevertheless he feels that Tillich's far-reaching analyses of faith 'end by disappointing the reader. The beautiful symphony ends on a false note.'[3] He is guilty of a philosophical distortion of faith inasmuch as his phenomenological approach does justice to neither the exclusiveness of Christian faith nor its historical structure.

So eminently just is Fr Tavard that he admits that Tillich's Christology may make the necessary corrections to his fallacious basic approach. The exposition of this Christology, he says, must correspond to the four levels of truth which Tillich distinguishes—the symbolic, the historical, the dogmatic and the ethical. Fr Tavard distinguishes two senses of the word 'symbol' in Tillich's work.[4] The first 'denotes the elements that have been associated with a revelation and that have retained some of the revelatory power then manifested'. The second denotes the pointers to reality which are our only way of expressing the ultimate ground of being. It is not at all clear to me that Tillich does in fact use the term 'symbol' in the first of these two senses, and significantly Fr Tavard gives no references for this point. I suggest that he has read this into Tillich's doctrine because of Tillich's insistence that symbols live and die. The distinction between a symbol and a sign is stressed, and Fr Tavard relates the participation in the reality

[1] Tavard, *op. cit.*, pp. 42-3.   [2] *Ibid.*, p. 49.
[3] *Ibid.*, p. 50.   [4] *Ibid.*, pp. 54-5.

symbolized to the first use of the term, and for this reason, his interpretation seems to me to be false. After this preamble, Fr Tavard comes to the central symbol of Christology, the term 'Christ'. Tillich's basic point is that Christ is the historical manifestation of Eternal Godmanhood.

> 'The problems raised by his explanation of symbolic Christology are twofold. In the first place, we should ascertain to what extent history backs up his interpretation, and, in the second, confront his world-view with the traditional Christian dogmas. What is the status of history in symbolic Christology? And what is the dogmatic meaning of the same Christology?'[1]

The important element in Tillich's Christology is that the Christ is the New Being able to conquer the situation of estrangement because he is primordially 'the principle of the divine self-manifestation'. This is borne out by applying the symbol of 'the Word of God' to the Christ. Tillich recognizes that the doctrine of the Christ dovetails into a doctrine of God as Three in One. The symbol of Christ as one of the Trinity means that 'the New Being which, in Christ, subjected itself to the conditions of existence without being destroyed by them is being-itself, the ground of all'.[2] Father Tavard praises the eloquence and reverence Tillich displays as he unveils the symbolism of the Cross but also confesses to 'a certain embarrassment: at times Tillich gives the impression of having discovered the fullness of the symbol of the Cross all by himself'.[3] Only in Protestantism, says Tillich, has the Cross been given its full place, but not even in all Protestantism is this now the case. The 'end of the Protestant Era' means precisely that institutional Protestantism is no longer the standard-bearer of the Protestant principle. It 'is merely on the defensive'.[4] However, the basic problem of Protestant institutions—that of elaborating positive forms of life whilst constantly denying their sufficiency—is so difficult, says Father Tavard, that Tillich's objections to institutionalism may be turned against him.

[1] *Ibid.*, p. 72.   [2] *Ibid.*   [3] *Ibid.*, p. 76.
[4] *The Protestant Era*, p. 230.

'If to institutionalize salvation often entails a withdrawal of self-negation, an undermining of the meaning of the Cross, is not Tillich himself transcending self-negation when he proclaims "the superiority of Protestant Christianity"? This pride in superiority is as arrogant as the "sacramental authority" of bishops and priests has ever been.'[1]

Furthermore, Tillich does not mention the transcendent meaning of the Cross as 'an act of divine cult'. So, concludes Father Tavard, he has once more 'been caught in the snare of ontology. He has ontologized the symbol of the Cross.'[2] From this follows the ontological distortion of the whole pattern of Christian symbolism. It seems to me that Father Tavard's criticism is fundamentally sound here, though I had not considered the distortion of the Christian theme to be so great. It is certainly true that Tillich tends to interpret whole schemes of symbolism and historical movements also as exemplars of metaphysical principles. To this extent I think there is an element of distortion in Tillich's interpretation of symbolism.

This leads us to Father Tavard's next problem—'Christology as History'. He distinguishes three historical problems raised by Christology—(a) whether the Christ was a historical figure whose life is historically documented, (b) the definition of the world-historical importance of Christology and (c) the influence of history on the forms of Christian doctrine. Of these it is the second which Father Tavard regards as the basic historical problem. So he devotes much of this chapter to an exposition of Tillich's conception of history, but makes only one comment on it. Tillich, he says, shows that the centre of history cannot be conceived of as either future or present; but since, in Tillich's analysis of time, the present is, in a sense, both the past and the future, 'this remark on the past character of the centre of history is not as striking as it may seem'. 'But it does affect Tillich's view of the self-consciousness of the Christ. For if the advent of the Christ in Jesus is the centre of history for us, it cannot have been the centre of history for Jesus.'[3] So we come to the Christological affirmation, and the significance of this is discussed in terms of salvation, self-negation and *kairos*.

[1] Tavard, *op. cit.*, p. 78.   [2] *Ibid.*, p. 79.   [3] *Ibid.*, p. 93.

The centre of history in the Christ as the final revelation, and the centre of history as the standard of all knowledge both converge on one point: the Cross.'[1] The meaning of history, as manifested in the Cross of the Christ, says Father Tavard, is precisely the Protestant principle,[2] and this he finds 'rather disappointing'.

> 'The sense of "let-down" recurs. If the meaning of history is that we must accept what we cannot avoid, there was really no need of the extraordinary situation of the Cross to let us know it. There was no need for Jesus the Christ to die in a supreme testimony to his unity with being-itself, if the result is only that we shall continue to do, with more awareness, what we have always done anyway. Yet this is what the matter comes to in Tillich's universe. We are in the truth even when we are not; we are in grace even when we are in sin; we are accepted even when we are estranged. This is Tillich's Protestant principle. It is, for him, the meaning of the Cross and the entire history of man illuminated by the word from the Cross. No doubt that it is a valuable insight. But is it worth all that has prepared it? Above all, is it worth the self-sacrifice of Jesus?'[3]

Finally, we have the historical problem of the historicity of Jesus which, in contrast to Tillich, most theologians would regard as the basic historical problem of Christology. Father Tavard, as we have already seen, agrees with Tillich, and once again he says so.[4] Yet he soon shows himself uneasy about Tillich's sceptical attitude towards historical investigation.[5] Even so, he offers only one criticism.

> 'Tillich is right in being sceptical of the historians' efforts to rewrite the story of Jesus—but for the wrong reason. Historians cannot re-write the story because it is already written: the historical value of the New Testament is plain enough. Historians have not been able to make its reliability improbable. Tillich has not been radical enough in criticizing liberal theology.'[6]

If Father Tavard feels a sense of 'let-down' after discovering what Tillich's Christological interpretation of history amounts to, I must confess to a similar feeling at seeing the extent of his

[1] *Ibid.*, p. 100.   [2] *Ibid.*, p. 101.   [3] *Ibid.*, p. 103.
[4] *Ibid.*, p. 105.   [5] See *ibid.*, p. 106.   [6] *Ibid.*, pp. 111-12.

agreement with Tillich on this point. It seems strange that he should have missed the frightful ambiguity in Tillich's thought here. He does not seem to have noticed that Tillich is intent on having his cake and eating it—he denies that history is relevant and yet maintains, as Father Tavard himself points out, that Christianity is historical.

If the examination of Tillich's Christology as history is, on the whole, rather uncritical the examination of Tillich's Christology as dogma clearly reveals Father Tavard's theological acumen, and he states his conclusions bluntly.

> 'Paul Tillich has failed to account for the biblical picture of Jesus and for the Christological dogma as the Church has always believed it. He has paid lip-service to the dogmas, by saying that "Protestant theology must accept the Catholic tradition insofar as it is based on the substance of the two great decisions of the early Church, Nicaea and Chalcedon." But when he himself tried "to find new forms in which the Christological substance of the past can be expressed", the Christological substance vanished. . . . Where the Council of Chalcedon, spearheading the Church, follows a ridge between two chasms, the Christology of Paul Tillich falls into both chasms one after the other.'[1]

How just and even charitable Father Tavard is can be seen both from the way in which he proceeds to test his conclusions by reference to Tillich's theory of the Resurrection of Jesus (only to find it is in keeping with his departure from the faith of Chalcedon)[2] and from his conviction that heretical though Tillich's theology undoubtedly is, his faith is Christian.[3]

Father Tavard praises Tillich's correlation of dogma and ethics. The dominant theme of his Christology dominates his ethics as well. The Protestant principle is the end of all law. Christian revelation does not give a new law and a new set of commands. It gives a new spirit in which any law may be accepted as a norm of behaviour because it is already transcended in spirit. This transmoral character of the ethics of the New Being is precisely the ethics we have outlined in the Bible. The centre of the ethics of the New Being is the supremacy of

[1] Tavard, op. cit., p. 132.   [2] Ibid., pp. 135-7.   [3] Ibid., p. 138.

love over law. This love is the love of God, Being-itself. 'There is', says Father Tavard, 'a close kinship between this and the Catholic doctrine of the supremacy of love',[1] but he finds in it certain negative elements which he proceeds to enumerate.

> 'The contrast between love and law is largely artificial. For in the concrete situation of the Christian who is totally committed to God, love never contradicts the law: it fulfils it. . . . The moral law of nature or of revelation cannot contradict the true love of God, and the true love of God always desires to follow the moral law. . . . Catholic ethics affirms both the supremacy of love and the divine origin of an objective moral law. Tillich affirms the first and ignores the second.'[2]

Father Tavard's conclusion is that the theonomous ethics Tillich has tried to build already exists in Catholic theology.[3] However, he does not discuss what seems to me the basic problem with regard to Tillich's ethics, i.e., whether he can avoid making ethics purely noetic. *Love, Power and Justice* was an interesting and important book because it revealed the abstract ontological interest which dominates Tillich's ethical and political thinking.

More than once I have had occasion to remark how just and constructive Father Tavard's criticism is, and this is again revealed in the concluding pages of the book. He surveys very briefly the attitude of contemporary Protestant theologians to Tillich's Christology,[4] and declares that his interest is less that of fixing a label on Tillich's work than that of trying to salvage what he can of Tillich's insights and incorporating them in an orthodox Christology. He sees the deficiency in the Tillichian solution—that it cannot ensure a connection between the philosophical conception of 'eternal Godmanhood' and the concrete existence of the man Jesus, and so 'the eternal always escapes history'. This dichotomy between the historical and the eternal, unbridgeable by Tillich's method, would cease to be, says Father Tavard, if the divine element in the Christ were presented not as a universal principle 'but as a concrete Being who is, by essence human in his very divinity'.[5] In this way,

[1] *Ibid.*, p. 155.   [2] *Ibid.*, p. 157.   [3] *Ibid.*, p. 159.
[4] *Ibid.*, pp. 164-7.   [5] *Ibid.*, p. 173.

he says, with due correction, Tillich's Christology can be integrated in an orthodox Christology. I wonder whether this solution of Father Tavard's is anything more than a clever linguistic formula such as Tillich himself might have produced. Nothing is achieved by pretending that we are saying two entirely different things about a piece of history when we say that the Word became flesh or that Jesus of Nazareth was the Christ. It is the merit of Tillich's Christology, to my mind, that this is emphasized. No more than Father Tavard do I think that Tillich's doctrine is sound, but I will have nothing to do with attempts to minimize the scandal of the Absolute Paradox. Having said this, we have come to the end of our survey of Father Tavard's book and the criticism made by other Catholic theologians. If this stimulates other theologians to similar minute and constructive criticism we shall indeed learn much from Paul Tillich.

SELECT INDEX OF NAMES

INDEX OF SUBJECTS